TOM RE

Wholesome
LEADERSHIP
the heart, head, hands & health of school leaders

Illustrated by Oliver Caviglioli

First Published 2018

by John Catt Educational Ltd,
12 Deben Mill Business Centre, Old Maltings Approach,
Melton, Woodbridge IP12 1BL

Tel: +44 (0) 1394 389850
Fax: +44 (0) 1394 386893
Email: enquiries@johncatt.com
Website: www.johncatt.com

ISBN: 978 1 911382 70 6

Set and designed by John Catt Educational Limited

REVIEWS

This is a must-read for all current and aspiring school leaders. Tom writes with great authenticity and skill, balancing theory, relevant first-hand experience and useful strategies to take away. This book is personal in style and very accessible – for me it was extremely useful, informative and incredibly relevant.

Jon Watson, Headteacher, North Yorkshire

Whether you are doubting entering primary school leadership, jilted by your current headship or would simply welcome the perspective of another colleague, you need to make this the first purchase on your planned reading list. Tom was a first class primary teacher and has been successful in headship.

Craig Jones, Principal, Haywood Village Academy

A book of humble wisdom from a master of evidence-based educational research and a self-help manual for the often lonely world of school leadership. Full of practical advice and guidance, it is a perfect dip-in, dip-out read for school leaders of varying experience and expertise. A must-read for every experienced or aspiring leader!

Julia Kedwards, Multi-Academy Trust CEO

At a time when the teaching profession is crying out for strong leadership, this book comes as a hugely useful roadmap. Filled with valuable insights from the author's own experience in leadership, interviews with inspirational school leaders and heavily informed by evidence, *Wholesome Leadership* is a must-read for anyone working in a leadership role.

Carl Hendrick, Head of Learning and Research at Wellington College and author of *What Does This Look Like in the Classroom?*

An utterly compelling account of leadership through the lens of research and individual leaders. All of them with their unique stories, insights and wisdom. Tom talks about Peter Hall Jones making him fall in love with the profession. Reading this book will make us all fall in love again...

Mary Myatt, education adviser, writer and speaker

This is a fascinating book packed full of insights about teaching and leadership. It addresses the challenges around creating practical and research-based school systems, building a strong culture and ethos, and staying true to your purpose in the face of changing national policies. The focus on primary education is particularly valuable in a field often dominated by secondary leaders.

Daisy Christodoulou, Director of No More Marking and author of *Making Good Progress: The future of assessment for learning*

Tom has written a great book, full of wisdom and insight. The book speaks both to the heart and the mind and truly explores the complexities of leading a school. Based on experience that comes from getting it right and wrong this is a must have for prospective and current school leaders that will help you challenge and explore the work you do.

Simon Smith, Primary Headteacher

What I really love about this book (and trust me, there's plenty) is how Tom has managed to combine effortlessly some really big, complex ideas with such simplicity. Obviously, the illustrations help, but the narrative is crystal clear and easy for any experienced or aspiring school leader to dip in and out of. Above all though, the book reeks of authenticity and warmth, which in today's ever-changing climate is very welcome indeed. (Oh, and any leadership book that quotes Han Solo, is fine by me and long overdue.)

Andrew Morrish, Chief Executive, Victoria Academies Trust and author of *The Art of Standing Out.*

In *Wholesome Leadership*, Tom Rees invites you to become the best version of yourself; the authentic leader you are called to be. I love the Five Fives grids as a way of moving from reflection, to action to impact in a sustainable way. Thoroughly recommended to current and future leaders.

Stephen Tierney, Headteacher, MAT CEO & Chair of Head Teacher Roundtable

This book fizzes with an authentic and human voice. Honest and useful – it will serve all leaders and those thinking about leadership really well. I'm pleased too that this distinctive voice is from our fantastic primary sector.

Ty Goddard, Director, The Education Foundation

Wholesome Leadership is a great read for leaders in any educational setting and at any stage of a leader's career. Tom Rees draws on his experience as an Executive Headteacher and Education Director at a multi-academy trust to set out a very clear and practical model for school leaders to develop an authentic approach to leadership.

The book acknowledges the complex nature of schools and never goes for easy answers. It is full of good sense and practical suggestions with reference to current research and theoretical models. What Tom provides is pragmatic advice that makes you think and consider your own practice. *Wholesome Leadership* is an accessible and insightful read and is highly recommended for those currently in leadership positions in school or looking to develop their leadership skills to move into a new role.

Andrew Percival, Deputy Headteacher, Oldham

This is an ambitious and inspiring book. It draws on values-based leadership from within education and beyond. The book reminds us that for both teachers and pupils, a great education is far more than a Progress 8 score. Rather, it enriches lives and advances society. Ultimately, *Wholesome Leadership* is a book about people. If Ministers had used it as a model for education reform over the past eight years, our system would be in a far better place. This is a book for every leader in every school in England.

Marc Rowland, Head of Rosendale Research School and author of *Learning Without Labels.*

This is a warm, brilliant hug of a book which was a pleasure to read from start to finish! With honesty, humility and humour Tom has written a clever joyful mixture of anecdotes, quotations and interviews as well as providing pragmatic models, helpful protocols and practical tips and tools which will have a positive impact in our schools. The pictures and diagrams by Oliver Caviglioli are another highlight in this book and uniquely include four visualised managerial processes that will be hugely useful to every senior leadership team!

Wholesome Leadership is a book I will certainly want to come back to again and again as well as using as a starting point for shared discussion with other members of the senior leadership team to help us reflect on and review our practice.

Rae Snape, Headteacher of The Spinney Primary School, Cambridge/ National Leader of Education

FOREWORD

Andy Buck
Founder of Leadership Matters

Every now and then, I read something that really chimes with me. Something that seems to capture what I think, but then challenges me to think even further. Something that resonates, but brings a fresh perspective. This timely book from Tom Rees does just that.

Writing can be a lonely and challenging business – especially if you are running a school at the same time, as Tom is. So it really has been a complete privilege to have been involved in talking about this book with Tom almost from its inception. Right from the start, I was taken with Tom's passion for school leadership and the difference it can make. But what really struck me was his depth of thinking and knowledge of leadership, and his ability to translate that into both a structure and tone that will be relevant to leaders in schools today.

It has been almost ten years since I led a school; but working closely with hundreds of heads and senior leaders every year, I see today's leaders under intense pressure from a broken accountability system and facing real difficulties recruiting and retaining teachers while at the same time trying to balance the books. This book is just the tonic they need. It doesn't shy away from these challenges – it is ruthlessly authentic. But with its beautifully simple yet powerful 'H4' model, it reminds us all why leading in schools is so important and so rewarding. By focusing on Heart, Head, Hands and Health, it takes a balanced approach to leadership that puts the fact that all leaders are human at its core. There is a deep humanity about this book that runs through every chapter.

It is also refreshing to have someone from a primary perspective writing about leadership in this powerful way. Speaking as a former secondary teacher and leader, I am only too aware that the voice of my own phase is overly represented. But at the same time, this is a book for all leaders in all schools. Tom's curation of both thoughts and personal views spans the whole educational spectrum. And what an impressive list of contributors he has pulled together, from Clare Sealy and Daisy

Christodoulou to multi-academy trust CEOs Julia Kedwards, Stephen Tierney and Andrew Morrish – plus his very own dad!

Spanning the perspective of self, school and system, this *tour de force* is both well informed and uplifting, full of practical advice and guidance rooted in Tom's front line role leading a school. You just know that what he talks about will be useful.

From a purely personal perspective, I learnt so much from this book. I had never heard of the idea of Gemba walks or the concept of Jidoka. Intrigued? Then you had better start reading – you're in for a treat!

Andy Buck

A NOTE FROM
THE ILLUSTRATOR

Oliver Caviglioli
Visualiser of teaching concepts and processes

It has been a great pleasure to work with Tom on *Wholesome Leadership.*
Our partnership has developed far beyond simply choosing and creating
the illustrations.

This is the book that I would have loved to read as a deputy or head
teacher. Management books can be either rather dull or too celebratory
of personal successes. By contrast, Tom's book strikes a very human tone
that is both touching and effective. His weaving of evidence, theory and
personal accounts is humble and authoritative at the same time. While
we have seen the inexorable rise of the generic manager – all targets and
checklists – Tom's writing and experiences are a wonderful antidote to
managerialism that resonate with maturity and reflection.

His interviews are full of practical wisdom, covering a wide range of
perspectives from a talented collection of practitioners. They alone are
worth the price of the book.

Throughout the book, readers will sense the vocation and
professionalism of Tom's approach to leadership.

Oliver Caviglioli

PREFACE

> **"** Do all the good you can, by all the means you can, in all the ways you can, in all the places you can, at all the times you can, to all the people you can, as long as ever you can.
>
> John Wesley

Education remains the answer to many of the world's questions and problems in this extraordinary and volatile 21st century.

With many different influences competing to blow the educational winds in the direction of political, commercial and ideological interests, authenticity of school leadership has never been more important.

Governments and ministers come and go; industries and businesses rise and fall; while high-powered voices in the system ebb and flow, along with their respective ideologies and hobby horses. Within this unpredictable and fluctuating educational narrative, school leaders must find the courage and integrity to do what is right for our young people.

At the heart of this, we should remember the primary purpose of education: education itself. Yes, there are other purposes, such as gaining qualifications and skills for future employment or preparation for adulthood; but these are secondary to the entitlement of future generations to a rich and wholesome education which, in itself, enriches lives, develops minds and advances society.

There is no more important job than the role of 'teacher' and fewer more fulfilling places to work than a well-run school.

Never has it been more important for good people to become or remain school leaders.

Tom Rees

CONTENTS

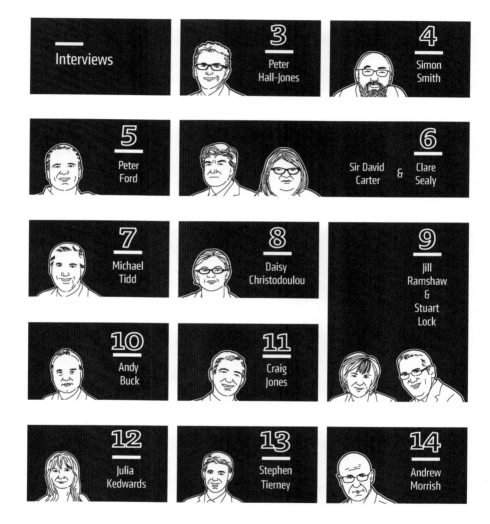

Interviews

3 Peter Hall-Jones

4 Simon Smith

5 Peter Ford

6 Sir David Carter & Clare Sealy

7 Michael Tidd

8 Daisy Christodoulou

9 Jill Ramshaw & Stuart Lock

10 Andy Buck

11 Craig Jones

12 Julia Kedwards

13 Stephen Tierney

14 Andrew Morrish

For teachers everywhere.

Never wish the days away,
One day we'll wish for them all back.

INTRODUCTION

Tom Rees
Author

DOES THE WORLD NEED ANOTHER BOOK ON EDUCATION?

This is a question I have asked myself many times; after all, a wealth of wisdom and opinion has already been published in books, articles and blogs, alongside the ongoing conversation that social media now offers us. There are four reasons why, in the end, I came to believe that *Wholesome Leadership* was a book worth writing:

- **Leadership shortage**
  Despite the critical importance of effective school leadership, recruitment and retention have reached crisis point. Recent research tells us that England already has a shortfall of 2,000 to 3,000 leaders in the system; that half the existing leadership pool is likely to leave the profession in the next six years; and that by 2022, England could require 19,000 new school leaders.[1] This could have catastrophic effects for an education system already fragile from stuttering structural reform. We must do more to attract teachers and professionals into the business of running and improving schools. We must think more carefully as to how we can keep them in these roles for the long term.

- **Breadth of the role**
  School leadership is a complex affair; yet training and development for leaders is often patchy, missing many essential points. Given the variety of hats that leaders wear each day, it is vital that the nuances are understood more widely, and that the role is not reduced to simplistic models of leadership that are not always transferable into school settings. This book presents a holistic leadership model for schools through the four domains of Heart, Head, Hands and Health to capture the breadth of leadership required in our schools.

---

1. Future Leaders, Teach First, Future Leaders, 'The School Leadership Challenge: 2022' (November 2016)

■ **Practical help**

So often, what is written and presented about education is academic, journalistic or influenced by politics and ideology which overlooks the important practical help that school leaders need. Having spent the last 17 years of my life as a school leader, I have learned much from successes and failures, the people I have met and the things I have read. The examples and approaches in this book are real and drawn from my experience as a teacher, school leader and parent of three. It was written over nine months while spending my days running a primary school and leading school improvement across a number of other schools. *Wholesome Leadership* is written about life on the front line, from the front line; it is honest and I hope it is helpful.

■ **A primary voice**

I write from a primary school perspective, although I believe that many of the leadership principles and approaches presented in this book are transferable across wider educational settings. Our system is awash with powerful voices and influences from secondary and higher education; we need to balance this so that the challenges and opportunities within primary education can be better understood. I have always believed that children's formative years afford the greatest potential for us to affect their lives for the better. I am a primary head and I write unashamedly from this view, with all the inevitable biases this brings.

Give me a child until he is seven and I will show you the man.

Aristotle

WHOLESOME LEADERSHIP

This book is intended as a companion for school leaders at all levels. Whether you are an experienced senior leader, a school governor or new to a middle leadership role, my hope is that you will find plenty to make you think within these pages.

Leading in a school is complicated. It requires us to know enough about many different issues and to be able to spin different plates without allowing the most important to come crashing down. No two days are ever the same in a school; and while this daily cut and thrust is demanding, for many it is the variety that keeps us in the job.

After the first two introductory chapters, this book is organised into the four sections of the Heart, Head, Hands and Health, each of which contains three chapters. Each chapter features research, advice and approaches, alongside some of my own experience and ideas and an interview with someone who has significant relevant expertise or experience. I am indebted to the interviewees for their insight and am sure you will enjoy their contributions!

Although I have primarily used the term 'leaders' within this book, this is not to neglect the importance of the managerial and operational functions of the role. Schools stand or fall by their operational effectiveness, and the effort made just to keep a school running on a daily basis should never be underestimated. Operational tasks are always a focus of the wholesome leader.

If I have one hope for this book, it is simply that it proves useful for you in your daily life.

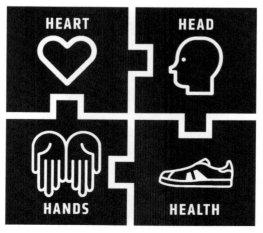

WHOLESOME LEADERSHIP – A MODEL FOR SCHOOL LEADERSHIP

Writing about the spectrum of school leadership issues is difficult without some kind of model to organise them. Therefore my next job is to explain the different aspects of the 'wholesome leadership' model, which has three dimensions:

- breadth of leadership;
- reach of leadership; and
- depth of leadership.

The breadth of wholesome leaders

Figure 1. H4 Leadership Model

 Know what you stand for. Believe in what you do and who you are. Create the right ethos and professional culture, and lead careful change effectively.

 Create good school improvement strategy rooted in research and evidence. Secure healthy accountability and develop the use of effective school improvement processes.

 Be visible and 'hands-on', walking the talk of your leadership. Be relentless in the development of staff and manage people well.

 Prioritise your own health and the wellbeing of staff around you. Develop interdependent relationships within and outside your school.

The 'H4' model captures the breadth of leadership, acknowledging that successful leaders manage to lead with Heart, Head, Hands and Health. Each domain plays a vital role in developing effective and sustainable leadership, and must be developed carefully and in balance with the others.

The depth of wholesome leaders

Within the H4 model, 'depth' refers to the substance and authenticity of leaders. I have adapted David Rock's 'Iceberg' model,[2] which shows that the observable aspects of leaders – such as their results and behaviours – are just the tip of the iceberg. Rock argues that while leaders often focus on results and behaviours, it is by delving beneath the waterline that they can make more significant connections with the people they lead.

2. Rock, D, *Quiet Leadership: Six Steps to Transforming Performance at Work* (HarperCollins, 2007)

The best leaders I have known achieve great results not because they micromanage behaviours of their staff or spend their lives obsessing over how to improve outcomes in the short term, but because they focus on the root causes of the challenges they face. Leadership with substance and authenticity, connecting to the values, beliefs, emotions and thought processes of others, is a far more powerful and effective approach.

As Andrew Morrish, former head teacher and CEO of Victoria Academies, often says: 'If I'm going to improve KS2 SATs results, the last thing I'm going to do is focus on KS2 SATs results.'

Although school leaders often spend time in the spotlight, the depth of their leadership is often demonstrated in the moments when no one is watching. It is at these times when decisions and actions affecting others are often made, and when the integrity and authenticity of decision-makers are tested. Only the individuals themselves will ever know the true extent of their integrity.

Figure 2. The 'Iceberg' model

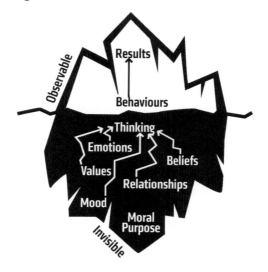

The depth of leadership in our system is of critical importance – particularly as we often find ourselves playing a game which rewards the wrong things. It is all too tempting to make short-term decisions in the name of chasing league tables or Ofsted grades at the expense of more important and fundamental responsibilities to society such as inclusion, supporting the most vulnerable and establishing a broad and rich curriculum. Our education system relies upon authentic leaders avoiding these potentially career-enhancing temptations to make the right decisions for the right reasons.

In the end, if we want to look back at our lives and know that we made a positive contribution to the world, then the authenticity with which we lead is important.

DEFINITION

Authentic[3]

adjective: authentic

- of undisputed origin and not a copy; genuine.
  "the letter is now accepted as an authentic document"
  synonyms: genuine, original, real, actual, pukka, bona fide, true, veritable

- made or done in the traditional or original way, or in a way that faithfully resembles an original.
  "the restaurant serves authentic Italian meals"

- based on facts; accurate or reliable.
  "an authentic depiction of the situation"
  synonyms: reliable, dependable, trustworthy, authoritative, honest, faithful; More antonyms: unreliable, inaccurate

- (in existentialist philosophy) relating to or denoting an emotionally appropriate, significant, purposive, and responsible mode of human life.

The reach of wholesome leaders

The three 'reaches' of leadership define different arcs in which we make an impact: self, school and system. These capture how successful leaders combine an investment in themselves alongside a commitment to improvement in their own schools and beyond their own gates – making a contribution to other schools and the wider education system.

Self: The saying goes that 'There's no 'I' in team; but there is a 'me' if you look closely enough.' Initially, leadership is very much a personal thing, requiring us to develop the knowledge, skills and resilience to do the job properly. It can also rely on us getting over ourselves, shaking off some of the hang-ups that we might have acquired and becoming aware of our own strengths and limitations. Even when leaders become experienced and proficient, it is important to maintain a state of continuous self-reflection and personal development. Without this, there is a risk that fresh challenges become stale and the reservoir of energy required to do the job becomes depleted.

---

3. Google Dictionary: www.google.co.uk/search?q=Dictionary#dobs=authentic

School: Leadership in the main is a selfless business and our main focus will usually be beyond ourselves and centred on the schools in which we work. The best leaders are those who are service driven, putting the genuine and long-term interests of their organisation above all other peripheral and personal goals. At the heart of most successful schools is a group of leaders who have a heartfelt commitment to their role, which is more than 'just a job'. This drive for continuous improvement must be checked or wellbeing and self-preservation can be compromised.

System: As we grow as leaders, we can start to contribute to the wider educational landscape. This may involve collaborating with teachers from other schools, supporting another school or playing a role in a multi-academy trust (MAT). Work across the system can also be as straightforward as sharing classroom practice or leadership efforts via a blog or with colleagues online. Many of the best professional development opportunities across schools have arisen through this less formal route in recent years.

In the last five years, the narrative of a self-improving system has become a reality, with leaders playing a much more central role in organisations such as MATs and teaching schools, and in school-to-school support arrangements. The 'system', as this final reach, is where our greatest impact can be made, as our ideas and practice have the potential to reach beyond the gates of our own organisations.

The best way to find yourself is to lose yourself in the service of others.

Mahatma Gandhi

Figure 3. The three leadership 'reaches': self, school and system

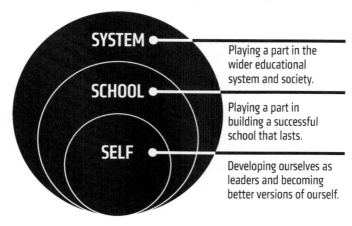

SYSTEM — Playing a part in the wider educational system and society.

SCHOOL — Playing a part in building a successful school that lasts.

SELF — Developing ourselves as leaders and becoming better versions of ourself.

PLANNING FOR LASTING CHANGE

FIVE FIVES – ACTION PLANNING FOR LASTING IMPROVEMENT

At the end of each chapter, you will find one of the 'Five Fives' planning tools to support your thinking as to how you can develop this topic towards long-term and lasting change. Within it, there is space for you to make notes on the different issues that are discussed in the book to help you plan the jump from ideas and theories into embedded practice.

The 'Five Fives' planning approach is one I've developed with schools and leaders. Its purpose is to help avoid fads and false starts by thinking about different actions at different future stages, to help bring about change which is carefully-planned, well-implemented and sustained. It can also be used as a way of agreeing timescales for actions following review processes or when giving feedback.

5 Minutes	Immediate action	What small steps towards change can you take now?
5 Days	Short-term action	What actions or discussions can you take in the next week to kick-start change?
5 Weeks	Short/Medium-term actions/change	What actions or follow-up meetings/discussions can you plan for in the next half-term?
5 Months	Medium-term actions	What follow-up and follow-through activities do you need to plan to ensure that the change isn't a flash in the pan?
5 Years	Long-term change	What might your change look like in five years? What structures, systems and processes will you need to adjust to ensure lasting improvement that becomes embedded in the fabric of your school and not just a passing fad?

Example: Five Fives grid for planning change in feedback and marking

This is an example of a Five Fives plan written from the perspective of a deputy head teacher on the train home from visiting another school, having seen a new 'minimal marking' policy in practice and being introduced to a number of ideas and further reading.

FIVE MINUTES: What immediate first steps can you take?

- Order Daisy Christodoulou's book on assessment (*Making Good Progress?*)*.
- Check diary for next week's meetings.
- Add 'marking update' for initial discussion at SLT

FIVE DAYS: What short-term actions can you take in the next week to kick start or plan change?

- Discuss current marking practices in conversation.
- Plan time to read the Education Endowment Foundation's 'A Marked Difference'
- Discuss marking approach with SLT.
- Update teachers at staff meeting with initial thoughts from the visit to Abington Vale.

FIVE WEEKS: What actions or follow-up meetings/discussions can you plan for in the next half-term?

- Read up on blogs from schools and teachers who are ahead of us on changing their marking policy.
- Review staff meeting to discuss current practices and gather views of staff about strengths and weaknesses of current practice.
- Create working party to start assessing different approaches to feedback from research.

FIVE MONTHS: What follow-up and follow-through activities do you need to plan to ensure that the change is not just a flash in the pan?

- Take feedback from the working group on its findings and consider its recommendations for changes to school practice.
- Provide revised guidance to all staff on marking approaches.
- Draft revised marking approach for new academic year.
- Write in marking/feedback specifically to next year's school improvement plan.

FIVE YEARS: What might your change look like in five years? What structures, systems and processes will you need to amend to ensure that your change becomes embedded in the fabric of your school and is not a passing fad?

- Adapt book scrutiny processes over the years.
- Change monitoring.
- Repeat annual marking/workload survey with teaching staff to monitor reported time spent on marking.

* Christodoulou, D, *Making Good Progress? The Future of Assessment for Learning* (Oxford University Press, 2017).

Section **1**

Wholesome leadership

Before we get into the Heart, Head, Hands and Health of leadership, here is an introduction to help understand the context in which school leaders work and an insight into the author, who wanted to be anything other than a teacher when he was growing up.

Chapters

The challenge

CHAPTER PREVIEW

Why is it that tradesmen can drive home confident that their work for the day has been completed, while teachers up and down the country spend their lives worrying about whether their different approaches are working, continually trying new initiatives to make learning stick?

What became clear to me in this brief dual life as head teacher and building site manager was that while we have worked out how to build houses that can stand for centuries, we still lack a shared understanding and confidence of 'what works' in our schools.

At the heart of this conundrum lies one of the biggest challenges for all of us involved in education: we can't see learning. Although there are many different definitions of 'learning,' it is widely accepted that this is something that happens in the brain as information transfers from working memory to long-term memory and is then applied in different situations. Learning, therefore, is invisible.

A further problem with policy making is that it is often heavily influenced by political ideology or personal political power, or bargained off to keep others happy within the same political party, rather than focusing on genuine improvements in education.

A lot of decision-making is not based on evidence, but on hunch. I had little coming to me from civil servants that presented the latest academic evidence. Too often, they just serve up practical advice about how the minister can do what he or she wants. But politicians are prone to make decisions based on ideology and personal experience.

David Laws

THE CHALLENGE

A few years ago, we built an extension on the back of our house. It was a big project and at one point we had to move our family of five to live with my parents for what we thought might be a fortnight and ended up being three months. With Adele (my wife) having spent hours watching *Grand Designs* and my natural assumption that I had the skills and knowledge to be able to take on such a task, we decided to manage the project ourselves, with most of the work carried out by a builder friend.

It was an exciting yet stressful time, which inevitably took considerably longer than planned and cost more than we could afford. The stress of trying to manage the project and help with the manual labour at weekends and evenings was compounded by preparation at school for an Ofsted inspection. Simon de Senlis Primary had been (rightly) judged as 'Requiring Improvement' 18 months previously, shortly after I was appointed as head, and we knew we would be re-inspected at some point in the summer term. While all logical thinking assured us that the outcome would almost certainly be positive, there is always an element of doubt and a great deal was riding on it. I felt that our staff and community really needed the public stamp of approval to recognise all the improvements that had taken place.

BUILT TO LAST?

Although it was difficult, there were some therapeutic benefits to living this dual managerial role of school leader and site manager. Seeing our dreams become a reality was both exciting and rewarding; lifting blocks and sweeping up in the evening offered enforced escape from the all-consuming world of 'Ofsted readiness'; and watching different tradesmen at work provided a welcome and refreshing new perspective to life. One memorable observation was of the confidence exuded by the many tradesmen as they carried out their different roles. The bricklayers knew that with a four-to-one mix of sand to cement, one inch of mortar would be enough to hold the blocks and bricks together securely; the carpenters knew that two-inch screws would keep the doorframes firmly in place; and the electrician slept well at night, knowing that once he had tested the circuits and tightened the final screws, his work was done.

I was so envious of this certainty that the job was 'done'. Why is it that tradesmen can drive home confident that their work for the day has been completed, while teachers up and down the country spend their lives worrying about whether their different approaches are working, continually trying new initiatives to make learning stick? And while I was having restless nights about whether teaching was really improving in my school, I didn't once wake up panicking in the night over whether my newly renovated house would fall down.

Over the six months or so that the project took, I must have watched between 25 and 30 workers come and go, all playing their separate roles. It amazed me how clearly defined their methods were; how there was no real debate or discussion about which approach would be better than another. Don't get me wrong, they still moaned a lot about how tired they were and blamed the previous workman for anything that went wrong; some days it looked as though nothing had progressed at all. But in their eyes, there was no sense of 'Did we get it right today?' as they packed up their tools at the end of the day.

AN INSPECTOR CALLS...

And then Ofsted came and everyone put on their best clothes and shoes and did their thing. We stayed late at school for two days, working harder than ever, and abandoned our families to make sure that we could answer any conceivable question or possible line of enquiry. The stakes are high with these inspections due to the public nature of the reports and the months of anticipation. There were many brilliant teachers in the school, yet despite their commitment and loyalty, the school had never been graded 'Good' by Ofsted in the eight years since it merged from lower to primary school. In another school or another context, many of these teachers would have been held up as bright lights in the local area and could have been advanced skills teachers or specialist leaders in education; I wanted this inspection to give confidence to these staff to spread their wings and fly in the future.

Meanwhile, at home, the building inspector came to visit. And I worried. But there was no sense of panic among the builders or concern that if it went the wrong way, this could be part of a career-defining disaster. After all, they had invited him along in the first place to check their work. The building inspector duly arrived with his tape measure and checked that the roof insulation was of the right thickness and the windows were set at the right depth, then got back in his car and drove off. A relief for me, but otherwise just another normal day applying processes that everyone knows work when building a house.

Back at school and after two days, I smiled and waved off the inspection team from the carpark. If an inspection has gone well, the walk from the farewell handshake with the inspectors down to the staffroom to share the feedback with your staff is a lovely moment to savour. Nice things were said and written; we opened the bubbly and celebrated and enjoyed all the stories that inspections always bring, reflecting proudly on the journey over the last two years. But amid this sense of accomplishment and elation, what was most evident in our language and behaviour was the feeling of relief. Relief that it was over; relief that the worst-case scenario behaviours that week had not taken place in front of an inspector; relief that the inspectors were not the kind of rogue and blinkered mavericks that everyone fears.

What became clear to me in this brief dual life as head teacher and building site manager was that while we have worked out how to build houses that can stand for centuries, we still lack a shared understanding and confidence of 'what works' in our schools. And while many people you meet make loud and confident claims about what great learning looks like, they are often wrong.

LEARNING IS INVISIBLE

So why is it so difficult? We have been teaching children in formal state education for well over 100 years now. Surely we must have worked out the right approaches to use in schools, so that we can get on and do the right things?

At the heart of this conundrum lies one of the biggest challenges for all of us involved in education: we can't see learning. Although there are many different definitions of 'learning', it is widely accepted that this is something that happens in the brain as information transfers from working memory to long-term memory and is then applied in different situations. Learning, therefore, is invisible.

And because we cannot see learning happening, we rely on signs that we associate with good learning to make judgements about when and where it is taking place, or 'proxies for learning'. Typically, such proxies are visible and therefore easy to check or measure; they can be outputs – such as assessments, tests and work in books – or inputs, such as planning, certain teaching approaches and types of learning activities. Either way, these proxies for learning can become the basis of expectation and accountability in schools and often find their way into checklists, minimum expectation documents and lesson observation sheets for leaders or managers to check.

All of this at surface level sounds reasonably sensible: leaders should check that the right things are happening in the classroom, just as site managers and building inspectors should check that the screws are being used in the correct way and the concrete in the foundations is the specified depth. But research conducted in recent years has made us question the validity of many classroom inputs as reliable proxies for learning. Learning styles, lengthy written comments for marking, use of mobile technology in the classroom, three-way differentiation in each lesson, writing 'WALT' ('We are learning to…') or 'WILF' ('What I'm looking for…') on the board are all examples of things which have been encouraged or insisted upon in schools even though their effectiveness is disputed by research.

In his inaugural lecture at Durham University, Professor Rob Coe said the following: 'Much of what is claimed as school improvement is illusory, and many of the most commonly advocated strategies for improvement are not robustly proven to work. Even the claims of school effectiveness research – that we can identify good schools and teachers, and the practices that make them good – seem not to stand up to critical scrutiny.'[4]

The challenge of understanding when good learning is taking place is significant and we cannot simplify it or rush it. To use Captain Blackadder's phrase, understanding which strategies are effective is as hard 'as finding a piece of hay in an incredibly large stack of needles'. We must take more care to draw useful and reliable inferences from the outputs of assessment, and more critical evaluation should take place of different inputs if we are to move towards a better understanding of 'what works' in schools.

However, this important evaluative and analytic type of school improvement activity is not yet common practice – partly due to the operational challenges that come with running buildings that house hundreds of children, but also due to the chaotic and volatile nature of our education system and the unhealthy relationship with accountability that has been normalised across our schools.

---

4. Coe, Prof R, 'Improving Education: A Triumph of Hope over Experience', inaugural lecture at Durham University, 18 June 2013, www.cem.org/attachments/publications/ImprovingEducation2013.pdf

STORMY WATERS

The current education system is prone to poor policy decisions by design, starting at the top. The Education Secretary wields significant power and influence over schools, with the ability to make sweeping changes to how they are funded, organised and run. Even former Education Secretary Michael Gove has been quoted as saying, 'I do think that education secretaries do have too much power.'[5] But this power is short lived: the average time in office of the 30+ secretaries of states since 1944 is just over two years. With the impact of education policy likely to take years to reveal itself – and often decades before it becomes realised across society – it is easy to see how legislation is made without proper accountability. In effect, this system affords as much stability as a school that has had a change of head teacher every two years for the last 70 years.

A further problem with policy making is that it is often heavily influenced by political ideology or personal political power, or bargained off to keep others happy within the same political party, rather than focusing on genuine improvements in education. In the last 10 years alone, we have seen radical changes and occasional U-turns to policies such as infant school meals, proposed grammar schools, free schools and full-academisation. These high-profile debates all cause uncertainty and create additional work in schools, while avoiding the important question of how to improve teaching across the country.

David Laws, former schools minister and current executive chairman of the Education Policy Institute, has talked openly about the poor quality of policy making from his time at the Department for Education (DfE): 'A lot of decision-making is not based on evidence, but on hunch. I had little coming to me from civil servants that presented the latest academic evidence. Too often, they just serve up practical advice about how the minister can do what he or she wants. But politicians are prone to make decisions based on ideology and personal experience.'[6]

CONFUSED GOVERNANCE

Lines of accountability are in a mess nationally, as the role of local authorities in school improvement has diminished due to the academies programme and the regional school commissioners (RSCs) have become established in overseeing the performance of academies. Ten years

---

5. Michael Gove interview with Anthony Horowitz, *The Spectator*, March 2014.
www.spectator.co.uk/2014/03/the-disturbing-certainty-of-michael-gove/
6. Wilbey, P, 'David Laws: The quality of education policymaking is poor', *The Guardian*, 1 August 2017,
www.theguardian.com/education/2017/aug/01/david-laws-education-policy-schools-minister-thinktank-epi

ago, local authorities assumed responsibility for governance and HR as the employer for most schools, and were also accountable for school improvement and providing continuing professional development (CPD). Today, a more complex web of accountability exists, with MATs, local authorities, RSCs and dioceses now holding different responsibilities for the governance of schools.

This ever-changing landscape means that very little educational policy has a chance to be embedded on the ground. School leaders are often too busy implementing knee-jerk reactions to different policy changes to remain focused on the important business of curriculum, teaching and learning.

The way that schools are held to account is also problematic and riddled with inequality. In my view, the existing system of high-threat inspections by Ofsted with an over-reliance on crude published data has become more a part of the problem rather than a solution to improving education over the last 20 years. While I believe that there is a need for a regulatory body and acknowledge recent efforts to shift the inspection rhetoric, the current Ofsted framework remains unfit for purpose and needs more radical reform.

It is impossible to talk about educational challenges without also highlighting the issue of school funding. While undoubtedly there are examples of where money has been wasted within education in years gone by, there is simply no fat left to cut in schools. Rising living and pension costs within these austere times are making it almost impossible to set balanced budgets in schools anymore without making unacceptable and sometimes dangerous compromises to provision. It feels like we have forgotten that education is an investment, not an expense.

The impact of these different challenges is that schools now sail in stormy and often unchartered waters. They have become far more complicated places to manage than they should be with further symptoms such as teacher recruitment and retention now reaching crisis point.

The importance of authentic and wholesome leadership has never been more important.

> *It is the set of the sails, not the direction of the wind that determines which way we will go.*
>
> **Jim Rohn**

Another teacher...

2 CHAPTER PREVIEW

A SELECTION OF QUOTES FROM THE CHAPTER

#WholesomeLeadership

As is the case for many, my school experience would be best summarised as 'mixed'. Some wonderful teachers, achievements and experiences on one hand balanced out the mistakes, mediocrity and missed opportunities on the other.

My predominant memories of the classroom are ones of restlessness and frustration.

There was only one thing I was sure of in life: I was never going to become a teacher.

My induction to the profession began in the car park with a greeting of 'Welcome to the madhouse' cried through a window by my new mentor, and included a welcome from one of the more long-standing teachers with the sage advice that social lives were overrated anyway.

And then somehow, in September 2008, I found myself standing outside the school gates of Little Harrowden Primary – a 30-year-old head teacher in a new Next suit brimming with enthusiasm, promise and naivety. What on earth do I do now...?'

Ten years of headship have brought the richest experiences and challenges to my life. When I am grey and wrinkly, I hope that I'll look back at these days with a warmth and appreciation.

ANOTHER TEACHER...

Everyone's story offers insight as to why they think and behave the way they do. Our previous experiences inevitably form the lens through which we see life and inform the biases we hold. I find this is particularly true in education, where – even at the highest level – debate and discussion are full of personal (often emotional) anecdotes and experiences. We are all products of our past.

Mine is no rags to riches tale – 'son of two teachers becomes head teacher' hardly classes as social mobility – but there were enough twists and turns along the way that I almost fell off the edge a few times. I hope this is not too self-indulgent...

EARLY DAYS

My early childhood memories of school are vivid. I remember my first experience of using the ceramic trough urinal in the reception toilets at Earls Barton Infant School, the aeroplanes on the hand-knitted jumper of a boy who sat next to me on the carpet on my first day and the boiled sweet jar in the head's office that you were allowed to choose from for every third library book you finished. I also remember the shock of being smacked on the hand with a ruler in my first year at school – a rare hangover from the days of corporal punishment in school – no doubt for talking too much.

As is the case for many, my school experience would be best summarised as 'mixed'. Some wonderful teachers, achievements and experiences on one hand balanced out the mistakes, mediocrity and missed opportunities on the other.

My predominant memories of the classroom are ones of restlessness and frustration. I still feel the physical sensations that accompany these memories from over 30 years ago. As I write these words and picture the images of 1980s classrooms, my feet are crossed, rubbing together tensely, I am forced to stretch my fingers and arms and notice my teeth clenched. I want to misbehave!

And I also feel these emotions and physical sensations today when I visit lessons or schools where children are not getting a good deal. I share the disengagement and frustration on children's faces and in their body language as I remember what it was like to clock-watch and wish away the hours.

But I also look back with a sense of great fortune at my childhood and much of my school life. I had some simply brilliant teachers along the way, whose expertise and commitment afforded me a precious collection of memories and experiences. Obsessions with good books; orchestra trips to play in French towns and villages; first sporting competitions; performing on stage; the thrill of our whole school becoming published authors; standing with the rest of the junior school cup-winning football team crying on our last day at school with Mr Blake. Such formative experiences shape our lives and I am grateful for the richness of mine.

And it is the same buzz and tangible sense of excitement I remember from these childhood experiences that I am fortunate to feel on a daily basis as I watch great teachers and leaders working their craft in our schools or see young teachers developing their skills and confidence in the classroom. The breakthrough moments, the concerts, the academic successes, the camaraderie – the wholesomeness that is being a part of a great primary school.

Two of my most influential teachers happened to be my parents: Mum was deputy head at the village junior school and Dad was head of music at the local secondary. As musicians, their impact reached far beyond the confines of the classrooms as they played their part in ensuring that music and the arts were alive and well in our local community. I say that now – of course, when you're growing up, having your parents working in your school is a complete embarrassment!

I blew hot and cold at secondary school. The classic underachieving 'bright boy' with an answer for everything, I frustrated my teachers (and parents) at times with a lack of application and rigour, and was generally dismissive of the importance of education. Despite this, I managed to achieve OK. I left as head boy, leader of the school orchestra and with a collection of sporting colours, including representing Northamptonshire at cricket.

Like many 18-year-old boys leaving a Wellingborough comprehensive school in the mid-1990s, the last thing I wanted to do with my life was to continue in education. The possibility of leaving school and starting work was liberating.

And so it was that, much to my parents' disappointment, I collected a mediocre set of A levels on results day, did not go to university and instead started a new life working in a builders yard selling bricks and cement, happily enjoying the daily banter and the opportunities that £100 a week could bring. There was only one thing I was sure of in life: I was never going to become a teacher. I had had enough of education, and the thought of following my parents, grandparents and great-grandfather into the profession was about as appealing as spending another year in the classroom.

ANOTHER TEACHER

Naturally, then, within 18 months I had enrolled on a teaching degree in Leeds. I quickly fell in love with the treasures of working in a primary school through some fascinating school experiences in some of the most challenging areas. My 'Road to Damascus' moment happened while sitting on a pile of timber on a bleak February afternoon in the builders yard, picking splinters out of my numb fingers. The reality of hard work through a cold winter had brought about a dawning realisation that there was more I wanted to pursue in life.

Training to teach in Leeds was a brilliant experience. My degree was in Middle Years, which took me to placements in primary schools across Leeds as well as a secondary experience in Doncaster. I have always had an affinity for Yorkshire – Mum grew up in Leeds and I have early childhood memories of my grandparents' house next to Headingley Cricket Club, where my grandad spent many hours of his life – and I loved the diversity and vibrancy of Leeds at this time. I met a proper Yorkshire girl, Adele (she even pronounced Bradford as 'Bratfud' back then), and we started applying for our first teaching jobs together. I think it was around this point that someone pressed the fast-forward button on life and it all started to get very grown up very quickly.

I had a really enjoyable year as a newly qualified teacher (NQT) at Windmill Primary School in Raunds, getting used to the pace of school life and the hours of planning and preparation that were to become a part of my life (along with an introduction to the staffroom politics that can exist in a primary school). My induction to the profession began in the car park with a greeting of 'Welcome to the madhouse' cried through a window by my new mentor, and included a welcome from one of the more long-standing teachers with the sage advice that social lives were overrated anyway. I learned a lot at Windmill and although I was only there for a year, I still feel part of that school and have friendships there that have lasted all this time.

At the end of the year, family circumstances took us back up to Leeds, where I spent three years working in Year 6 at a high-performing, multicultural city school – a complete step change to rural Northants. As well as the obvious differences within the local community, I was struck by the professional culture of the school: there was a real sense of drive and high expectation, and I learned so much from teachers of the highest calibre whom I still use as a benchmark for what 'great teaching' looks like.

It was here that I fell into a leadership position – more through coincidence than design (more about that later) – and then was fortunate to be supported to get a post with Leeds City Council working as an advanced skills teacher (AST). Of all of the different acronyms that I have held, working as an AST was the most enjoyable and useful, as I had one day a week just to work alongside other teachers who, for a variety of reasons, needed some support in the classroom. It was great fun and really rewarding, and I learned so much from being inside the classrooms of other teachers in other schools.

WELCOME TO HOLLAND

It was at this point that Adele and I decided to get married and teach abroad. We both had a bit of an itch to travel and see the world, so we applied for jobs in Dubai. Our grand plan was to teach there for four or five years, travel the world in the holidays and come back with some money in the bank and a great suntan. But it didn't work out like that.

It started brightly – we were young and DINKY (double income, no kids yet), and it felt so exciting living in the luxury and opulence of Dubai. Weekends were spent in the desert or at beach clubs, and evenings having dinner at one of the many five-star hotels. The school experience was really interesting and such a contrast to teaching in England. But all that glitters is not gold; and before long, we started to get glimpses into some of the exploitation and prejudice on which the city is built, seeing workers from India and Sri Lanka being treated in ways that felt alien to us in the UK. It started to feel a bit hollow – like a city still trying to find its soul – and I remember England feeling like a very 'green and pleasant land' when we returned in the holidays.

And then along came Freddie – perhaps a bit earlier than was written in the life plan – and everything changed again.

One of my favourite pieces of writing is called 'Welcome to Holland'.[7] It is written by the mother of a child with Down's syndrome and describes the process of coming to terms with a child's disability as getting

7. Kingsley, EP, 'Welcome to Holland' (1987), www.our-kids.org/Archives/Holland.html.

on a plane expecting to go on holiday to Rome, but instead touching down to find out you have arrived in Holland. The author compares the experience of raising a child with a disability to the realisation and disappointment of not being able to see the Coliseum, gondolas in Venice and Michelangelo's David, and learning to appreciate your new surroundings: 'It's just a different place. It's slower-paced than Italy, less flashy than Italy. But after you've been there for a while and you catch your breath, you look around ... and you begin to notice that Holland has windmills and Holland has tulips. Holland even has Rembrandts.'

Our arrival in 'Holland' came unexpectedly in the delivery room at Kettering General Hospital. Freddie's almond-shaped eyes and a mother's instinct gave the game away to Adele, who called it within seconds of his birth. We'd had no idea.

We returned to Dubai with our precious bundle and started our different life. But despite the best intentions of everyone, illness and complications with Freddie meant that a premature return to the UK was inevitable.

> *If you spend your life mourning the fact that you didn't get to Italy,*
> *you may never be free to enjoy the very special,*
> *the lovely things about Holland.*

Emily Perl Kingsley

LEAVING THE DESERT

After our time in the sun, I returned to deputy headship in Northamptonshire and experienced first-hand the challenges of working in tough communities without the kind of funding and support structures of the cities. Arriving with the confidence that I could handle difficult behaviour and understand high needs, it was a humiliating experience to start with, as my new class regularly wiped the floor with me. It was a tough but rewarding time, and a good reference point to remind me how difficult genuine school improvement is in communities that have been systemically failed by society over generations and whose challenges continue to be neglected and underfunded today. There are no magic bullets to solving these problems.

And then somehow, in September 2008, I found myself standing outside the school gates of Little Harrowden Primary – a 30-year-old head teacher in a new Next suit brimming with enthusiasm, promise and naivety.

It was a funny time stepping up to headship. Having jumped successfully through the hoops of interview, I spent months dreaming, talking and planning about what it would be like. I met the staff, appointed a few new faces and duly delivered the most energetic training day of my life, making dreams and promises about the future. And then, at some point on the morning of the first day, the adrenalin faded. The nervy hustle and bustle with parents at the school gate was over, and after visits to see the children and teachers who were now officially 'mine' came a dawning moment of realisation at the magnitude of what I was now responsible for and the potential implications if I messed up: 'What on earth do I do now...?'

THE BEST JOB IN THE WORLD?

I think that in total, over the last 20 years, I have visited or worked in more than 100 schools in different countries and continents, learning something new from every teacher, classroom and setting along the way. I have been involved in some genuine successes, with many achievements I am proud of, and have worked with some of the most amazing people who carry out astounding work every day. I have listened to children sing and watched them perform on sports fields; celebrated successes that no one believed were possible; and had the privilege to stand at the front of the hall and lead assemblies with my school community. I will treasure the memories from these years forever. There is no other job like it.

But alongside these great times have come testing challenges and spectacular lows. Dealing with death and tragedy within the school community, realising that a colleague was defrauding the school and trying to keep the school afloat under intense financial pressure are examples that spring to mind. Standing at the funerals of children, parents and colleagues is a reminder of the harsh reality of life and our fleeting existence. As well as these external tests, I have worked through my own challenges with the job, battling with periods of anxiety and experiencing complete burnout at one stage.

These days, though, I sleep well at night. I can look in the mirror and have confidence that I (mostly) know what I am doing and can handle (almost) anything that comes my way tomorrow. I no longer agonise over difficult meetings or conversations, and it has been a long time since I've panicked over what shirt I should wear on the training day or what the staff will think of me if I wear trainers rather than shoes.

Most importantly, I have learned that a successful career is of secondary importance to a happy family, and am more committed than ever to finding the right balance in life so that I can be a good enough dad to Freddie, Stanley and Ellen.

Ten years of headship have brought the richest experiences and challenges to my life. When I am grey and wrinkly, I hope that I'll look back at these days with a warmth and appreciation. As Granddad used to say, 'It's all part of life's rich tapestry.'

Section 2

Leading with your Heart

*Know what you stand for.
Believe in what you do and who
you are. Create the right ethos
and professional culture and lead
careful change effectively.*

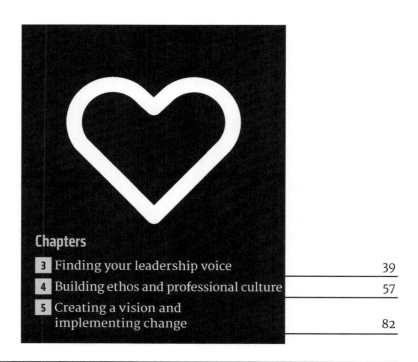

Chapters

Finding your leadership voice

3 CHAPTER PREVIEW

The 'super-head' narrative is not only unhelpful, but also untrue. Often the success in these 'turnaround' schools is short lived as it's built on the character of a leader or leaders being present and hands-on.

Although leadership is ultimately about influencing others, the starting point is to understand ourselves better.

We often hear people talk about their values and beliefs as though they are interchangeable terms, but what do they mean and what is the difference between the two?

At its heart, we should remember that our role as teachers and leaders is one of public service.

In the end, people will remember us for who we are more than what we did.

AND ONE FROM THE INTERVIEW INSIDE

*I don't think any leadership skills are 'naturally inherited';
I think leadership skills are learnt. I'm not sure leadership
skills can be taught, but they can be learnt.
Leadership is largely about confidence.*

Interview with Peter Hall-Jones

FINDING YOUR LEADERSHIP VOICE

> " People can't live with change if there's not a changeless core inside them. The key to the ability to change is a changeless sense of who you are, what you are about and what you value.
>
> Stephen Covey

It is January 2002 and I am in my second year of teaching in a thriving multicultural Leeds primary school, which has just survived an Ofsted inspection.

In fairness, we did more than survive: to achieve 'Very Good with Excellent Features' was a pleasing and well-deserved outcome for what is a mostly brilliant school. In terms of the wellbeing and morale of the team, however, 'survived' feels like an accurate description. I have never experienced anything quite like it in terms of stress and anxiety in a workplace; but also the strong sense of camaraderie that the work has brought to our team. Despite the friction that exists between some, this is a group of people who all want the school to do well and are dedicated to their work. Late nights and weekends for most of October were tough but rewarding, and I have never seen the corridors and classrooms look so pristine!

Here in 2002, for those too young to remember, an Ofsted inspection is more of an occupation than a smash-and-grab raid. A team of eight came to stay for the whole week and three months' notice was given, which means that every plan, set of minutes, display and marking comment produced since September has been written primarily for external eyes. The process has taken its toll on the staff and two senior leaders have stepped down from the senior leadership team (SLT), leaving a vacant Key Stage 2 coordinator post for which no one has applied, despite two rounds of internal ads.

And so, despite my complete inexperience and lack of credentials or qualifications, I find myself in the head's office expressing an interest in the role.

I have to build up the courage to go in and have the initial chat. The first time, I walk straight past her office and pretend I am going to the photocopier. On the second occasion, I do an about-turn, as though I have forgotten something back in my classroom. Finally, I knock awkwardly on her door and then mumble something about knowing that it is a bit of a long shot, but that potentially I could be better than no one at all and perhaps some of my experience captaining a cricket team might be useful.

So somehow, after only 15 months of teaching experience and just three months at the school, I find myself responsible for a key stage full of experienced and highly capable teachers whose Yorkshire plain speaking and occasional abrasiveness (which I will come to love) are already proving a challenge. They know the politics, the families and the children better than me, and I get the feeling that some are enjoying seeing the enthusiastic new kid on the block flapping around.

I have a job description that tells me what I need to do; but who is it that I'm supposed to be?

WHO ARE YOU?

Although leadership is ultimately about influencing others, the starting point is to understand ourselves better. Building self-awareness is essential in ensuring that we understand what we want to achieve in our life and, most importantly, how we go about it.

I believe that the vast majority of school leaders come into the job with a clear sense of purpose; but without a sense of leadership identity to guide our daily behaviours and decision-making, it is easy to lose this focus. There are three important questions that we should ask ourselves along the way:

- Who am I?

- Who do I want to become?

- What do I want to be remembered for?

Taking on a new role can bring a shift in self-perception and an adjustment in existing relationships, particularly for those who are stepping up a level in the same organisation. Inevitably, this can make the heart beat faster – we all want to prove to ourselves and to others that we can do a good job. New questions and doubts can creep into our daily thought patterns. Am I credible? Can I do this job? How should I talk? What should I wear? I'll never be able to do that like him/her…

For the self-aware, leadership can be a self-conscious business, especially when starting a new role.

WHAT DO YOU STAND FOR AS A LEADER?

At the heart of our everyday actions and decision-making lie our values and beliefs. These act as our moral compass that guides us in all we do. We often hear people talk about their values and beliefs as though they are interchangeable terms, but what do they mean and what is the difference between the two?

DEFINITION

Values and beliefs

- Values are a set of principles or a moral code that helps us to define what is important in life (eg, being honest and hardworking).
- A belief is an internal feeling that something exists or is true, even though that belief may be unproven or irrational (eg, that walking under a ladder brings bad luck or that there is life after death).

Our values are likely to endure and stay with us for life: some things that I value specifically –such as honesty, hard work, cooperation and collaboration – are enduring and have not changed much throughout my working career. With experience and age, however, our values can evolve. Since having a child with Down's syndrome, for example, I have more empathy for families affected by disability. Working in a school with particularly high levels of deprivation has likewise altered my values, making me think more compassionately about the difference that we can make to those in society with the greatest need.

Our beliefs, on the other hand, are likely to change as we go through life and are presented with more experiences or evidence that changes our minds. As a child, I used to believe in Father Christmas, until at the age of around ten I was sadly presented with enough evidence to make me change my mind. I also used to believe that I would win the National Lottery and play cricket for England, until the reality of this not happening and rational thought eventually got in the way.

Progress is impossible without change, and those who cannot change their minds cannot change anything.

George Bernard Shaw

Within schools, several of the beliefs that I have held over the years have also changed. Early in my teaching career, I believed that detailed daily lesson planning was a sign of being a good teacher. These days, I believe that experienced teachers don't need to produce lengthy written plans to teach effectively. When the iPad came out, I believed that this would revolutionise the classroom (I think I wrote a blog post about them being a 'game-changer' in education); now I'm far less sure about their place in the primary classroom.

I also used to believe that leadership was something that you were either naturally good at or not. Now I believe that, like most things, leadership is developed through training, time and conscious practice. It is important to recognise that our beliefs can and will change throughout our lives, as otherwise we can find ourselves entrenched and resisting reason. At the end of this line are the leaders who are so defined by their beliefs that they become obstructive; where once they may have been part of the solution, they become the problem.

The best leaders I know are defined by their enduring values and, while they may have strong and passionate beliefs, they remain open to change over time as they are presented with new experiences or evidence that contradicts their beliefs.

TAKE A LOOK AT YOURSELF AND MAKE THAT CHANGE

When I was in my mid-20s, a good friend gave me a copy of Stephen Covey's *The 7 Habits of Highly Effective People*[8] at a time when I was struggling a bit with direction in my life. I was initially sceptical, as I had never read a self-help book in my life before; back then, Harry Potter and John Grisham were about all that was on my reading list. It might sound a cliché, but I think that book really did change my life. Although I have read lots of books about education and leadership since, I have revisited this one several times over the years – each time taking something different from it. One key theme is the 'inside out' approach: the concept that any change starts from within. Covey lists 'Beginning with the End in Mind' as one of his seven habits and it is a great way of thinking about our values and beliefs.

---

8. Covey, S, *The 7 Habits of Highly Effective People* (Free Press, 1989).

I'm starting with the man in the mirror, I'm asking him to change his ways. And no message could have been any clearer. If you wanna make the world a better place, take a look at yourself and make that change.

Michael Jackson

Try this visualisation exercise to help with this important business of working out what you stand for, adapted from Covey's chapter on 'Beginning with the End in Mind'.

Imagine your leaving party

- Think ahead to the day when you finally retire from teaching. Picture the occasion in the school hall. Perhaps there are a few sandwiches and cakes on a table on one side, teas and coffees on the other. Imagine yourself mingling in the room with colleagues you have worked with over the years, family and friends. Now someone calls everyone to attention and a few key colleagues step forward to say a few words about you and your contribution.

- Write down the names of a handful of people who you imagine might talk about you. Include someone you haven't met yet.

- One by one, think about what you hope they will say and write down as many of the words and phrases that feel most important to you. Don't feel embarrassed to write down praise or accolades – remember, the point of the exercise is to identify what you hope people might say, so this should be positive!

- Once you have a page full of phrases and words, circle or highlight those which are most important to you.

These words that you have identified can then become the basis of your 'to-be' list – a much more significant list than the thousands of 'to-do' lists to which we can easily become enslaved. Once we can work out who we are or who we want to become, we can go about living and leading like that for the rest of our lives.

In the end, people will remember us for who we are more than what we did.

LEADERSHIP STYLES

The model set out in Table 1 explaining six different leadership styles is commonly used within schools and businesses, and was brought to prominence through Daniel Goleman, who is widely renowned for his work on emotional intelligence.[9] Each style has a different impact on the emotional state of the organisation and the individuals within it.

Goleman argues that self-awareness and intra-personal skills are critical and examines the effect that these different styles have on emotions in the workplace. Many of us can quickly think of managers or leaders we have worked with who lacked the 'people skills' to be effective in their roles. The most successful leaders are always those who have become adept and handling people well.

Many people with IQs of 160 work for people with IQs of 100, if the former have poor intrapersonal intelligence and the latter have a high one.

Daniel Goleman

Table 1. Goleman's six leadership styles

Six leadership styles	Modus operandi	Style	When style works best
Coercive	Demands immediate compliance	Do what I tell you	In a crisis, to kick-start a turnaround, or with a problem employee
Authoritative	Mobilises people towards a vision	Come with me	When changes require a new vision, or when a clear direction is needed
Affiliative	Creates harmony and builds emotional bonds	People came first	To heal rifts in a team or to motivate people during stressful circumstances
Democratic	Forges consensus through participation	What do you think?	To build in or buy consensus, or to get input from valuable employees
Pacesetting	Sets high standards for performance	Do as I do now	To get quick results from a highly motivated and competent team
Coaching	Future	Try this	Strengths

Source: Leadership that gets results (Goleman, 2000)

---

9. Goleman, D, *Emotional Intelligence* (Bantam Books, 1995).

Question: Which of these leadership styles do you feel that you naturally fall into? Which do you recognise in other leaders? Which do you feel are most effective and why?

Of these six styles, research carried out by the Hay Group suggests that four have a net positive impact on the workplace climate, with the other two overall having a negative effect.

Table 2. Impact of leadership styles on workplace climate

Leadership style	Overall impact on climate
Coercive	−0.26
Authoritative	0.54
Affiliative	0.46
Democratic	0.43
Pacesetting	−0.25
Coaching	0.42

Here, we see that coercive and pacesetting leadership styles were found to have a predominately negative effect on the workplace climate, whereas authoritative, affiliative, democratic and coaching styles were made a positive contribution.

The two overall negative styles on workplace climate are commonly used when leaders have not yet developed a secure sense of their leadership identity. Typically, therefore, they try to influence others either through their status to enforce change (coercive) or by trying to lead from the front at an unsustainable pace, working every hour given and hoping that others will follow suit and become the same type of teacher or leader (pacesetting). Both of these styles inevitably lead to failure. Coercion – while useful in certain turnaround situations, fire drills and other life and death moments – breeds resentment among staff and can lead to toxic staff cultures where compliance rules and commitment and creativity are stifled. Pacesetting, by contrast, often means that while the leader is calling all the shots and trying to get everyone to keep up with their expectations, others cannot think for themselves or contribute to the strategy and therefore become burnt out or disillusioned.

SITUATIONAL LEADERSHIP

The remaining four styles that have an overall positive effect are a good starting point for us to reflect on the way we lead. These leadership styles should not be seen as permanent states of being, more as different tools to be used at different times. Goleman likens these styles to having a range of golf clubs in the bag which can be selected to suit particular conditions or situations. Just as seasoned golfers can switch clubs to play the conditions, skilled leaders can use the right leadership style at the right time with the right people to get the right result. But even those leaders who are skilled in situational leadership are likely to still develop one or two prominent styles which will inevitably contribute to their overall approach. This is where self-awareness is important: skilled leadership is not necessarily about being able to deliver in each style, but about being able to recognise our strengths and weaknesses so that we can ensure that others within the team have strengths to balance against ours.

For example, one really effective head teacher I have worked for led with an authoritative style: the vision and strategy were sound and well thought out, and there was real clarity in the school. He had also built a great culture in which there was harmony among the staff, who really bought into the place as a result of affiliative and democratic leadership styles at times. But coaching leadership was a deficit area for this head: other staff were not being developed enough to progress either within the school or at other schools. Over time, the head became self-aware of this and invested in the coaching abilities of others in the SLT so that they could develop the future talent in the school. No one can be all things to all people, but people still need all things.

KEEPING YOUR UNDERPANTS ON THE INSIDE...

One of the most unhelpful narratives around education in recent years is the notion of turnaround leaders – often hailed in the press as 'hero heads' or 'super-heads'. The story goes that schools in difficulties can be rescued by these astonishing individuals who, after transforming a school in a matter of months, can then move on to bigger and better things, safe in the knowledge that now the school has been 'turned around', things are plain sailing for those left behind.

The 'super-head' narrative is not only unhelpful, but untrue. Often, the success in these 'turnaround' schools is short lived, as it is built on the character of a leader or leaders being present and hands-on. I have the utmost respect for those who go into schools in special measures or difficulties, but it can often be a much simpler job to do the turnaround work as long as you are strong enough to make tough calls and tackle difficult staffing issues. More challenging is to stay and see the job through over a period of years after the quick wins have been secured and honeymoon period has passed. Wearing capes and underpants on the outside of your trousers should be saved for Comic Relief, if at all.

In fact, the more we dig, the more we discover that the most successful leaders might not be the charismatic extroverts that society has led us to believe at all. The most successful leaders are often those who recognise that their role is to bring out the best in those around them, at times playing second fiddle to the talented but less experienced leaders in their ranks. Jim Collins described the most effective leaders as 'Level 5 leaders': people in whom 'genuine personal humility blends with an intense professional will'.

HERO LEADERS?

The best leaders, in my experience, are not necessarily those who sit at the top of the league tables or have the most glowing inspection reports. They are not those who spend their time on the speaker circuit or those with the loudest and most authoritative voices. Nor are the best leaders necessarily those with the best titles or the most expensive shoes, or those sitting at the most impressive desks. Of course, these things in themselves are not markers of bad leaders – it's just that they are not useful proxies of genuinely good leadership.

Despite what the media says, the greatest leaders I know aren't super-heads, trouble-shooters or turnaround specialists. They don't move from school to school, leaving a trail of overnight successes in their wake; they haven't discovered a revolutionary new approach; and they don't have a magic formula that they can sprinkle on schools which 'just works'.

More often, the best leaders I know are those who have remained committed to an important challenge and have seen it through over a significant period. Rather than seeking the headlines or limelight, they are happy to do tireless work in the shadows, knowing that the measure of real success lies not today but in the future, and in the sustainability of their approaches and through their successors. The best leaders I know are human beings with compassion, humility and intelligence. If they do have a 'secret sauce', it is often that they were once committed and successful teachers themselves and have managed to retain their enjoyment of teaching throughout their careers.

Management is doing things right; leadership is doing the right things.

Peter F Drucker

SERVICE LEADERSHIP

At its heart, we should remember that our role as teachers and leaders is one of public service. Regardless of which school, trust or local authority we might feel we belong to, ultimately we are all paid by the taxpayer to serve all children in our country. Competition between different schools or groups of schools is simply a motivational game that we are often drawn into playing and does not necessarily have the desired impact; a focus on whether we are doing better or worse than each other prevents us from thinking about whether we are getting better or worse overall.

Life's most persistent and urgent question is,
'What are you doing for others?'

Martin Luther King

In my first headship, the school log books were still kept in the school safe from the days when part of the head's role was to record what happened each school day. These were not only a fascinating resource to share with the children when studying the world wars, but also a great way to get some perspective on life. Once I got over the fact that every head teacher up to around 1960 had far better handwriting than mine, I enjoyed reading the entries from the past. There were wartime days when school started late in the morning to allow everyone to sleep after night time air raids; days when the number on roll doubled due to evacuees; days with almost no attendance due to outbreaks of infection in the village; and family names through the years which brought home the importance of school to the community over the generations since it opened in 1661.

Although leading a team or sitting in the head's chair can sometimes feel like being at the centre of the universe, perspective such as this is a reminder that heads and leaders are simply the temporary custodians or stewards of a school, which in turn is an important but relatively small cog in something much more significant.

That said, there is nothing wrong with seeing leadership in schools as a career. We need talented and driven people in our system, as long as this ambition is checked by a sense of values and underpinned by a commitment to the wider cause. And if we must aspire to heroism as a desirable concept, perhaps we could see real heroes as those who dedicate their lives to the service of the families and communities they serve and to making a little positive dent somewhere in the universe.

Rank does not confer privilege or give power. It imposes responsibility.

Peter F Drucker

AN INTERVIEW WITH PETER HALL-JONES

As a young student in 1997 arriving at my first teaching practice in inner-city Leeds, I was greeted at reception by a tall, enthusiastic and energetic head teacher who quickly enthralled me into his mission. Until this initial fortnight at Little London Primary, I really wasn't sure that teaching was for me. By the time I left, I had already fallen in love with the challenges that working in both a primary school and a deprived community offers.

Little was I to know that this head teacher, Peter Hall-Jones, would continue to inspire me long after this experience and I am pleased that we have remained in touch for the 20 years since then. These days, Peter travels the world coaching and developing leaders in schools, businesses and governments. I spoke to him to find out more about how leaders develop their sense of identity.

TR: One of the things that I know you spend a lot of time doing is helping people to find their identity as a leader. How do you go about starting this type of work with school leaders in particular?

PH-J: The school leaders I work with have usually identified one (or more) of the following three main reasons that leads them to work with me:

- an irritability or dissatisfaction with merely 'killing themselves' on the 'stuff' that fills their inbox, diary, days, evenings and weekends;

- an inconvenient (often blurred and bruised) belief or aspiration of school, education or themselves as something bigger and better; or

- a degree of crisis or victimhood through perceived 'bullying' by one or more of the different stakeholders, opinion holders or establishment drivers for so-called 'improvement'.

There are other reasons why colleagues choose to take time on developing their leadership self; but all routes and reasons often lead to a paper-cluttered, data-wallpapered, spreadsheet-ever-ready, file-laden room with us facing each other over cups of coffee, digestive biscuits, a box of tissues and a mutual shared love of learning, kids and staff.

With this purpose in place – to better live out and lead towards a greater goal – our journey can begin. So my work in helping to develop a leadership identity starts first with a discussion around 'How it is' and 'How we would like it to be'.

TR: *We often hear the phrase 'natural leader' or 'born leader', which I think can be a barrier for those who feel that they might never live up to the standards of others. How much of leadership do you think is to do with naturally inherited skills or instinct and how much can be learned?*

PH-J: I don't think any leadership skills are 'naturally inherited'; I think leadership skills are learned. I'm not sure leadership skills can be taught, but they can be learned. Leadership is largely about confidence:

- confidence in what is right;

- confidence in a vision and values;

- confidence in self;

- confidence in others; and

- confidence not to assert certainty.

So for me, confidence is the root of leadership: appropriate, humble, compassionate, 'just' confidence. As Lou Tice puts it, 'You can't have too much self-esteem, but you can wear it inappropriately.' So confidence that is borne out of knowledge, insight, experience and love – confidence that is shared with compassion, respect, empathy and a belief that (again as Lou Tice says), 'They are clever enough if I am good enough.'

This confidence as agency or self-efficacy is evident in pretty much everyone I have ever met. The humblest and smallest of people quietly and self-consciously show it in so many fields.

The loudest and most seemingly confident leaders to me are often those most anxious about their right or base to lead from. They often seem to overcompensate for this anxiety with 'bombastic certainty', which – though sometimes initially attractive and reassuring – can quickly become intimidatory, arrogant and thus ignorant. Ironically, this ultimately inauthentic leadership is unlikely to cause others to follow, but rather encourages the 'follower' to attack, undermine or move away from the leader (and her or his goals).

TR: I know that you work with leaders from within education and across industry. What are the main lessons that schools can learn from leaders outside of the education sector?

PH-J: That we are not alone; that we are not unique; that we are not first.

My daughter recently came home and told me that all people share 91.9% of common DNA. She may have got this wrong – at 14, she's prone to exaggeration – but all of us have more in common than in difference. Leadership at home is not that different from leadership in the workplace. All my work with leaders across all sectors around the world points to this commonality, which is as reassuring as it is exciting, for it celebrates the skills of the most effective school leaders and gives us the confidence to share our learning and hunger with others. Equitably.

I sometimes wish that school leaders could be as sublimely/ruthlessly efficient and aligned in our systemisation of process as many of the leaders I have worked with in commerce and industry. But such certainty can soon become unattractive and ignorant; and in cases where leadership becomes certain and arrogant, I guess many businesses go bust.

However, the systems and tools, acronyms and software often used in commercial and industrial leadership – which serve as evidence of investment in leadership development – are perhaps less evident in schools. When school leaders spend money on leadership development, there is a perception that they are 'taking it away from the pupils'. Investing effectively in leadership is something that commercial leaders do more confidently than I think many school leaders believe they can 'morally' afford to do. This, for me, is perhaps the single biggest difference. I think that many school leaders can learn from and ponder this.

For me, the most credible and sustainable leaders across all sectors, scales and societies are those who choose to enjoy the life-affirming struggle towards unobtainable perfection. Those humble leaders who know it is about 'considered options', 'imperfect choices' and decision-making based around a clear vision and strong values. As a coach, I am privileged and relieved when our conversations reach the practical alchemy of resolving these imperfect positions; the application of values to decision-making is where the learning (for us both) takes place.

Bringing school and other leaders together as we do to discover their unique solutions through shared and common experiences enables such coaching conversations and relationships to occur in non-competitive, respectful communities of interest and discovery. Through these conversations, leaders from industry and commerce learn as much from the school leaders as school leaders learn from them.

TR: Peter, as someone who has both challenged me and inspired me over the years to look at my style and approach, I'm really interested in how you found yours! You always seem so confident in what you do; did it come naturally to you or were there times as a school leader when you were full of self-doubt and needed help?

PH-J: Thank you, Tom. However:

- I found 'it' first evolved while I was leading;

- I'm still enjoying looking for 'it' while living; and

- I sometimes, annoyingly, lose 'it' when under pressure.

I am confident in my values of loving and valuing people as intrinsically good, but understanding that they may be damaged. I do have a clear vision of a better world – by my terms and values.

As a leader, as much as any other human, my values are and were challenged and my subsequent actions shaped daily through pragmatic, real, often unanticipated, sometimes unimaginable challenges. I saw myself as a leader, not a manager; and I know I have high self-efficacy when it comes to influencing and effecting others.

On a daily basis, all of the above was challenged, threatened, bruised and occasionally celebrated.

I learned whose opinions to sanction. I learned who I wanted to be sanctioned by. I identified markers, behaviours, responses, actions, achievements and goals that I would choose to measure myself (us, the school) against. I worked out what my contribution, and that of others, to the alchemy was.

I discovered – somewhat later than most – the game of Tetris. I learned what shape brick I was and got better at offering to fill only those gaps that my brick would best fit. I got better at working out and seeing what shape brick others were and the gaps they might best fit too. I encouraged them to do so, and got better at showing them the bigger picture and how it was aided by them filling a gap elegantly and importantly.

I slowly (honestly!) began to listen more and talk less. I tried to sanction the negative feedback as purposefully as I tried to sanction the positive.

Doubt was the driver of innovation. Innovating was more fun and healthier than wrestling the negative.

I didn't eat that well. I didn't sleep that well. I chose to call this 'creative energy', not 'stress'; but I didn't manage to completely convince myself – or others – all the time!

TR: Thanks for sharing your thoughts, Peter – it's been great, as always, to talk to you. Finally, if you had three pieces of advice to give to leaders starting out on their journey and finding their feet, what would they be?

PH–J: First, never use a sentence that starts with:

- I should...

- You should...

- We should...

- I must...

- You must...

- We must...

- I have to...

- You have to...

- We have to...

That's because each of these sentences pretty much has to end with the words '...or else'! Live your life, lead and let others be motivated by 'want-tos'. There are no 'have-tos' beyond, I think, blinking and dying (perhaps there are some others). Lead by finding the reason and the motivation for others as to why they would 'want to...'. It's that simple.

Second, remember that they really are clever enough if we are good enough. It's down to us.

Third, while it's your (chosen) job to get things done, that doesn't mean you have to be the one to do them. There may well be others who can do them better or with more credibility. Lead like a GP: ask, listen analyse, diagnose, prescribe – but get someone better qualified or more experienced to deliver the medicine/surgery/therapy/injections.

IN SUMMARY – FINDING YOUR LEADERSHIP VOICE

- Are you clear about what you stand for as a leader? Have you defined the values that you stand for and are you clear about the educational beliefs that you hold?

- What is it that you want to be remembered for in life? In your job? As a leader?

- Are you self-aware of your leadership styles? Can you use different styles of leadership in different situations? Do you have any deficit styles of leadership that you need to ensure are balanced across the team you work in?

- Among all the different styles you use and hats you wear, can you keep a sense of authenticity and 'you' within your work? The unique range of skills, experiences and interests that only you have is important, and playing to your strengths is definitely allowed in leadership.

FIVE FIVES GRID FOR PLANNING

FIVE MINUTES: What immediate first steps can you take?

FIVE DAYS: What short-term actions can you take in the next week to kick start or plan change?

FIVE WEEKS: What actions or follow-up meetings/discussions can you plan for in the next half-term?

FIVE MONTHS: What follow-up and follow-through activities do you need to plan to ensure that the change is not just a flash in the pan?

FIVE YEARS: What might your change look like in five years? What structures, systems and processes will you need to amend to ensure that your change becomes embedded in the fabric of your school and is not a passing fad?

Building ethos and professional culture

4
CHAPTER PREVIEW

The words 'ethos' and 'culture' are well used by leaders in education – we all seem to know that they are important, but they are seldom written into development plans or worked on deliberately.

Most of us can point to examples of initiatives or processes in the past that we did 'for Ofsted' or 'for the SLT,' knowing that they were pointless.

An over-focus on consistency and conformity (often driven by a perception of what Ofsted is looking for) leads to a culture of compliance, where people carry out processes without really understanding why.

I remember worrying that I couldn't fall in love with the job because I didn't know what the place was really about. It took the first year for me to really get my head around it.

AND ONE FROM THE INTERVIEW INSIDE

Ethos is the glue; it's something I feel very strongly about. When somebody comes to our school it's the thing I want them to feel from the moment they walk through the door till the moment they leave. It's the thing I want them to step away thinking about.

Interview with Simon Smith

BUILDING ETHOS AND PROFESSIONAL CULTURE

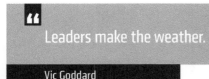

> Leaders make the weather.

Vic Goddard

WORKING ON THE SOIL

The most important things in any school are its ethos and professional culture. Together, they affect the mood, performance and commitment of every individual; they are the 'soil' in which all other things grow. Where the soil in a school is fertile, staff become more motivated, disciplined and connected to the cause. But in stony soil or where acidity is too high, growth is harder and developments can be short lived as roots fail to become established and leaders turn to a series of short-term rescue measures.

The words 'ethos' and 'culture' are well used by leaders in education – we all seem to know that they are important, but they are seldom written into development plans or worked on deliberately. Instead, when schools need improving, it is more common to see a series of short-term initiatives focused on boosting outcomes or jumping through the next inspection hoop rather than identifying the heart of an issue. Booster groups, off-rolling, a narrowed curriculum and a wealth of other school projects are often short-term interventions focused on trying to improve the current year's data or prepare for the next external inspection.

When gardeners see that plants and flowers are not growing healthily, they know that becoming frustrated with the plants themselves or bemoaning the weather is unlikely to help, and that rescue interventions will have a limited effect. Instead, they are better placed to work on the soil – to understand the type, its acidity, the moisture levels and its depth, and to work in the nutrients. This is the best indication of how well things will grow. For real long-term improvement to happen in a school, we must work on the root causes of the big issues, which can be slow, attritional and at times dirty work.

As leaders, it is our job to work on the soil.

The culture precedes positive results. It doesn't get tacked on as an afterthought on your way to the victory stand. Champions behave like champions before they're champions: they have a winning standard of performance before they are winners.

Bill Walsh

AN INTERVIEW WITH SIMON SMITH

For some thoughts around the importance of ethos and culture in a school, I spoke with Simon Smith, principal of East Whitby Primary School. I have followed Simon's blog with interest since he took up headship at the school in 2015 and have always enjoyed the authenticity with which he writes about leading a school.

TR: I've been following your very honest and inspiring blog about life as a primary head for the last few years. You often write about the ethos and culture in your school – how important are these to you and why?

SS: Ethos is the glue; it's something I feel very strongly about. When somebody comes to our school, it's the thing I want them to feel from the moment they walk through the door until the moment they leave. It's the thing I want them to step away thinking about. Ethos and culture are about a collective understanding of what we do, the reasons we do it and what we are trying to do. If the ethos is right, it acts as a lens on the work you do; it helps you to make those difficult decisions; equally, it helps you to say no.

For me personally, it comes back to my moral core: I remember a head teacher a lot wiser than I really challenge me on what it was I believed and made me nail my colours to the post. That discussion has guided every decision I have made since and has often kept me going when the going gets really tough. The ethos of a school is the extension of your moral purpose; equally, it's an extension of everybody's beliefs and hopes.

TR: Almost every leader talks about the importance of ethos and culture in their school, yet this is often an area that doesn't explicitly get worked on – rarely featuring on school improvement plans, for example. What deliberate actions and strategies do you employ to build the ethos and culture at your school, and how do you keep these going among all the other pressures and demands on your time?

SS: We actively put this front and centre last year. Different situations demand different things. When I first came to my current school, there were so many priorities that we had to address – behaviour, in-class teaching, communication, curriculum, assessment and expectations – that, sadly, ethos and culture were put on the back burner. The school had a common thread of caring, but this was actually used as an excuse for low expectation. I suppose, looking back, that the seeds of the school ethos were being shown at that point.

When my new deputy joined (my old one had retired after 38 years at the school), the time felt right to begin exploring what we were really about. Most of the work was about creating a dialogue around the ethos and the culture. We interviewed staff, designed a questionnaire for children and parents, held meetings. We read lots of stuff: Mary Myatt's and Ron Berger's books were very useful in challenging our thinking around expectations. Then we actively took it to staff and children; we talked about what it meant in our classroom, in the playground, everywhere. The key bit was then we followed it up; we stuck to it; we held fast; we demanded/expected. It became a mantra. We enquired into the impact of our ethos and we now use it as a lens on our work. If doing something new doesn't enhance our ethos, then we don't do it.

TR: From reading your blog, it's clear how much emphasis you place on developing the right culture within your school. Where did this come from and is it something that you've always believed in? Have you experienced working in schools where it's been both right and wrong?

SS: I was very lucky: the first school I worked in had a fantastic, well-established culture and as an NQT it was really easy to step into that. It was evident that this was something that had been developed and built over time; the consistency of the head teacher and the staff had allowed that culture to build. There was a real team ethos and a supportive network around me. I never worried about getting stuff wrong, because the culture was there to pick me up; this really allowed me to fly, teaching-wise.

The second school I worked in had no such culture; I was seconded to a school in special measures and within weeks I was on the leadership team. This was great as it let me see a head teacher build a team, a culture and an ethos. This was in a tough school in Middlesbrough (89% eligibility for free school meals), and the head teacher essentially created an 'our school against the world' culture that everybody – staff, pupils, parents – bought into. I have never laughed as much as I did at that school.

Both of these schools helped me to understand what I want from a school, but also why culture is worth the effort. Seeing and feeling it when it works really helped me to understand the what and the whys of its importance; until then, I hadn't really thought about it. Equally, I then worked in a school where the culture was wrong for me. That's an important distinction, I suppose: the culture may be right for the school, but may not be right for you. I had only one choice in that situation, and that was to get out. I stepped away from teaching at that point and became a local authority literacy consultant. This gave me the opportunity to go into lots of schools. In the best, you could feel the culture and ethos from the moment you walked through the door. More often than not, the head set the tone of that culture; but staff and pupils were completely on board, it was threaded through everything. A wise head in Hartlepool once talked to me about the 'golden threads'. If a school ethos is right, it is exactly that.

TR: I was interested in a particular blog post you wrote about joining your school and managing to take the existing staff with you as you implemented lots of change at the school. How did you manage this? Often, a new head with a new vision will result in at least some staff turnover.

SS: I was lucky! It wasn't something I expected to be able to do; it was at best an aspiration. I spent a lot of time initially wandering into classrooms, listening and watching. I got to know staff, parents and pupils. This exploration of the school meant that I developed a clear picture of where we were and an idea of the key challenges and priorities. It meant that staff knew that any decision I made came from a place of knowledge about the school's circumstances.

The chief issue was behaviour: it was challenging and this was impacting on the wellbeing of staff and pupils alike. A new behaviour policy was devised and quickly embedded. Patterns of behaviour were analysed and minor but high-impact changes were made: we restructured lunchtimes, for example, so that all year groups were not on break together. Meanwhile, I made sure I was visible in school and visibly supporting behaviour. I also spoke to parents and we put the onus on them helping us to get it right. The impact in class was almost instant: teachers were able to teach and behaviour improved. The previous behaviour issues were not the fault of staff, as many a 'turnaround head' may assume – it was purely down to the systems. Teachers' confidence was low. To move forward, we had to be honest about where we were, what we were good at and also where we struggled. This took time. I got in classes, I planned with people and we tackled issues together, head-on. It was a process of incremental improvement. And it was a partnership, not a series of top-down changes. Professionals had to feel trusted and valued at whatever stage in their career.

TR: While it's clear that lots of what you have done has been successful, we all make mistakes along the way. Could you share any times when you got things wrong and what you learned from those experiences?

SS: I've genuinely made as many mistakes as I've got things right; I just don't shout about them. There have been plenty of times when I got stuff wrong. One thing I learned very early on in my career is to have the humility to put your hands up and say sorry when you get it wrong. We all need to be able to make mistakes and learn from them. This was/is my first headship, so I made quite a few mistakes. I was particularly guilty of jumping on bandwagons before thinking of the implications. That's something I don't think I do now; but sometimes this led down blind alleys, often meaning increased workload for staff and pretty poor pay-off for the children. I was, for better want of a term, a little too reactive at times, responding to events rather than planning effectively for them. As we've tightened up around our ethos, that is a lot rarer. If it doesn't build on the things we're trying to achieve, then I take a deep breath and say, 'Thanks but no thanks.'

TR: It's been great to talk to you, Simon. Finally, if you had to offer three tips to school leaders as to how they can create the right culture and ethos in their schools, what would they be?

SS:

1. Know your own drivers. What are the things that make you tick? What is your personal moral core? The ethos has to fit within your own beliefs or you can't possibly deliver on it.

2. Get everybody's voice; understand your school and its community. How does the work you do match the aspirations of the wider community?

3. Be relentless about it. Don't compromise on it. Let it be the lens through which you measure your work.

And a cheeky fourth! Define it, celebrate it. We found that defining our school in three words was a great way of distilling down what we were truly about and believed in.

FROM COMPLIANCE TO COMMITMENT AND CREATIVITY

Whatever it is that we lead on in school, it is important to get buy-in from others. Whether it's a new approach to behaviour, a change to break-time supervision or a revised marking policy, we all want people to go along with the plan and do what they are supposed to. 'Consistency' is often talked about as the holy grail in schools, but it is so much more than that. An over-focus on consistency and conformity (often driven by a perception of what Ofsted is looking for) leads to a culture of compliance, where people carry out processes without really understanding why. A crude drive for consistency – often in the form of checklists or non-negotiables – can reduce opportunities for staff to think intelligently and prevent professional growth. Consistency for the sake of consistency is not the answer.

Of course, minimum expectations in a school are needed, usually to do with behaviour and safeguarding; but in a profession such as teaching, where approaches are nuanced depending on the subject or age group which is being taught, the culture must allow for the expertise within the school to be applied with some freedom and sense of professional trust. Without this, managerialism can take over, as Martin Robinson captures brilliantly (and tragically) in the following blog post, entitled 'The 51-year Lesson Plan'.[10]

---

10. martinrobborobinson.wordpress.com/2014/02/04/the-51-year-lesson-plan/

It takes a lifetime to plan, not five minutes. Wherever you plan your lesson, whether it's in your head, on paper, or online, a lesson plan is a struggle, a labour of love, hate, and compromise. It is open to constant revision, it is a dialogue with the past, present and future and will always take longer than the writing of a few words.

An example:

In a school in which I taught the head of D&T was told off for having the following written in his planner:

'Dovetail Joint'

Apparently as a lesson plan it was not detailed enough, it didn't include differentiation, it didn't include assessment, it didn't include levels and he, a very experienced teacher, was told he had not put enough thought into his planning.

Pardon my French but couilles!

He'd been teaching kids to do dovetail joints for years, he knew better than any detailed written lesson plan would ever recognise! This is the sort of silly bureaucracy that wastes so much energy and stresses out experienced staff needlessly.

Then someone pointed out that dovetail joints are unnecessary in the twenty first century and he should be teaching 'how to use a staple gun' or how to read Ikea instructions, brandish Allen keys and a screwdriver. I pointed out we always need Classics and craft and the dovetail joint is a sign of beauty and care that connects us to our past and to quality.

A bit like an old teacher.

Most of us can point to examples of initiatives or processes in the past that we did 'for Ofsted' or 'for the SLT', knowing that they were pointless. It depends on the culture and ethos of the school whether staff feel they can question these and suggest alternatives, or whether they simply tick the boxes publicly and then get on and do what they think is right when no one is watching.

We can find out how fertile the 'soil' is by trying to answer the following simple question: how much do people buy into their work at the school?

Stephen Covey offers us the following levels of buy-in, describing different degrees of commitment that we might see from staff:

- rebel or quit;

- malicious obedience;

- willing compliance;

- cheerful cooperation;

- heartfelt commitment; and

- creative excitement.

Clearly, one of our most important jobs here is to ensure that we can build higher levels of commitment among staff to our school's mission and strategy. If staff bring heartfelt commitment or creative excitement to their work, the job of leading becomes much easier and any approach or initiative is likely to be more successful.

One initial challenge is that it can be difficult to work out exactly where different people's commitment sits on this scale. Those at the two extremes are fairly easy to spot: the rebels tend to make themselves known quite quickly and those with creative excitement are often keen to share their ideas with you. But the middle ground is a place where people generally do what is asked of them, without fuss or opposition, even though their hearts may not really be in it.

Question: Take a minute to reflect on some of the key staff you work with and consider their level of commitment. Is this level of commitment constant or does it change depending on what policy or initiative you are thinking about, or even perhaps on who is leading it?

I always find this exercise interesting and it is good to talk through with other leaders in your school to see how your opinions might differ. Sometimes we become concerned by those staff who offer initial resistance and vocal challenge to initiatives – particularly in situations such as staff meetings. But in my experience, it is often the same people who offer initial challenge and resistance that become the greatest advocates in the long run. The process of challenge and questioning allows for a better discussion and leads to reasoning things through. In fact, if there are no difficult questions, it can be a sign that staff are sitting more around the 'willing compliance' or 'cheerful cooperation' stage of commitment, where they will go along with the ideas without resistance, but without the full commitment that is so important in high-performing schools and organisations.

We can think of these different levels of commitment in four stages (ignoring the rebels or the quitters):

- Coercion: People are forced to do things.

- Compliance: People do what they are told to.

- Commitment: People believe in what they are doing.

- Creative excitement: People believe in what they are doing, have agency to contribute to school improvements and are innovative in their approaches.

Figure 4. The four levels of commitment

ETHOS AND CULTURE

The terms 'ethos' and 'culture' are often used interchangeably, but have subtly different meanings which can be defined in a school context as follows:

- **School ethos:** The fundamental character or spirit of the school; the underlying sentiment that informs the beliefs, practices and thinking of the staff.

- **Professional culture:** The beliefs, attitudes, relationships and habits within and between staff – 'The way we do things around here'.

We can think of these two definitions in the following simplified terms:

ETHOS
What we're here for.

CULTURE
The way we do things here.

ESTABLISHING ETHOS

Many external factors influence a school's ethos. Small village schools, for example, have a very different character from large urban schools; those of particular faith have their own distinction; and some private schools can be entirely different places from typical state schools. Even within each of these different categories, schools can vary significantly in their character and spirit. One school might encourage busy classrooms first thing in the morning, with active learning and plentiful opportunities for talk; while another might insist that children line up in silence in the playground for uniform and planner checks before heading to their classes in silence, where they focus on daily retrieval practice in silence.

Schools also vary in the amount of time and effort spent on defining their ethos. In some cases, the ethos will be deliberately crafted and painstakingly upheld; in others, it will be more organic and a natural product of the staff within the place at that particular time. But a school ethos is too important to be left to chance; it must be worked on consciously and continuously by leaders. In all the schools I know with a distinct character, it exists because leaders have worked hard to define and uphold it.

Kings' Dubai

They were the most bizarre few months of my life: waving goodbye to my class in Leeds in July, getting married in August and then a week later finding ourselves standing at Dubai airport in 50 degrees of heat to start a new life as part of a team opening a new school.

The owner of the school – a local Emirate businessman who had been privately educated in the UK – had a very clear ethos that he wanted to establish based on this experience and had spent millions on the most incredible building, which looked more like a Porsche showroom than a school. Built for just 300 primary pupils, Kings' Dubai came complete with a swimming pool, five-star toilets and the sports facilities of a university – I had honestly never seen anything like it. But although the building made a statement and provided us with inspiration, bricks and mortar are never enough to establish the ethos of a school and it was the job of the new head and deputy to inject character and sentiment into the foundations of this grand design. In the first fortnight before the school opened, there were lots of meetings, social gatherings and opportunities for them to try to establish what the ethos of the school would become. There was a lot of attention to detail. Quite specific dress codes, high-quality resources and talk about how we needed to bring together the high expectations and standards from the private system alongside the innovation that some of us brought from the state sector – all part of creating the specific ethos that existed in the minds of the owner and the senior team.

This ethos became really well established – perhaps more so than at any other school I have worked in. It had a real sense of character and individuality, which became reality over time and as a result of many different actions and interventions. But I will never forget the first full staff meeting as a real defining moment in us understanding how Kings' would be different.

As the building was not yet finished, we were at the owner's offices hoping to get our hands on essentials such as pupil lists, planning formats and timetables. Imagine our surprise when the deputy head walked round and handed us each a watercolour set and sketch book. We then spent the next hour and a half being taught in the use of watercolours – learning technical specifics around brush grip, colour mixing and how to build up blocks of colour slowly.

There were a few sideways glances – partly due to many of us not being great at painting, but mainly because there was a sense that we should have been focusing on the practicalities and logistics of meeting new classes. Shouldn't we be making sure that we have registers, books and pencils sorted, rather than learning to paint?

The staff meeting wasn't really about improving our painting skills; it was a line in the sand that said that art is important, high expectations matter and our curriculum approach would be about doing fewer things better. 'Less is more' became one of our mantras. Going back and learning to paint again also showed us all that even a 'creative' subject relies on the basics being taught really rigorously – it wasn't just something that we could look at as an add-on within the curriculum.

As a result, a tangible sense of character emerged within the staff of what the school was about. Some of the following points became part of what we termed 'The Kings' Way', and in many cases became beliefs that were taken on from Kings' and lived in our practice as we left:

- Art is important and is a defining part of our character.

- Everyone can learn to paint well if they are taught properly and have time to practise.

- You achieve the highest outcomes if you simplify what you are doing and focus on doing it really well.

- Excellence comes where basic skills are secured through high teacher subject knowledge, expert modelling and regular opportunities to practise.

- We will have sky-high expectations within the classroom and a genuine commitment to excellent outcomes.

Simon de Senlis

Defining the school's ethos is important, as it gives a sense of purpose to everyone who works there. In the first school in which I was head teacher, I found the ethos very easy to find and preserve. The school had existed since 1661 and part of it was housed in an 18th century building next to the village church, which dates back to around 1190. The school was a central and focal part of the village, and the previous head had worked hard to establish a sense of drive and ambition within the school and had introduced new technology and fresh ideas within the curriculum. The ethos of the school was clearly about preserving the history and traditions of the school's past, but with an aspiration, openness and energy for the future.

When I started at Simon de Senlis, however, it took me a while before I could really define the ethos of the school. The building was relatively modern and nondescript, and initially felt a bit soulless. I was also uninspired by the school's motto, 'Excellence for all', which I didn't think was translated in either the practice or outcomes for children. I remember worrying that I couldn't fall in love with the job because I didn't know what the place was really about. It took the first year for me to really get my head around it.

One thing I came across was an adopted school song – the hymn 'When a Knight Won His Spurs'. An additional fourth verse had been written by the founding head teacher, Roger Samson, who sadly died shortly after leaving the school some years before. I loved the verse and also the sense of importance that the song had for those staff who had taught with Roger:

> *With hope as my spur and with truth as my sword, I can venture through life to its greatest reward.*
>
> *To be honest and earnest in all that I do, And to know that my life Lord is of value to you.*

In that first year, we ran a curriculum project named 'When a Knight Won His Spurs'. It focused on creative writing and art based on the legend of 'Simon' – a Norman nobleman who, according to history, had been the Earl of Northampton and was responsible for building Northampton Castle and two prominent churches in the town. The children's outcomes from this project were amazing and we celebrated these through an art gallery to which we invited friends and ex-staff of the school. This shared experience helped us to build the ethos of the school and brought a sense of identity and community to us. Since then, we have sung all four verses of 'When a Knight Won His Spurs' on the last day of every term at Simon de Senlis.

Question: Can you describe the ethos of your school? Can you define it in a single sentence? Trying to articulate an ethos in a limited number of words makes us choose each word carefully and be more precise.

CREATING PROFESSIONAL CULTURE

While ethos is critical in establishing the character of the school, it is no sign of success on its own. Schools of all different characters and identities can become successes or failures not due to their particular religious denomination or their 'traditional' or 'innovative' ethos, but due to the quality of professional culture within the staff.

Over the years, I have seen a real range of staff cultures in schools – from the most diligent and professionals who seem to work together like poetry in motion, taking any challenge in their stride, to the most unprofessional and toxic cultures where personal relationships take over and get in the way. At its worst, an unhealthy culture can result in staff being so preoccupied with adult issues that these take precedence over the children.

To return to the model set out in Figure 4, the type of culture we are aiming to develop in a school should avoid coercion and move beyond compliance to a place where staff feel wholeheartedly committed and have creative excitement for their work. In order to achieve this, there are four aspects which I believe are important to understand and develop within our teams:

- healthy relationships;

- disciplined thought and action;

- teacher agency and innovation; and

- solution-focused thinking.

I present these four aspects in figure 6 below as the '4 Planks of great school culture':

Figure 6. 4 Planks of great school culture'

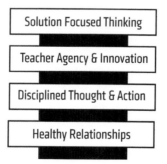

| Solution Focused Thinking |
| Teacher Agency & Innovation |
| Disciplined Thought & Action |
| Healthy Relationships |

Healthy relationships

Relationships among educators within a school range from vigorously healthy to dangerously competitive. Strengthen those relationships, and you improve professional practice.

RS Barth

Relationships between staff in a school are at the heart of a thriving professional culture; when teams and partnerships click, you can almost feel the buzz and synergy that are generated within a school and see the benefits in the classroom.

Many complex factors make up relationships in a school. In Figure 7, I present four component areas of healthy staff relationships.

Figure 7. The components of healthy staff relationships

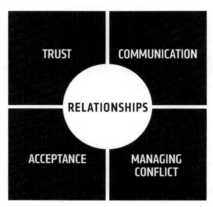

Trust: Trust is at the heart of all effective professional relationships and a key factor in all successful teams. When we have high levels of trust in those around us, our job becomes much easier; we have faith that people will do what they say. Building trust among teams takes time and happens as a result of many small but important deposits that we make with each other every time we keep our word. Trust should never be taken for granted, however, as it can disappear much more quickly than it can be rebuilt. It is therefore important to pay attention to two simple but often overlooked principles:

- Do what we have said we will do.

- Never criticise someone who is not present to explain their perspective.

Communication: In a world where we are bombarded with different information, it is easy for messages to get lost. Often, friction can occur when messages are not received, or are forgotten or misinterpreted. In the wrong culture, this can lead to blame and defensive behaviour. Over-communication is helpful – that is, communicating more than we think we need to, such as following up emails with reminders in briefings of a deadline for reports or curriculum letters, or taking a quick walk around school to give everyone a heads-up in case they had forgotten about the visitor or change of assembly time tomorrow. Good over-communication can also help to build trust, as a friendly reminder helps others to remember that we are on the same side and want each other to succeed.

Acceptance: Every team consists of a diverse number of individuals. There will be different personality types; introverts and extroverts; those with and without children; staff of different ages and interests. Where relationships are not strong, this diversity can be a cause of divisiveness as different cliques emerge. The best relationships exist when people recognise each other's individuality and this is viewed positively, rather than being a cause of frustration. There is a sense that everyone can bring something to the party and, rather than being frustrated that people don't all 'think like me', people value and enjoy each other's different strengths.

Managing conflict: Conflict is draining and rarely associated with positive relationships; but if we don't bring concerns or issues to a head, we never resolve things. Honesty at the point of contact is a useful mantra that I have seen embedded in a school and encourages staff to always talk honestly and openly to others when they are face to face. A 'good disagreement' is a positive and useful exchange and avoids arguments – which, as Dale Carnegie says in the original self-help book, *How to Win Friends and Influence People*[11], are impossible for leaders to win. Carnegie says that if leaders win arguments due to their status or rank, then they never really win as the other party is likely to harbour resentment at losing, which is likely to lead to lower levels of commitment. As Benjamin Franklin said, 'A man convinced against his will/is of the same opinion still.' To win also implies that someone has lost and there is no benefit to any leader in having a culture in which there are 'losers'.

> *You can't win an argument. If you lose it, you lose it;*
> *and if you win it, you lose it.*
>
> **Dale Carnegie**

Developing and repairing relationships: While personal and private relationships are an individual's business, the way we relate to each other professionally is part of our job, so these relationships can and should be worked on deliberately within a school or any professional environment. Working on shared beliefs and behaviours is an essential

---

11. Carnegie, D, *How to Win Friends and Influence People* (Simon and Schuster, 1936).

leadership task. This work cannot be limited to training days in September, but should be evident every day of every week that a school is open.

But even with a shared ethos and healthy professional culture, rarely do all relationships remain plain sailing: the combination of work pressures and human nature makes conflict inevitable from time to time. When this happens, we should feel the same sense of urgency to resolve the situation that Formula One mechanics do when trying to get the car back on the track from a pit-stop. As long as resentment or animosity exists between staff, this will be the overriding thought process and it is likely that children will not be getting the best deal in their classes every day as a result. Whether it is something as informal as a good heart-to-heart conversation or something more formal, perhaps even requiring professional mediation, repairing a broken relationship should always be considered a high priority.

Disciplined thought and action

In schools, when we talk about discipline, we might initially think about children's behaviour or perhaps a 'disciplinarian' leader who leads with 'the stick'. In *Good to Great* by Jim Collins[12], a 'culture of discipline' is highlighted as one of the eight things that exist in truly great companies. Collins says: 'A culture of discipline is not just about action. It is about getting disciplined people ... who engage in disciplined thought and ... who then take disciplined action.'

One of the questions we ask on our staff survey each year is: 'Do staff consistently implement school policies?' In the first year I was at Simon de Senlis, only 38% of staff agreed with this statement. In effect, therefore, it didn't really matter how good the policies in the school were, as the perception was that fewer than half of the staff were carrying them out anyway! This is an example of where many perfectly capable individuals were failing to be effective together because a culture of disciplined thought and action did not exist.

Avoiding bureaucracy: Establishing a culture of discipline has therefore been a key focus at the school. In many cases, our default response is to introduce systems of monitoring and checking; however, this can create very time-heavy processes which don't necessarily address the underlying issue of poor self-discipline. In *Good to Great*, Jim Collins defines this as the 'bureaucratic death spiral' and goes on to emphasise the importance of establishing a culture of discipline:

---

12. Collins, J, *Good to Great: Why Some Companies Make the Leap and Others Don't* (William Collins, 2001).

The purpose of bureaucracy is to compensate for incompetence and lack of discipline – a problem that largely goes away if you have the right people in the first place… Most people build their bureaucratic rules to manage the small percentage of wrong people on the bus, which in turn drives away the right people on the bus, which then increases the percentage of wrong people on the bus, which increases the need for more bureaucracy to compensate for incompetence and lack of discipline, which then further drives the right people away, and so forth.

How often do we see this in schools? Processes such as book scrutinies or planning checklists can become totally overwhelming for everyone, despite the fact that concerns exist only about certain individuals. Collins goes on to describe the alternative to trying to improve performance without having to monitor everything that moves: 'Avoid bureaucracy and hierarchy and instead create a culture of discipline. When you put these two complementary forces together – a culture of discipline with an ethic of entrepreneurship – you get the magical alchemy of superior performance and sustained results.'

Of course, there must be regular checks of important things and every experienced leader will know how painfully true the old saying is that when you start to assume that something is happening, you make an 'ASS' out of 'U' and 'ME'. But this doesn't mean that we need to bury everyone in time-heavy processes which lead to managers sitting at desks typing up monitoring sheets and teachers feeling swamped with complex and over-burdensome monitoring. Instead, we should audit regularly the important 'must-dos' and create regular opportunities for low-stakes checking and evaluation of other areas. If there are issues around lack of discipline, focus on the people, not the systems to rectify this.

Teacher agency and innovation
Building on the foundations of healthy relationships and a disciplined culture, it is important to consider how much self-direction can be afforded to teachers when it comes to their professional development.

'Teacher agency' can be defined as teachers having more ownership of their own professional improvement and contributing to the improvement of others.

In the last ten years or so, we have seen much more of this in the UK as it has become more common for staff to learn more from the work of other teachers through social media or by reading teacher blogs; or by attending professional development events in the evenings or at weekends. Approaches such as lesson study, team teaching and even visiting classrooms in other schools are also becoming more common. We are getting better at having the confidence to encourage teachers to learn from each other rather than simply following procedures and approaches dictated through schemes or government publications, or promoted by 'experts'.

Agency, not autonomy: One of the phrases I have heard increasingly in recent years is 'earned autonomy'. I have used this myself to describe the process of allowing effective teachers or leaders to get on and do the job in the way they think is best without interference from above.

The problem with earned autonomy is that it can give people the impression that once they hit a particular standard (often when they are declared a 'good' teacher or when their children are making 'good progress'), people will stop checking up on them so much and they will be free to use different methods or approaches as they wish. I have seen this end badly at different levels – usually where people or schools stop doing the things that made them successful in the first place and try something else, perhaps in the name of innovation or because chasing an 'Outstanding' Ofsted judgement suggests that you need to be something very different or unique.

Effective teacher agency is subtler than simply saying that staff are free to make a declaration of independence from the systems of the school. It is about having the freedom to play a more self-determining role, but within agreed existing structures and on an existing platform of healthy relationships and disciplined thought and action.

Innovation: While innovation, like creativity, can be interpreted by some to mean 'wacky ideas', the best innovative practices are usually developed within a very disciplined culture. In truly innovative schools, staff are afforded the opportunity to try different approaches or to think differently about how to solve new challenges in their classrooms. Often, teachers need encouragement to think innovatively about things. Whether it is simple things such as timetable changes or new ways of planning or giving feedback, a coaching conversation that gives 'permission' to try these things out can be empowering to staff.

| DEFINITION

Innovation[13]

noun: innovation

■ the action or process of innovating.
  "innovation is crucial to the continuing success of any organization"
  synonyms: change, alteration, revolution, upheaval, transformation, metamorphosis, reorganization, restructuring, rearrangement, recasting, remodelling, renovation, restyling, variation.

Innovation is becoming more and more essential within our system as we try to continue raising educational standards across the country with less money and fewer teachers to go around. These challenges, in the right conditions, can act as 'creative constraints' and make us think more innovatively about how to achieve our goals, perhaps using collaboration opportunities or new technologies to solve challenges such as recruitment or analysing data.

An important point about innovation is that it is not a licence to try anything out that hasn't been thought through. So much is published now through research bodies such as the Education Endowment Foundation (EEF) or via educational books and blogs that there is simply no excuse for us just getting together in a meeting or a staffroom and coming up with a bright idea to put into practice that has not yet been tested or tried out in another school. On almost every issue – whether it's revising approaches to the teaching of reading, behaviour management or communicating with parents – we can build from the successes and mistakes of others.

The early bird may catch the worm, but it's the second mouse that gets the cheese.

Solution-focused thinking

Sometimes in schools we can become consumed by the problems in front of us and, occasionally, this can slide into spirals of negative thought. Of course, it's OK for people to offload at times; but we must not allow our schools to become places where somehow the default setting for individuals or teams is one of perpetual gloom. Evolutionary psychology offers an explanation as to why, as humans, we are prone to focusing on negativity, as the focus on threats was once essential for us to stay alive: a focus on a lack of food, outbreak of illness or threat of a predator would then sharpen our responses and give us a greater chance of survival.

13. Google Dictionary: www.google.co.uk/search?q=Dictionary#dobs=innovation

But thousands of years later, these thought processes can easily become 'doom cycles' that drain energy and can lead to toxic staff cultures.

In order to create a culture where commitment and creativity rule, leaders can establish a resilient 'default positive' – where problems are seen as challenges to be enjoyed and not as being insurmountable. Of course, we don't want to oversteer away from defeatist negativity and into wide-eyed optimism or naivety, as this can lead to a failure to address difficult issues.

A solution-focused mindset is a form of strength-based working and can be a refreshing alternative to the typical 'deficit' model, where our focus is drawn to finding the things that are wrong and then trying to fix them. Strength-based working is a powerful habit to develop and helps in those familiar situations where, at the end of a long day, you find yourself either round a table or in an office somewhere focusing on all the things that need improving. It must be led and modelled by leaders through actions which sound simple, but can be difficult to apply in practice.

Here are five examples of opportunities to flip from deficit to solution-focused thinking:

■ Use coaching questions to flip conversations from focusing on the problems to the solutions. For example, if the discussion is getting stuck on the things that went wrong in class this morning, ask 'What are our options?' to get others thinking about solutions.

■ Focus on the opportunity for personal growth. A tough inspection or set of meetings with governors might be coming up, but it will be an opportunity to develop different facets of leadership through the experience.

■ Try to see problems as challenges and opportunities – this can be a subtle but transformational change of language. Where possible, enjoy the challenge of problem solving rather than lamenting the hard work.

■ With every decision, there will be pros and cons. If you feel that the discussion is focusing too heavily on the cons, shift it on to the potential benefits of each option, rather than the risks.

■ A colleague leaving is always an opportunity for another to grow. Although initially it might feel like someone might be irreplaceable, think positively about the opportunities to develop someone else in the space they leave behind.

'Chop wood, carry water'

Throughout this journey of nurturing a culture in our organisation beyond compliance and into commitment and creativity, one of our key roles as leaders is to remain constant and connected to creating the 'good soil' of ethos and culture: checking the acidity, digging it over, adding the fertiliser and watching for the weeds. This is the important and often unseen work of wholesome leaders which enables the right conditions for personal growth and sustainable school improvement.

An ancient Zen saying goes: 'Before Enlightenment, chop wood, carry water. After Enlightenment, chop wood, carry water.' And it is in the simplest but most important tasks – such as being 'on the gate', making tea for staff at parents' evenings and enjoying playground duties – that we can maintain this connection. There are many ways in school to chop wood or carry water; and of course, for many, this comes through the greatest part of working in a school of all – teaching. It is in these seemingly normal and small things that we can stay connected to the soil of the organisation. The day you walk past litter on the playground or a coat on the cloakroom floor and catch yourself pretending not to see it, you know it's time to reconnect with what matters!

TEN BUILDING BLOCKS FOR GREAT STAFF CULTURE

1. **Build trust** over time through small but important actions, such as doing what you say you will and never criticising someone who isn't there.

2. **Over-communicate** the same important messages to help make sure that everyone hears the main things.

3. **Accept others** and the strengths and weaknesses they bring to the team.

4. **Manage conflict well** with each other. Make sure that differences of opinions can be explored professionally and without defensive behaviour or judgement.

5. **Avoid arguments** as a leader, as you will never win. As Franklin said, 'A man convinced against his will/is of the same opinion still.'

6. **Develop disciplined thought and action** among the staff. A culture of discipline removes the need for time-heavy monitoring processes that breed compliance rather than commitment.

7. **Allow teacher agency** so that professionals feel empowered to unleash their knowledge and expertise in the classroom in a supported environment.

8. **Encourage innovation** that is carefully thought through and research based. Value new ideas from across the team.

9. **Remain solution focused** and 'default positive'. See the many challenges that come your way as opportunities to grow through.

10. **Chop wood, carry water**. Remain connected to the core purpose of the school through simple but important jobs, no matter how high you climb or how impressive your job title.

IN SUMMARY – BUILDING ETHOS AND PROFESSIONAL CULTURE

■ Is there a clear and tangible ethos in the school? Are the character and spirit well defined and understood by its community?

■ How healthy is the professional culture in the school? Is the 'soil' rich and fertile, so that people and ideas can grow?

■ Are there healthy relationships among the staff? Are trust, communication and acceptance of others well established and can you 'disagree well'?

■ Has a professional and disciplined culture been established? Remember, if staff have both disciplined thought and action, there is no need to create bureaucratic management processes of constant checking.

■ To what level does teacher agency exist in the school? To what extent are teachers allowed ownership of their professional development and contribution towards school development? How is this different across the range of experience and competence within the school?

■ Is there innovation in the culture of the school? Are staff encouraged to take managed risks and to try new ideas within sensible parameters? Is there an open dialogue around this or is it something that happens when leaders aren't looking?

■ How solution-focused is the culture? Can you observe more of a focus on problems or solutions in the language of the staff?

FIVE FIVES GRID FOR PLANNING

FIVE MINUTES: What immediate first steps can you take?

FIVE DAYS: What short-term actions can you take in the next week to kick start or plan change?

FIVE WEEKS: What actions or follow-up meetings/discussions can you plan for in the next half-term?

FIVE MONTHS: What follow-up and follow-through activities do you need to plan to ensure that the change is not just a flash in the pan?

FIVE YEARS: What might your change look like in five years? What structures, systems and processes will you need to amend to ensure that your change becomes embedded in the fabric of your school and is not a passing fad?

Creating a vision and implementing change

5 CHAPTER PREVIEW

The starting point for leaders in any organisation is almost always to think about what the future might look like and to bring direction to the work of others.

Often in a rush to create an action plan or just to get on and implement something as a response to a particular challenge, leaders in schools risk working on the practical 'what' without paying enough attention to either the 'how' or 'why'.

Not making time for proper informal consultation is a false economy. Unless ideas are tested early and thought through as a result, the job of implementation is nearly always more problematic and time consuming. As the old saying goes, 'Act in haste, repent at leisure.'.

With appreciative inquiry, more time is spent focusing on gaining a deeper understanding of the organisation, conducting root cause analysis and then engaging staff as owners of school improvement..

Great schools ensure that their compelling, cohesive and coherent vision is woven into the fabric of school life and culture. It's always on the lips of leaders. It starts every meeting and is the yardstick against which progress is measured. The whole community can articulate in their own ways why their school exists and why anyone and everyone should care..

Interview with Peter Ford

CREATING A VISION AND IMPLEMENTING CHANGE

> **❝**
>
> Great things are done by a series of small things brought together.
>
> Vincent Van Gogh

BRINGING DIRECTION

It almost goes without saying that establishing and implementing a vision is at the heart of leadership. The starting point for leaders in any organisation is almost always to think about what the future might look like and to bring direction to the work of others. 'Future' can be a helpful umbrella term for us to think about in schools and trusts, as it catches various different processes in which we are involved, such as visioning, action planning, change management, project management and recruitment. When considering this wide range of activity, leaders spend a large proportion of their time thinking about the future.

DEFINITION

Change[14]

Noun

- an act or process through which something becomes different.

FIRST AND SECOND CREATIONS

In *The 7 Habits of Highly Effective People*[15], Stephen Covey tells us that everything is created twice: once as an idea or vision and the second as an actualisation, when a vision becomes reality. Initiatives in schools

---

14. Google Dictionary: www.google.co.uk/search?q=Dictionary#dobs=change
15. Covey, S, *The 7 Habits of Highly Effective People* (Free Press, 1989)

have the potential to fail at each of these points, either because the idea wasn't any good in the first place or due to poor implementation. It is important to work on both the first and second creations of vision and delivery – ideas and implementation – in order to lead positive change.

- **Vision:** creating and clarifying a better version of the future with others in the school.

- **Delivery:** the implementation, follow-up/follow-through and dogged determination to turn vision into reality.

FINDING OUR 'WHY'

In his widely popular book, *Start with Why*[16], Simon Sinek suggests that organisations find it easy to talk about what they do, but harder to explain how they do it and rarely know why they do it. In his 'golden circle' model, he presents the simple idea that we should always 'start with why' before thinking about the 'how' and the 'what'. Establishing our 'why', Sinek argues, is therefore the most important part of leadership, as it establishes our *raison d'être*.

> *People don't buy what you do; they buy why you do it. And what you do simply proves what you believe.*
>
> ### Simon Sinek

This is so true in schools, where it can be difficult to think strategically if our headspace is taken up with all the day-to-day operational issues. Often in a rush to create an action plan or just to get on and implement something as a response to a particular challenge, leaders in schools risk working on the practical 'what' without paying enough attention to either the 'how' or 'why'.

---

16. Sinek, S, *Start with Why: How great leaders inspire everyone to take action* (Penguin, 2011).

Figure 8. The golden circle

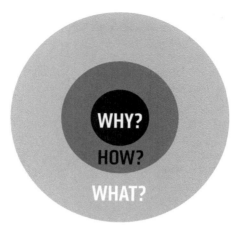

Source: Simon Sinek, *Start with Why*

Why? How? What?

Creating clarity around the vision and direction of our school is crucial, as it helps to connect our daily work to the bigger picture and wider ambitions of our organisation: our 'why'. Terms such as 'vision', 'mission', 'strategy' and 'targets' are all used frequently by leaders – sometimes interchangeably. There are many interpretations of what some of these terms mean and five minutes on Google will reveal countless different pyramids and hierarchies associated with vision, mission and values statements. Table 3 presents my interpretation of some of the different language involved and examples of how these terms can be interpreted through the stages of why, how and what using Sinek's overarching terms and with many ideas I learned through working with change management specialist Graham Smith, one of the directors of our academy trust.

Table 3. Interpreting the school's vision through why, how and what

	Term	Meaning	Example
WHY?	Vision	The overarching view of how we might change the future. Can be brief and should not need revising often. **Why do we exist?**	Educational excellence: enriching lives, creating opportunities. (Northampton Primary Academy Trust)
WHY?	Strapline/motto	A simple phrase or statement which captures the essence or spirit of the organisation and attaches people to the vision and mission. **Why are we here?**	'Making a dent in the universe.' (Simon de Senlis Primary School) 'Achieving extraordinary things.' (Northampton Primary Academy Trust)
HOW?	Mission	A short statement that tells us about how the organisation aims to achieve its vision. **How we will create/achieve in order to bring about the vision that we aspire to?**	'To create a MAT of highly effective and sustainable schools.' (Northampton Primary Academy Trust)
HOW?	Values	As the enduring core values, these ways of being or working are the things we hold dear. These should not need revising often, as they are the enduring values that remain constant **How do we do things**	• Aspiration and ambition • Community • Collaboration • Integrity • Innovation • Hard work
HOW?	Goals and objectives	Specific and aspirational priorities that need to be achieved for the mission to succeed. There will probably be several of these. **How will we know that we are achieving our mission?**	For all children to be able to read at an age-appropriate level by the time they leave primary school. For all children to have learned a musical instrument by the age of 11.
HOW?	Strategy	The tactics and approaches that we will use to achieve our goals (more about this in Chapter 6). **How can we best achieve our goals?**	Establish an evidence-informed approach to the teaching of reading across our schools, including the development of early language. Develop high levels of teacher subject knowledge in reading alongside strategies for enjoyment and wider reading.

WHAT?	Targets	The measures or success criteria that we will aspire to in the shorter term that will help us to achieve our long-term goals. **What will we achieve in the short term to know we are on track to achieve our goals?**	Currently, 65% of children read at an age-related level in our schools. We aim to increase this by 10% each year until all but those with significant and recognised learning difficulties achieve it.
WHAT?	Action plan	A plan which identifies the practical small steps of action that need to take place and the resources required **What specifically will we do and when to achieve our targets and goals?**	Many forms of action plan exist within schools – the only thing they have in common is that someone will always disagree about their format. However, they should include plans over a period of one to two years, and state the targets, actions, cost and measures of success, as well as identifying who is responsible for delivery and for monitoring/checking.
WHAT?	Job List	The short-term actions and priorities that need to happen in order to deliver on the action plan. **What are the tiny steps we need to take this week towards delivering the mission?**	• Book training venue. • Share reading for leadership time from *Reading Reconsidered*.* • Write training programme for senior leaders across schools. • Create staff survey to ascertain existing confidence levels across staff of teaching reading.

* Driggs, C, Lemov, D and Woolway, E, *Reading Reconsidered: A Practical Guide to Rigorous Literary Instruction* (John Wiley & Sons, 2016).

Management is efficiency in climbing the ladder of success; leadership determines whether the ladder is leaning against the right wall.

Stephen Covey

AN INTERVIEW WITH PETER FORD

When I first took on the headship at Simon de Senlis, I found it a challenge to discover the 'why' in the school. It surprised me how hard I found this process, as I had assumed that things like this would be straightforward in a second headship. Having worked previously with Peter Ford, I asked him to come in and support me and the leadership team to help us 'reimagine' the school. Over a year, Peter coached me through a process where we thought a lot about the vision, values and mission of the school. Within this period, we also had an Ofsted inspection which resulted in a 'Requires Improvement' judgement and felt the usual pressures to deliver a quick turnaround. Despite this, we were determined to prioritise the bigger-picture, longer-term work to secure the future culture and ethos of the school. We named this project 'Simon de Senlis Reimagined'.

TR: When you worked with us on 'Simon de Senlis Reimagined', you encouraged us to think more and act less – slowing us down a bit as we were thinking about the new vision for the school. While I found this frustrating at times, in hindsight it was really helpful, as it enabled us to think harder about the specifics of the change we wanted. How important is it for leaders to think more and avoid rushing to action?

PF: Leaders naturally tend towards action and problem solving. However, the discipline of exploring perspectives and thinking deeply about complex change is always time well spent.

An effective school vision is compelling, cohesive and coherent. Communicating vision draws the hearts and minds of a community together and drives action. However, vision generally starts life hidden away in the heart and mind of a leader – an amalgam of nascent ideas, experiences and assumptions. Making these internal thoughts and emotions visible is a crucial developmental milestone. The subsequent deep dive, interrogation and discussion of what a leader believes, bringing the embryonic vision to life in exemplar stories and crafting its precise language, are worth investing time in.

Leaders who take the time to deeply understand their own perspectives on a school's vision – or on any important change initiative, for that matter – are better placed to introduce it with both passion and clarity to their community for feedback. A community that is afforded the same luxury to explore, discuss and question vision is one that is empowered to take ownership from the outset.

TR: You've worked in such a diverse range of places, including schools, local government and some of the world's largest multinational companies. What similarities do you see in the challenges that all of these organisations face when trying to work out what their future looks like?

PF: The most common challenge lies in the tension between successfully executing 'business as usual' while simultaneously investing ongoing energy in exploring the strategic implications of far more ambiguous and distant longer-term horizons.

It can be tempting to view the future as a never-ending succession of tomorrows that relentlessly appear over the short-term horizon. Managing the day to day is, of course, important to success in the short term. Building forward-thinking agility into organisational culture determines relevance over the long haul.

History is littered with once-successful companies that failed to embrace changing futures. One of the saddest is the story of the CEO of Blockbuster Videos, who passed up the opportunity to buy Netflix in 2000. The company's video rental *status quo* was buoyant. Its future was not.

Effective organisations strike a balance between present realities and future possibilities through inspired professional development, research and the implementation of shared processes for innovation and problem finding. Effective leaders ensure that the responsibility for 'working out' the future is shared, viewed through the lens of a coherent vision, and that time is allocated to make it a sustainable process.

TR: Another of the things I learned from working with you was to be better able to receive feedback on my ideas. I can still hear your voice saying, 'Hold your ideas lightly' when carrying out consultations or testing out ideas on people. How difficult is it for people to manage this and how can you help people who find it difficult to receive feedback?

PF: Demystifying the dark art of feedback is at the heart of building a community culture that leverages the collective smarts of its members to improve ideas, experiences and outcomes.

The secret is not to leave feedback up to chance, personality types or the alignment of the stars. Develop a common understanding of its potential, along with shared routines for framing, giving and receiving feedback.

Accompany this shared foundation with an appreciation and implementation of rapid prototyping in the course of testing ideas. Rapid prototypes are 'quick and dirty' iterations of thinking made visible. Think five or ten-minute outputs, or testing a six-month pilot project with an initial 30-second pitch to stakeholders. People are more emotionally inclined to receive (and give) robust feedback on ideas when the time invested feels minimal. Identifying suitable 'minimum viable prototypes' helps people to 'hold their ideas lightly' and to prioritise which to invest time in developing and testing at greater fidelity.

Organisations that combine commitment to feedback with an ability to prototype effectively often become fertile breeding grounds for ongoing innovation.

TR: A big problem with change is that so much time can be invested in the first creation of developing a vision statement or plan without this becoming reality. How do the best schools you've worked with ensure that the second creation happens too?

PF: Investing time and energy in creating a vision for the future that gradually retreats from hearts, minds and action to end up as a tagline on a school's letterhead or website is a tragedy.

There is no blueprint for avoiding this danger. Leaders know their own communities and are best placed to tailor activity, monitor processes and celebrate milestones along the journey set out by the vision.

However, successful second creation will always have vision at its core. Great schools ensure that their compelling, cohesive and coherent vision is woven into the fabric of school life and culture. It's always on the lips of leaders. It starts every meeting and is the yardstick against which progress is measured. The whole community can articulate in their own ways why their school exists and why anyone and everyone should care.

TR: As always, Peter, it's been brilliant to talk to you. Finally, what three pieces of advice would you offer to leaders who are trying to develop their vision for change in their schools?

PF:

1. Craft your vision to be compelling. Will it touch hearts and minds and drive people to action with the same passion that you feel? Put your assumption through the 'So what? Who cares?' test by asking a five-year-old and a 14-year-old pupil what it means to them. The results may be validating or enlightening.

2. Think through some of the practical implications that might result from embarking on your vision for change. Celebrate current strengths and communicate clearly to stakeholders what is not going to change, to encourage a sense of perspective and stability.

3. Decide what you are going to stop or do less of, to make room for the change initiatives. Communicate this to colleagues. It will be music to their ears. Most schools are operating at capacity, so every new initiative adds to workload. It's like pouring more water into a full bucket.

If the implementation of vision really is the 'main thing' then its outworking will have to take priory over some existing – and probably effective – activity. Understand and address this dilemma early or your vision will quickly join the never-ending list of general priorities in school. When everything is a priority, nothing is.

IMPLEMENTING CHANGE

Leadership is the capacity to translate vision into reality.

Warren Bennis

This next section of the chapter deals with the important business of implementing change and making a vision a reality. This 'second creation' is an area of leadership that I feel is often overlooked, so I have been encouraged by recent developments such as the EEF's guidance document, *Putting Evidence to Work: A school's guide to implementation*[17], which pay more attention to the nuts and bolts of implementation

Implementation is what schools do to improve: to change and be more effective. And yet implementation is a domain of school practice that rarely receives sufficient attention. In our collective haste to do better for pupils, new ideas are often introduced with too little consideration for how the changes will be managed, and what steps are needed to maximise the chances of success.

Education Endowment Foundation

---

17. EEF Implementation Guidance Report (2018), educationendowmentfoundation.org.uk/public/files/ Publications/Campaigns/Implementation/EEF-Implementation-Guidance-Report.pdf

Here are eight practical steps to building vision and delivering effective and lasting change:

1. Beware the visionary.

2. First, do no harm.

3. Apply appreciative inquiry.

4. Consultation.

5. Avoid compromise.

6. Take small steps of change.

7. Manage change well

8. Stay connected.

Beware the visionary
A sense of purpose and direction in a school is vital in increasing staff motivation and, clearly, a compelling, well-articulated vision is an important part of this. If there is a problem with the term 'vision', it is that it promotes the idea of a 'visionary leader' or the less-helpful 'hero leader'. School improvement, like test match cricket, can be a game of attrition; schools get better one day at a time, one person at time. Successful leadership comes through small, sensible and pragmatic changes with painstaking attention to implementation, rather than an overambitious vision or transformation.

Remembering the challenges faced by staff on the front line is important when thinking of the future, so that pragmatism doesn't give way to idealism. While there is a place for visionary thinking in education, in some cases it can become a fast train to Bonkersville: a place where a vast gulf exists between the leader's ideas and the reality of implementing them within the challenges of day-to-day school life. Like many leaders, I have had my share of 'bright ideas' over the years which sounded great in an office somewhere or on the drive home, but were never practical. When I look back, I am grateful to colleagues who had the honesty and courage to challenge these and rein me in when needed.

Vision without implementation is hallucination.
Thomas Edison

First, do no harm
One of the first lessons learned by medical students is 'non-maleficence'

– the concept that when deciding on a course of action with a patient, the first priority should be to avoid doing something that may make the condition or problem worse. 'First, do no harm' is a useful mantra for us to hold on to in school, where we can often feel pressure to make decisions or find answers quickly due to either real or perceived pressures of external accountability. It is important for us to develop the discipline to resist implementing new ideas too hastily, as this can often lead to us causing more harm than good.

Any change will inevitably bring with it unintended consequences or implications for staff. Sometimes these can be positive: we may discover, for example, that by improving engagement in reading with a particular child, their behaviour also improves; or perhaps that by working on a new online homework system, money is saved on books and photocopying. When this happens, it is a bonus. Sometimes, however, unintended consequences are negative and can undermine the change or initiative to the point where leaders end up backtracking or making U-turns. An obvious example of this could be implementing a new assessment system hastily due to pressure from governors who want something 'concrete' by which to measure progress. Putting something in place quickly without ensuring sufficient reliability or validity of assessment could then cause more harm as potentially damaging decisions are made based on poor data. Often, the unintended consequences of change lead to additional stress and additional workload for staff.

Apply appreciative inquiry

I was first introduced to 'appreciative inquiry' at the National College of School Leadership on an early headship qualification as a process that could be applied in school when considering and planning change. It is a simple but powerful model which is described as 'the search for the best in people, their organizations, and the strengths-filled, opportunity-rich world around them'.[18] With appreciative inquiry, more time is spent focusing on gaining a deeper understanding of the organisation, conducting root cause analysis and then engaging staff as owners of school improvement. Although initially time consuming, the process allows us to ensure that any planned change is well thought through and can avoid some of the trauma that unintended consequences can bring. 'Measure twice, cut once', as the wise carpenter says.

---

18. Stavros, Jacqueline, Godwin, Lindsey, & Cooperrider, David. (2015). Appreciative Inquiry: Organization Development and the Strengths Revolution. In Practicing Organization Development: A guide to leading change and transformation (4th Edition), William Rothwell, Roland Sullivan, and Jacqueline Stavros (Eds). Wiley

The appreciative inquiry process can be broken down into the following four stages:

1. **Discover:** Immerse yourself in the question or problem. Find out more about current strengths, as well as the opportunities for change.

2. **Dream:** Generate ideas with others about what the future could look like. Define the vision, values and mission.

3. **Design:** Agree the strategy and work out how and when change will take place. Define the project by creating clear action plans and share these widely.

4. **Do (deploy):** Implement the change, acting as mission control and evaluating success along the way.

Examples of leadership activities that might take place throughout the appreciative inquiry process are set out in Table 4.

Table 4. Application of appreciative inquiry process

	Activities	Mindset	Questions you might ask
Discover	• Consult with staff • Promote informal discussion • Ask questions and carry out surveys • Visit other schools and leaders • Read widely around the issues	Open Inquisitive Curious	What works well here? Where can we improve?
Dream (Why?)	• Ideas sessions with staff • Drawings, notes • Discussions • Write vision and mission statements	Imaginative Holding ideas lightly	What might be? What are other alternatives?
Design (How and what?)	• Develop strategy • Write action plans and define actions • Take feedback • Design prototypes and trials	Rigorous Testing Open to feedback	What do you think to this? What are the alternatives?
Deliver	• Implement change • Collect ongoing feedback and adapt approaches • Hone, tweak, review • Coach, monitor, check	Focused Project management Mission control	How is this working? What are the side effects? What do we need to tweak?

Although typically appreciative inquiry is presented as a four-stage model, like many leadership tools it can become a mindset and a way of working. When leaders adopt this mindset, they can keep staff engaged in creating and owning the why, what and how for the future of the organisation. Altogether, it is a much more positive way of being and leading

Table 5. Problem-solving mindset versus appreciative inquiry mindset

Problem-solving mindset	Appreciative inquiry mindset
• What is wrong here?	• What is right here?
• What are the weaknesses to improve?	• What are the strengths to build on?
• What are the solutions?	• What does better look like?
• How can I get people to buy into my ideas?	• How can people here own and become the solution?
• We need a quick turnaround.	• Any change must be lasting.

Avoid over-steering: By using processes such as appreciative inquiry, we can try to avoid some of the flip-flopping decision-making which is so prevalent in education. State schools in England have existed in a state of constant flux for as long as I have been teaching.

Whether it's government initiatives, curriculum reboots or staff turnover, change often feels like the only constant. Despite this, we should avoid being driven by reaction, as this can lead to policy and practice that lurch from one extreme to the other or 'educational over-steer' – a common and destructive phenomenon which exists across our schools.

If you have ever tried to play one of those car racing games in an arcade, you will know the feeling well. You try to turn left, but you do it so hard that before you know it, you're out of control and have crashed into the barrier on the right. Scarred by that experience, you quickly pull the wheel too vigorously in the other direction and hit the barrier you were trying to avoid in the first place.

| DEFINITION \

Over-Steer[19]

verb (intransitive)

■ (of a vehicle) to turn more sharply, for a particular turn of the steering wheel, than is desirable or anticipated.

---

19. Collins Dictionary: www.collinsdictionary.com/dictionary/english/oversteer

Training as a teacher in the late 1990s, I was a child of the literacy and numeracy strategies in which clear and rigorous primary instruction was the order of the day. Mass coverage of objectives up and down the country was dissected into crisp four-part lessons with precisely timed starters – I once got a target from a lesson observation that my plenaries should be limited to between eight and ten minutes! And then at some point in the mid-2000s came a general departure from this rigour to the freedom of 'creative curriculum', the lure of learning styles and a crescendo towards the revised national curriculum, which was delivered to my desk as a head teacher in 2008 and then thrown out in 2010 due to a change in government. Today, some years after a further national curriculum revision in 2014, the wheel is being pulled down hard to change direction yet again.

We must avoid chasing every initiative and counter-initiative in pursuit of transformational change.

Consultation

Consultation is a vital process to become familiar with before implementing any change; it can really help us to understand different opinions and perspectives, as well as understanding any potential reaction and barriers to new plans or policies.

DEFINITION

Consult: Origin

■ Early 16th century (in the sense 'confer'): from French consulter, from Latin consultare, frequentative of consulere 'take counsel'.

Consultation is at the heart of the appreciative inquiry model, where staff are 'part of the conversation' of creating and then becoming the new future. Consultation does not require a vote or imply a democratic process, but rather asks that people's views and opinions are taken into account on a subject before a decision is made. When used well, it can help to introduce change carefully and successfully. There are many different uses of the word and, in school, different consultation activities can be grouped into the following categories:

■ **Formal-formal:** Formal consultations which follow a set process. Typically, these are legally required and concern significant changes such as becoming an academy, changing particular school policies or changing school uniform.

■ **Informal-formal:** Where a policy or idea is shared and discussed with the school community, and feedback is taken and considered before a final decision is made outside of any formal or legal process (eg, through meetings, surveys etc).

■ **Informal–informal:** Ongoing discussions, conversations and ideas that are tested informally, often in an *ad hoc* way which can be part of an open and consultative style.

If you are working on something exciting that you really care about, you don't have to be pushed. The vision pulls you.

Steve Jobs

Formal consultation can be time consuming, but if processes are not followed correctly, you can end up paying the price further down the line. The most important and obvious thing to say about formal consultation is simply to follow the process exactly, within the correct timescales and with the right people. But in terms of navigating potentially tricky and controversial processes, the best advice I was ever given was to undertake plenty of informal consultation before it gets to the formal stage. This allows opportunities for discussion and for concerns to be raised in a low–stakes situation, where answers can be researched and provided to alleviate those concerns. It can also afford leaders the opportunity to change direction or adapt a potential approach before it goes wrong, and therefore avoid embarrassing U–turns or new policies that just fizzle out.

One really effective formal consultation process that I was part of was when Simon de Senlis became an academy. There were the legal processes which we had to follow, but my governing body was brilliant in pushing hard that we go well above and beyond these requirements and really engage the community with all the different options informally. Four options were on the table: remain as a local authority school, convert as a standalone academy, join a local collaborative MAT or join one of the several sponsors. It was clear that most of the governors felt that we should try to join the local MAT; but rather than making a decision and then going through a token consultation, they were keen to hear the voices of the staff and parents.

We held several information meetings in which we shared all the facts and the different views and options (formal–informal), and gave the opportunity for all of the initial issues raised, such as pensions and contracts, to be discussed. As a result, when we held the official parents' meetings and Transfer of Undertakings (Protection of Employment

Regulations) meetings with the staff, they were incredibly positive and did not raise any problems for the SLT and governors. The greatest benefit was not just that the process was smooth, but that the overall conversion process was seen as a great opportunity which put wind in our sails at a potentially delicate time and which underpins the strong relationship we have with our MAT today. It was the informal work at the initial stage that made the formal part a success.

Informal–informal consultation, meanwhile, is a low–stakes approach to testing ideas and collecting feedback, and includes activities such as corridor conversations, open discussions in staff meetings, ideas boxes and *ad hoc* meetings. It is an important approach in which leaders can 'take the temperature' in the organisation, and is part of the democratic and affiliative leadership styles we explored in Chapter 3. For some, these approaches come naturally and leaders may not even be aware that they are using them; others can find the consultative approach challenging to employ, as it can provoke feelings of vulnerability and a perception of being criticised. Asking for feedback is an opportunity to hear the opinions of others, which can be uncomfortable and reveal inconvenient truths; but all feedback is a gift, particularly if it enables better decision-making in the long run.

Of course, it is not possible to do this for every different issue and sometimes there are decisions that just need to be made. But not making time for proper informal consultation is a false economy. Unless ideas are tested early and thought through as a result, the job of implementation is nearly always more problematic and time consuming. As the old saying goes, 'Act in haste, repent at leisure.'

Avoid compromise

A less effective use of consultation that I experienced was with a leadership team which had initially written a bold curriculum document including an 'Excellence in Arts' afternoon, which then lost its way through implementation due to compromise. The concept was that specialist teachers would be brought in to teach areas of the arts so that all children would receive specialist teaching in these areas on one afternoon each week, to make sure that there was real quality. The rationale and vision were great; the implementation was not. Rather than seeing children receiving high-quality teaching in the arts, the reality was that lots of staff took planning, preparation and assessment (PPA) time; some non-qualified staff ended up delivering sessions which they were confident in rather than the arts subjects that had been planned; and there was not enough budget to resource the sessions.

Overall, it was a fairly mediocre experience.

Looking back at the annotated vision statement and meeting notes, it is apparent how, over the course of meetings and discussions, ideas had been added such as 'What about science?', 'Life skills', 'Opportunity for PPA cover' and 'Origami'. There were also notes showing that the costs of specialist teachers had been researched and then reduced due to budget pressures. Through consultation and discussion, the plan had become watered down, trying to be too many things to different people, and had lost its original vision. It is a good example of where a consultation became a compromise which ended up making a potentially effective initiative.

Trying to keep everyone happy is a mug's game; sometimes we have to nail our colours to the mast.

Take small steps of change
Regardless of how enthusiastic and committed to change a staff may be, lasting positive change takes place not with the speed and fanfare of a firework display, but rather with the steadiness and certainty of a rising tide.

Every day, small steps of change are carried out in each of our schools by staff through their daily work. Slowly, when guided by the right vision, this collection of individual and team action is what makes a difference. These individual actions come in many different shapes and sizes. They may or may not be part of a strategic plan; sometimes leaders may not even know about them. They might be a series of lessons or meetings on a particular topic; they could take the form of a particular drive or initiative, such as seeking consistent behaviour approaches; or they may simply be a single relationship that is being worked on between a teaching assistant and a new child.

Each of these different actions – while different in size, impact and complexity – plays an important role in contributing towards improving the bigger picture. When coordinated well and guided by the North Star of a clear, overarching vision, small individual activities can build momentum and rhythm and become the powerful collective action that moves the school forward.

Manage change well
However carefully we plan and manage implementation, the process can always ruffle feathers and elicit emotional reactions from staff in schools. Although this can be uncomfortable, it is a normal part of

any change cycle. Staff will often experience fear, anger and resistance to change as shown in Figure 9, which is adapted from the Kubler-Ross change curve.[20] This curve reminds us that when any change is implemented, it is normal for staff to experience feelings of denial, fear and anger before they can move through the process of acceptance and eventually into relearning and integrating new ways of working.

This is another reason why the culture is so important to get right. If leaders have failed to build trusting relationships, staff can become overly fearful of change. If relationships have become too friendly or informal, sometimes leaders can be too hesitant to implement change due to concern about the emotional reactions of others. Again, it is the important and delicate balance of professional culture and relationships which provides the right conditions for change to take place.

When we analysed staff morale from the wellbeing surveys in schools across our trust, we were able to draw a direct correlation between the schools in which most change was taking place (change of leadership, staff turnover, challenge from Ofsted) and lower reported morale. Therefore, it is important that we keep the momentum through periods of implementation – delays or U-turns halfway through are likely to leave staff morale low, as they don't get to move through the empowering stages of relearning and reintegration.

Figure 9. Transitioning through change

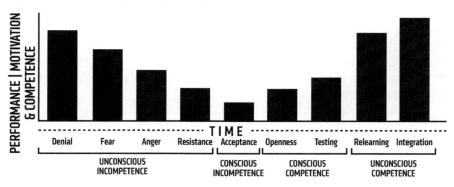

20. Kübler-Ross, E, *On Death and Dying*, (Routledge, 1969)

Powerful and effective leaders are guided by the future they want. And more than this, the leader is strongest when that Future is powerfully connected to what he or she cares about.

Steve Radcliffe

Stay connected

One quite specific change that stands out for me was improving the quality of handwriting in our school. The catalyst for this initiative was that the first year I joined as head, the handwriting was so bad that several of the Year 6 team and I spent hours during SATs week transcribing answers after the tests were finished so that they could be read by the markers. Not only was it a waste of time, but these were often high-achieving children who were perfectly capable of handwriting from a physical and cognitive perspective – it was humiliating for them! It seemed ridiculous that these children had been at the school for seven years and couldn't write legibly. I swore (literally) then that I would not allow children to come through the school in the future without us at least having taught them this fundamental skill.

This lack of attention to children's handwriting until recently is an example of how external accountability shapes the curriculum. Because the quality of handwriting used to make up just 3% of the overall assessment marks for English, it gradually became less of a priority in primary schools. 'Handwriting's only worth three marks' was a phrase you would often hear pass the lips of Key Stage 2 teachers. It is another good example of why our vision in school needs to be greater than whatever particular educational wind is blowing at that time. Developing a 'fluent hand' has always been, and should always be, part of the core purpose of a primary school. There are things we should hold onto – despite what is or is not valued in high-stakes testing.

This dissatisfaction with the state of handwriting coincided with a chance meeting with Margaret Williamson, author and owner of a rigorous research-based handwriting approach. Quickly, we were able to work on our strategy, get expert advice from Margaret and implement training to mobilise our troops. As is often the case, it cost more and took longer than we had initially predicted. As with many projects, after some early initial success, things slipped a bit and 'mission fatigue' crept in. These are the hinge points in leadership, when it's easy to let things slide backwards to the way they were if you are not careful as other priorities take over. Because it was so important to me, I found time and space to re-energise the mission and push forward until the approach was embedded as it is today.

The reason that this stands out for me was the personal connection I had with the issue and the fact that my emotional experience from seeing the quality of writing in Year 6 connected me to this change. It is an example of why a first-hand connection with the future is important at times of change.

IN SUMMARY – CREATING A VISION AND IMPLEMENTING CHANGE

- Is there a clear sense of direction in the organisation which is underpinned by a clear vision, mission and set of values?

- Is the 'why' of the school established? Is there a tangible sense of why the school is doing what it does?

- Is the strategy well thought through so that the right things are prioritised to deliver the 'why'?

- Is enough attention paid to the implementation of change or a vision? Is implementation seen as an ongoing process rather than a one-off event?

- Are projects/implementation plans managed well to avoid problems with too many or competing priorities? Can leaders keep 'the main thing' the main thing?

- Are change processes such as appreciative inquiry applied to work through the challenges of identifying and implementing change?

- Are the emotions of change understood and are staff well led and supported through times of change?

FIVE FIVES GRID FOR PLANNING

FIVE MINUTES: What immediate first steps can you take?

FIVE DAYS: What short-term actions can you take in the next week to kick start or plan change?

FIVE WEEKS: What actions or follow-up meetings/discussions can you plan for in the next half-term?

FIVE MONTHS: What follow-up and follow-through activities do you need to plan to ensure that the change is not just a flash in the pan?

FIVE YEARS: What might your change look like in five years? What structures, systems and processes will you need to amend to ensure that your change becomes embedded in the fabric of your school and is not a passing fad?

Section 3

Leading with your Head

Create good strategy rooted in research and evidence. Secure healthy accountability and develop the use of effective school improvement processes.

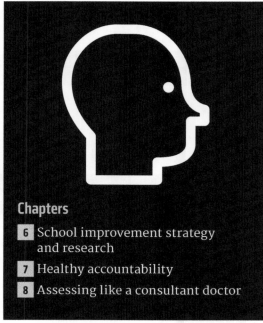

Chapters

School improvement strategy and research

6

CHAPTER PREVIEW

Genuine school improvement work should be less about accountability labels and more about understanding the genuine strengths and weaknesses in a school and using root cause analysis and research to inform sensible ways forward.

It is a reminder of how versatile leaders must be if they are to see a job through from turnaround to sustained success – perhaps a suggestion that those with different strengths could be used more effectively in schools depending on the job required.

In many cases, when a school goes belly up, it is not because the staff are inept at what they do – they have simply spent their time working on the wrong things, choosing superficial initiatives or projects over the real issues.

In recent years, the use of research and evidence has found a more prominent place in education — and not before time.

Build the strategy around the future you want to create, not the past you are trying to change. – Sir David Carter

The research from cognitive science about memory and the importance of things such as retrieval practice and spaced practice is really robust and longstanding; it's not just another flash in the pan. – Clare Sealy

Interview with Sir David Carter & Clare Sealy

SCHOOL IMPROVEMENT STRATEGY AND RESEARCH

> **"**
>
> Thinking is the hardest work there is, which is probably why so few people engage in it.
>
> Henry Ford

When I became head teacher at Simon de Senlis, I found it a real challenge stepping up to the added complexity of a bigger school with more staff to lead. In particular, I became frustrated with how long it took to implement new approaches and policies compared to my first headship of a smaller one-form entry village primary. Leading a small school presents many challenges, including the limited number of people to delegate to and share leadership responsibility with. Leaders of smaller schools often juggle a number of roles alongside full-time teaching commitments and many heads find themselves spending plenty of hours a week in the classroom. This has many benefits: you get to know every child by name and build closer relationships with parents, grandparents and siblings in the playground. You also get to form more personal relationships with staff and it is easy to get things done quickly with the right team in place.

My first headship was a perfect balance – a predominately non-teaching role which enabled me to learn the ropes with a small and supportive team while still getting some weekly time in the classroom. After a tricky first year with some prickly staffing challenges, things really started to fly. With three of the seven class teachers as part of the SLT, it was relatively quick and easy to implement necessary changes; and communication was straightforward, as I could visit each class within a 15-minute circuit.

This combination helped to establish some really good and consistent practices across the school and you could feel things improving day by day. The school went from strength to strength and I look back fondly at an enjoyable time in a great school with great people.

But the move to a large urban primary meant a change of approach. As the school was an inclusive two-form entry school with a separate special provision unit, the staff size jumped to around 70 – more than double the size of team I was used to. I found leading this number of staff a new challenge: change was much slower to effect and consistent approaches much harder to achieve. High numbers of part-time staff presented another challenge in ensuring good communication and consistency, with five of the seven year groups having job shares and several others in different specialist or additional roles (I later learned that these flexible working approaches could be more of a help than a hindrance). I had assumed that with a headship under my belt, it would be easier second time around; yet in many ways, I found it more of a challenge.

Size matters in any organisation and leading a bigger team is a totally different job. Eventually, I realised that I was no longer able to maintain the same kind of personal relationship with each individual and that I would need to curb my natural desire to lead from the front. While it may have been useful early on to show commitment to sport and the arts, running clubs and being at the centre of curriculum projects was unsustainable, and I was in danger of becoming a bottleneck to others who had the potential to lead in these areas.

Time passes quickly and today, with responsibility for the education strategy across 11 schools, my role has changed again. Trying to influence teaching approaches across more than 500 staff while still having your 'name on the sign' of a school as Executive Head demands different skills and strategies.

Above all, what I have learned during this time is the importance of good strategic thinking and planning. If the strategy is right, the day-to-day job of running the school is much easier and our chances of raising standards are higher. We have to pick the right wall to rest the ladder against before we start climbing. But creating the right strategy takes a lot of careful thought, an understanding of research and time – three things in scarce supply when leading on the front line in a busy school.

FOUR STAGES OF IMPROVING A SCHOOL

One problem with lots of school improvement activity is that it is often based on the language of Ofsted. Phrases such as 'getting to good' or claims to deliver 'outstanding' practice are commonplace on training courses and used widely by those planning and leading school improvement. This obsession with accountability labels and a need to judge and categorise often comes at the expense of genuine school improvement. It is the same problem that we experienced in schools with assessment levels – generic terms, loaded with consequences of accountability at the expense of proper diagnostic evaluation and lasting improvement. Genuine school improvement work should be less about accountability labels and more about understanding the genuine strengths and weaknesses in a school and using root cause analysis and research to inform sensible ways forward.

In his time as National Schools Commissioner, Sir David Carter has led important work on school improvement in the last couple of years, attempting to shift the conversation away from a focus on Ofsted judgements by introducing more helpful language that describes where schools are on their improvement journey. In his 'Four Stages of Improving a School' model, Sir David identifies four phases of a school's development: stabilise, repair, improve and sustain.

Figure 10. The four stages of improving a school

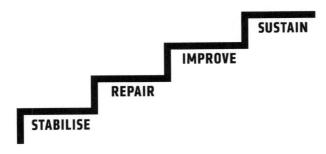

Source: National Schools Commissioner Sir David Carter

Thinking about schools in these terms can be useful in shifting the conversation away from a ranking process and on to the actual school improvement job in hand. Each stage reflects different challenges and requires specific leadership approaches. It is a reminder of how versatile leaders must be if they are to see a job through from turnaround to sustained success – perhaps a suggestion that those with different strengths could be used more effectively in schools depending on the job required. Table 6 describes some of the specific challenges and the types of leadership required that are identified in this model.

Table 6. Four stages of improving a school in action

Phase	What is the job?	What leadership is required?
Stabilise	Fixing what is broken Focusing on the urgent priorities Uncovering the reality	Calm and reassuring Highly visible Decisive
Repair	Taking control from the chaos Reactive decision-making Making the school feel 'normal' Short-term 'wins' while building a longer-term strategy	Implementing change Monitoring and evaluation Still visible Mentoring people Short-term planning
Improve	Becoming more proactive Embedding strategies and approaches Ensuring that outcomes can 'never be as bad again'	Shifting from management to leadership Rigorous tracking and monitoring Developing others through mentoring and coaching Medium-term planning
Sustain	Securing excellence Giving capacity to the system Ensuring lasting success	Confident and innovative delivery Distributed leadership/succession planning Longer-term planning (three to five years)

Source: Adapted from the work of Sir David Carter in his time as National Schools Commisioner

AN INTERVIEW WITH SIR DAVID CARTER

For further insight into this model, I was privileged to be able to talk with the author himself, Sir David Carter.

TR: Schools are often defined by their Ofsted judgements and it is my belief that too many of us talk about our schools by definition using the terms 'Requiring Improvement', 'Good' or 'Outstanding'. Why did you decide to propose this model rather than using the Ofsted terminology?

DC: Mainly because I wanted to develop a new narrative about school improvement that is more reflective of the stage of the improvement journey that a school is on. Deep, secure improvement takes time, and trusts and MATs need to be able to assess the quality of the strategy in relation to the outcome for children – especially when there is a time lag as the outcomes catch up with the improvement plan. I also liked the idea of finding a way to describe the improvement journeys that teams within schools are on, so that leaders and governors think harder about the in-school variations as well as the between-school variations. The Ofsted judgements are key parts of public accountability and I am not trying to create a new set of categories. However, a judgement for the whole school for the purposes of public accountability is a snapshot in time based on the validated outcomes from recent times. When regional school commissioners are working with MATs to focus the improvement, their strategy should consider the capacity of the trust to get better outcomes; the model I have been advocating provides a framework inside which that conversation can take place.

TR: Have you seen leaders using this model in their schools and trusts, and how do you anticipate that they might use it in the future?

DC: I have, and it is good to see so many CEOs in MATs find a use for it. I have also heard from chairs of MAT boards that it has been helpful for them in setting expectations for their leaders. Some trusts have looked at the improvement trajectories and worked out where they believe their schools are, and as a result have developed a far more bespoke school-by-school improvement strategy that recognises the different challenges and improvement curves that their schools are tackling.

TR: I particularly like the fourth stage, 'Sustain', as an alternative to 'Outstanding' because this implies that successful schools should continue to do the things that made them good in the first place, rather than trying to do something different or innovative to become 'Outstanding'. Is this a deliberate steer for successful schools to become more focused on giving capacity to the system rather than trying to focus on becoming 'Outstanding'?

DC: Sustaining improvement is the key. Outstanding schools, in my experience, rarely stop thinking about what needs to be done next, but building a narrative around sustaining high performance within a culture of continuous improvement is important. I would add that the best schools sustain their improvement by looking to work and support other schools, which adds capacity to the system as well as to their own performance. 'Outstanding' as a judgement for public accountability is fine; but the improvement journey I have described – from Stabilise through Repair and Improve to Sustain – enables leaders to reflect on where each of their teams, departments, year groups and so on are on this continuum.

TR: In the model, you describe different styles of leadership that are required at different phases of development. How able do you think individuals are to adapt to these different styles, or do you think that we should be moving leaders around in the system dependent on the challenge?

DC: This is one of the great advantages that MATs have. A head teacher needs to be able to look around the table and know that the capacity of the team is built around people who bring something different to each debate. This is a healthy and robust part of the development of the team. I think the skills required to lead a school from deep failure to secure performance are as valid and important as those needed to keep a brilliant school outstanding. It is not a competition to see which experience is more valid. I just make the point that having people in a leadership team who have worked in an outstanding school alongside someone else who has been part of taking a school from special measures to 'Good' adds incredible capacity to the improvement strategy. The best CEOs understand this and find ways to capitalise on the strengths of the leaders they employ in order to maximise their experiences for the benefit of as many children as possible.

TR: It's been great to talk to you, Sir David, to explore this model of school improvement further. If you had to give three pieces of advice to school leaders on thinking about school improvement strategy, what would they be?

DC:

1. Build the strategy around the future you want to create, not the past you are trying to change.

2. Recognise the strengths of the school as well as the weaknesses, so that you bolt improvement on top of secure practice.

3. Not much changes unless teaching improves! Make sure that the strategy does not become disconnected from classroom practice, so that the daily experience of children becomes the test of whether the plan is working.

A simple view of school improvement

Understanding the different stages of school improvement is a helpful starting point and the next piece of the puzzle is to work out what specifically needs prioritising for the school to improve. Many complex threads run through a school, and it is easy to become overwhelmed, distracted or confused by different challenges and priorities and to lose focus on the strategy.

The obvious is that which is never seen until someone expresses it simply.

Kahlil Gibran

Too often, we can over-complicated the answer to the fundamental question of 'What do we prioritise to improve this school?' I have already argued in the first section of this book that the starting point in a school is to establish its 'Heart' – the culture, ethos, vision and values of the place. Within this wrapper of wholesome leadership, we have to get our heads around the specific things to work on. To do this, there are six questions that I think leaders should always continue to ask themselves:

1. Are the children safe?

2. Is behaviour well managed?

3. Is the curriculum well organised?

4. Is good provision made for the vulnerable?

5. Is teaching effective?

6. Are children achieving well?

These questions underpin the following simple view of school improvement, which I term the vital organs.

The vital organs of school improvement

Humans have five organs essential for survival – the brain, heart, liver, kidneys and lungs – known as the 'vital organs' of the body. If any of these organs becomes damaged or diseased, restoring it to good health is a priority. This is obvious and sensible: a haircut won't fix a brain tumour, bicep curls won't cure liver disease and trying to battle lung cancer through cosmetic surgery is likely to be counterproductive. Despite this, we often see schools which have run into trouble simply by working on the wrong things – either distracted by operational priorities or with a weak school improvement model that is likely to be dominated by 'magic bullets' rather than being underpinned by common sense, experience or any credible research that says it works. In one notoriously difficult school that I worked in, I watched as a new MAT invested thousands in a rebranding exercise with garish new signs and a change of uniform, and then simply expected teachers to do a better job in the classroom. Needless to say, the school didn't improve as a result of this 'cosmetic surgery'.

Figure 11. The vital organs of school improvement

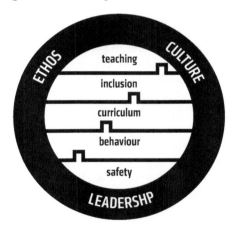

In many cases, when a school goes belly up, it is not because the staff are inept at what they do – they have simply spent their time working on the wrong things, choosing superficial initiatives or projects over the real issues. The 'vital organs' model identifies the most significant strategic issues to work on and aims to avoid 'cosmetic surgery' school improvement. It is a semi-hierarchical model, suggesting that the lower levels should be put in place first while recognising that there will always be flexibility within any model. Working too high up the model without the foundations in place is like building a house on sand. Despite any external pressures to get there quicker, it is important that we take our time to improve a school properly.

Safety: It almost goes without saying that the first priority for anyone working with children is to make sure they are kept safe. That is why the first of the vital organs that needs attention is the systems and processes that keep children safe. It is inevitable that at some stage in our careers we might make a mistake or drop an important ball along the way, but we should do everything we can to make sure that this does not put a child at risk.

Over the last decade, the emphasis on safeguarding in schools has increased significantly and, as a result, there are many layers of compliance. Alongside the compliant areas of safeguarding, an important task is to build a culture of wellbeing and safety into school life – not only through staff processes, but also within the curriculum, so that children can become more aware of potential danger and educated about risks and behaviours and actions that can help to keep them safer. Safeguarding can often be seen as a set of processes that we carry out when something goes wrong, rather than a part of ongoing training and education to reduce risks of harm in the first place. Thinking proactively and investing in programmes such as protective behaviours, online safety and anti-bullying, for example, are all valuable in this area – as is a well-developed personal, social and health education curriculum, which should be a priority for us all.

Behaviour: Behaviour is the next of the vital organs for us to pay attention to. It is the one that can have the greatest impact on teaching, standards and the wellbeing of staff and students, as well as minimising disruption to the flow of the school day and reducing large amounts of staff time spent following up issues with parents. The prize of consistently excellent behaviour across a school is invaluable.

As well as the more obvious high-profile challenges with behaviour in a school, low-level disruption should be a continual focus, as it can really hijack learning in the classroom. Five minutes wasted dealing with behaviour in every lesson equates to 25 minutes a day, two hours a week or over 80 hours in a school year (more than three full weeks). Considering the impact that missing three full weeks of school can have on education can help to sharpen our attention to avoid disruption in the classroom.

Behaviour can be a tough nut to crack and should be a clear and present priority for us in every school, all of the time. In the same way that fitness quickly drops when we take a couple of weeks off from exercise, behaviour soon slips if we become complacent or consider it 'sorted'. We should never underestimate the impact that we can have on behaviour (and therefore on learning, morale and the wellbeing of those around us) as a leader. Status does matter in an organisation and getting our hands dirty playing our part in the reinforcement of daily routines, modelling the standards expected and supporting messages from busy classroom teachers is one of the most important things that we do every day.

Teachers alone, no matter how skilled, cannot intervene with the same impact as a school leader. The key task for a school leader is to create a culture – usefully defined as 'the way we do things around here' – that is understood and subscribed to by the whole school community.[21]

Tom Bennett, Chair of Department for Education Behaviour Group

Curriculum: With safety and behaviour in good health, the next of the vital organs to pay attention to is the curriculum. 'What to learn?' is perhaps the most fundamental (and difficult) question to answer in a school. It is easy to avoid challenging conversations about curriculum, as they open familiar cans of worms such as which subjects are more important than others and which knowledge or skills should be prioritised. 'How to organise it?' runs a close second. The challenge of balancing curriculum entitlement is a fiendish puzzle and the job of packing all subjects into 27.5 hours is like fitting a quart in a pint pot.

In recent years, there has been a tendency for schools to prioritise more general 'teaching and learning' approaches or 'pedagogy' before tackling these difficult curriculum questions – perhaps because of the perceived benefits of specific teaching approaches; maybe it just feels easier. But just as we would not expect a group of great singers to perform in harmony without someone first composing the music, organising the score and conducting the choir, can we really expect the outcomes in a school to be optimal unless we have first organised the curriculum well – thinking in more depth about what should be taught, why and when? Often the curriculum is squeezed as a response to short-term pressures to improve standards at the end of a key stage. We must

---

21. 'Creating a Culture: How school leaders can optimise behaviour', assets.publishing.service.gov.uk/government/uploads/system/uploads/attachment_data/file/602487/Tom_Bennett_Independent_Review_of_Behaviour_in_Schools.pdf

be brave as school leaders and see curriculum breadth and richness as a route to raising standards, not an alternative.

There are many different views as to what should be 'on the curriculum' and the issue is subject to political pressure and influence from industry, as well as the different personal views of those within the school community. Because of this diversity of opinion and schools of thought, there can be no 'right' answer to the questions that organising the curriculum throws up (although there are definitely wrong ones), so inevitably we will never achieve consensus on what 'a curriculum' should look like in every school. But this does not mean that we should stop trying. An ongoing pursuit of school leadership should be to develop a curriculum that is broad, rich and rigorous. In the end, it is not that our answers are 'right', but rather that our thinking, discussion and rationale are right (or wrong).

For years, the phrase 'broad and balanced' has been used to describe a desirable curriculum in schools but I wonder about the 'balanced' part. What does it really mean? Table 7 sets out some questions to consider when working on the curriculum, organised into the areas of 'broad', 'rich' and 'rigorous'.

Many (probably all) of these ideas around curriculum have been developed through reading and discussion with other educators as part of a more prominent debate about the specifics of the curriculum in recent years. This has been spurred on, in part, by Ofsted since the appointment of Amanda Spielman as Chief Inspector. One example of a school leader thinking differently about the curriculum is Stuart Lock, who I heard speak at the Education Festival in Wellington in both 2016 and 2017 on the subject. His blog post 'Pedagogy is overrated' is one of my favourite reads and provokes us to think more closely about the what of the curriculum.

All young people are entitled to the knowledge that allows them to join the community of educated citizens as adults.[22]

Stuart Lock, Executive Principal – Bedford Free School

---

22. mrlock.wordpress.com/2017/06/23/pedagogy-is-overrated/

Table 7. Questions to inform a broad, rich and rigorous curriculum

BROAD	■ How effectively is each subject being taught across the school? It is a challenge to achieve satisfactory breadth, but our goal should be for the curriculum to be a rich tapestry in which the integrity of each subject is preserved.
	■ What is the level of expertise within each subject in the school? This is a particular challenge in a primary school, where there are fewer subject specialists.
	■ What specifically should be learned within each subject? Just the national curriculum or also other things outside of the national curriculum – and if so, what? Why are they important? Simply 'delivering the national curriculum' suggests that not enough thinking has taken place about what children in any school should learn.
	■ How is the curriculum organised using time allocation over a year, long-term plans and weekly timetables? The devil is often in the details of the mechanics of curriculum organisation.
RICH	■ How are the specific elements of the curriculum identified so that it is clear what the key things are that need to be taught and learned? Have you achieved clarity on these 'fewer things in greater depth' in your school?
	■ Are there opportunities to adapt the curriculum around your particular context? For example, are there specific geographical or historical features of your location that lend themselves to being topics or subjects for children to learn about?
	■ How are subjects protected from slipping to the sidelines? Some subjects, such as the arts, are easy to sideline due to the absence of accountability around them and often low staff expertise. These should be regarded as just as important as others. They should be protected and promoted not because of tenuous links to better standards in English or maths, but in their own right. Music for the sake of music; dance for the sake of dance. These subjects are part of the cultural inheritance that education should bring.
RIGOROUS	■ How different is the 'planned curriculum' to the taught or 'enacted curriculum'? In primary schools, the enacted curriculum can often affected by variables including resources, disruptions and the skills or confidence of the class teacher, who may prioritise different subjects and avoid others. Agreed ways to monitor the delivery of the curriculum are important here.
	■ How effective is any form of 'thematic' or 'creative' curriculum approach in ensuring that rigorous teaching of each subject takes place? While making natural links between subjects is sensible and has value, it often creates an illusion that a particular subject is being taught sufficiently, when in fact it is not.

- What model of curriculum leadership exists to ensure that each subject continues to be driven forward? Is there the subject expertise to hand out different subjects to many different teachers or does this give the illusion of delegation rather than the reality of not much happening?

- How are different subjects assessed? It is impossible to look at the issue of curriculum properly without considering how to assess what has been learned. Sorting out assessment so that it is both meaningful and manageable is a big discussion on its own; the next chapter deals with this in more detail.

Inclusion: The next of the organs to pay attention to is inclusion – an umbrella term in this model for those groups of children who typically do not achieve well within our education system. This includes those with convenient labels and tags such as special education needs and disabilities (SEND), children who are 'looked after' and those classed as 'disadvantaged'. It also includes those without such tags who, for a number of different reasons, have other barriers or issues in their lives that make school life more difficult to cope with.

There are moral, professional and educational reasons why the health of this organ is important in a successful school.

- **Moral:** We know that many in life are subject to conditions, family circumstances or life events which render them at a disadvantage to others. It should be the calling of all within the profession to do all that they can to help these individuals to achieve the best they possibly can through the highest level of care and most skilled teaching.

- **Professional:** All teachers and leaders have both professional and legal responsibilities through the SEND Code of Practice and Teachers' Standards to ensure that the right provision is in place and that particular actions are taken to support the most vulnerable.

- **Educational:** If one of our goals as educators is to raise academic standards across the country, it is in areas such as SEND and provision for the disadvantaged that the greatest opportunity exists to ensure that each generation sees more people from these groups leaving school as literate and numerate young people with good prospects of employment and happy and successful futures.

Although there is a strong argument that provision for the disadvantaged should come as an earlier priority in the model, it is generally the most vulnerable who stand to lose the most in schools where behaviour is poor and the curriculum weak. In contrast, where schools have really well-established good behaviour, children with SEND can often benefit from the structure and consistency of response; where the curriculum is rich and rigorous, this can provide opportunities for the less advantaged to build knowledge, skills and experiences that they would not acquire through wishy-washy curricular approaches and narrow experiences. Additional strategies and provision for the vulnerable are more achievable in settings where the previous organs are all functioning well.

Inclusion is a difficult thing to get right in schools and, sadly, there are too many cases where schools fail to invest properly in this vital organ, choosing to encourage a more privileged intake and avoiding the inconvenience and expense of inclusion. It is a test of the ethics of leaders as to how much time and energy they are prepared to invest in the most vulnerable in our society.

The true measure of any society can be found in how it treats its most vulnerable members.

Mahatma Ghandi

Effective teaching
One of the key differences of the vital organs model of school improvement is that it flips the archetypal school turnaround model on its head. Typical turnaround approaches can work on the basis of identifying weak teachers and focusing on improving their deficit areas to create an increasing percentage of teachers who can be genetically categorised as 'good or outstanding'. This can often result in teachers being 'moved on' and replaced by new teachers who can 'hack it'. The reality is that there simply is not a pool of super-human teachers waiting in the wings who are willing and able to fill the increasing gaps in our teaching staff to carry out the extreme demands that class teaching usually makes. We have to think more about how we can simplify teaching to make it both attractive and sustainable.

Within this model, teaching is placed on top of the foundations of secure safeguarding, good behaviour, a well-organised curriculum and provision for the vulnerable. This is not because teaching is considered less important; on the contrary, the actual process of teachers delivering the curriculum is the 'main thing' that makes learning happen. The job of the other organs is to remove all other distractions and create the optimum environment for teaching to take place.

The main thing is to keep the main thing the main thing.

Stephen Covey

In schools where all the other vital organs are in good health, an unadulterated focus on teaching is evident. It is in these environments that the outcomes look after themselves.

What about outcomes?

Often, outcomes or standards are the starting point for school improvement as leaders find themselves under pressure to deliver short-term improvements, particularly in contexts where achievement data is low. This immediate pressure to raise standards can be counterproductive if it steers schools away from the important and fundamental 'vital organs'.

There are many ways that outcomes can be boosted quickly through things such as last-minute one-to-one tuition and booster groups, narrowing the curriculum or reducing class sizes in high-stakes testing years. There are also real issues in the system with the manipulation of teacher assessments as starting points for progress measures and, at secondary school, with curriculum provision being driven by subjects that make the Progress 8 score look good rather than by the genuine educational value that these subjects hold.

Where data is improved in this way, it is simply an illusion of improvement rather than the more difficult work of genuinely raising standards. It is the equivalent of trying to get a green front lawn by spraying it with dye rather than taking on the slower, more laborious work of scarification, feeding and regular cutting and cultivation, which can take many seasons. This type of 'cosmetic surgery' school improvement mentioned earlier in the chapter is one that I hope more leaders will avoid in the future. Improving a school properly is hard work and takes time. It also takes conviction and for leaders to hold their nerve when immediate results don't follow. If the vital organs of a school are all functioning well, the score should take care of itself[23] in terms of outcomes.

Outcomes do not appear in the model as one of the vital organs themselves, but are rather an indication of how well the vital organs are functioning and how healthy the ethos and culture are within a school. It is important, too, that we consider a wider view of outcomes than just pupil achievement. Measures such as staff recruitment and retention,

---

23. Walsh, B, *The Score Takes Care of Itself* (Portfolio, 2010).

satisfaction surveys and attendance rates are good indicators of the overall health of the school, along with anecdotal evidence such as what supply teachers (really) think about behaviour in the school or the opinions of parents/teachers new to the school and their comparisons with previous experiences.

> *Even when you have an organization brimming with talent, victory is not always under your control. There is no guarantee, no ultimate formula for success. It all comes down to intelligently and relentlessly seeking solutions that will increase your chance of prevailing. When you do that, the score will take care of itself.*

Bill Walsh

Keeping the vital organs in good health

In order to ensure that a school's vital organs remain in good health, each requires regular 'health checks' through ongoing monitoring and evaluation. This should include a number of school improvement processes alongside clear accountability, which I elaborate on in Chapter 7.

Often, school improvement falters for one of the following reasons:

■ Regular health checks and monitoring are missed.

■ The right people don't sit down regularly enough to evaluate findings from monitoring and agree next steps.

■ Steps for improvement are identified, but don't become reality due to a lack of follow-up and follow-through activity.

To avoid these pitfalls, it is important to establish what I call the 'engine room of school improvement': a model set out in Figures 12 and 13 which ensures a continuous focus of review, action and follow-up and follow-through. This aspect of leadership within a school is essential in ensuring that all of the different aspects of school improvement are in good health.

Figure 12. Rigorous school improvement cycle

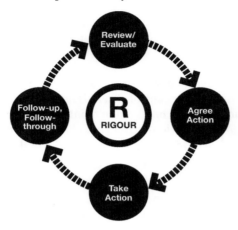

The engine room of school improvement

■ Teams should be assigned to each of the vital organs, with clarity of accountability and individual roles.

■ The size and number of different teams will change depending on the size of the school and SLT. In my two-form entry primary school of 440 children, for example, we have a learning leadership team which focuses on the of behaviour, curriculum and teaching and learning, with separate safeguarding and inclusion teams (see Figure 13). Other teams have responsibility for things such as business and finance. In smaller schools, there may be a fewer number of teams with more responsibilities.

■ The purpose of creating different teams is to ensure that the focus on the vital organs does not get lost in more generic agendas such as recruitment or operational challenges. These should be picked up separately.

■ Weekly or fortnightly meetings should be scheduled for each team, which are documented and returned to each time it meets. These meetings form part of the engine room model and create momentum in school improvement through reviewing actions, evaluating and then agreeing new actions for the next week/fortnight.

■ The role of the head or SLT is to ensure that each of these different teams is meeting regularly and carrying out its role. The head will usually also be a member of some or all of these different teams.

Figure 13. Leadership structures: The engine room of school improvement

USING RESEARCH AND EVIDENCE

When working on the vital organs of school improvement, we should choose approaches that give the best chance of success. This sounds obvious, yet the wide variety of approaches used across different schools suggests that we have not yet worked out what these are. Just as we would expect a doctor devising a plan to restore health to our liver or lungs to use an approved, well-tested method, we must do more to ensure that our approaches in school are those which are proven to be successful. This is where an engagement with research is essential.

In recent years, the use of research and evidence has found a more prominent place in education – and not before time. When I look back at the past, I recognise that too many decisions were made at all levels in schools based on whims and fancies rather than real knowledge of 'if and why' something works.

Fads such as learning styles, conversational marking and obsessions with graded judgements of lessons or measuring progress within 20 minutes are all real examples that have been either promoted or legitimised by Ofsted and willingly accepted by schools. Their impact on workload has been significant and has eaten into the lives of teachers, despite no substantial evidence to support a positive impact on learning. Education is prone to such fads and it is to be hoped that a more robust scrutiny of research and evidence in the future will help us to avoid similar mistakes.

Approaches in school must be formed as a result of careful consideration and engagement with what is proven to work – not just hunches or fads that are fancied by leaders at a particular moment in time.

In his foreword to *What Every Teacher Needs to Know About Psychology*[24], Professor Rob Coe of Durham University writes the following:

> *In the last few years there seems to have been a significant growth of interest from teachers and policy makers in research evidence and a scientific approach to understanding and improving education. In the space of a decade in England, randomised controlled trials in education have gone from being almost unheard of to being commonplace. A number of robust and accessible summaries of relevant research have become widely known by teachers. Social media, led by teacher bloggers and tweeters, have helped create communities of teachers who want to engage with research and discuss the ideas and their implications. There is an appetite for research evidence and an increasingly critical and sophisticated research stance.*
>
> *What we still lack is the translation of all this theory into scalable models for practice. Even if teachers know about, for example, Bjork's idea of 'desirable difficulties', they still have to work quite hard to plan their own teaching to incorporate spacing, interleaving and retrieval practice into the learner's experience. They must work from first principles, building the tools they need to use. The landscape is still one where a few pioneers forge a route through a challenging environment, working hard to gain every step of the journey. We don't yet have the infrastructure of roads, railways and settlements that would allow mass travel, but slowly and inevitably it will come.*

It is clear that we still have some distance to travel in schools in developing approaches that are better informed by evidence and research.

---

24. Didau, D and Rose, N, *What Every Teacher Needs to Know About Psychology* (John Catt Educational, 2016).

AN INTERVIEW WITH CLARE SEALY

One 'pioneer' who has forged a route in her school as a result of her engagement with research is Clare Sealy, head teacher of St Matthias Primary School in Tower Hamlets, London. Clare has become well known within the research community in England and has applied several principles from her reading around cognitive science at her school. I enjoyed questioning her about her journey over the last few years and what she has learned.

TR: Your engagement with research is really interesting and the amount of interest in your blog is evidence of how refreshing and insightful many of us find your evidence-informed approach at St Matthias. Where did it all start for you?

CS: I've been teaching 28 years, but until four years ago I don't think I had read any educational research since the stuff I had to read when doing my PGCE. Looking back, it seems incredible; but I think this is fairly standard across the profession. What changed things for me was actually Ofsted – or perhaps I should say my last Ofsted inspector, rather than Ofsted itself, as she gave me some good advice despite this being 'forbidden'.

We had a 'Good' inspection and the official report was positive (if fairly bland). But more useful was the 'shadow report' – the things she said to me off the record, which included the highs and lows that didn't fit the overall judgement. These were incredibly helpful and formed the basis of our school development plan for the next couple of years.

One thing she mentioned, which at the time didn't seem that important, was that I should definitely go on Twitter. I hadn't realised that Twitter could be used for serious purposes before that; I thought it was all people twittering on about what they'd had for lunch. She told me to follow her – not because she ever said much herself, but because she posted thought-provoking links which would start me on a journey. So that is exactly what I did. And what a journey! It's not in Ofsted's remit to give advice like this, but without her I might never have discovered the world of educational blogging.

The thing about blogs is that they usually provide links to other blogs, which provide links to others blogs and so on; so very soon, I was reading all sorts of things by all sorts of people. What absolutely flummoxed me was that actual teachers based in real classrooms could cite all sorts of educational research, with proper footnotes and everything. In particular, I recall reading Kris Boulton write about reading cognitive psychology and feeling like he had discovered 'the cheat codes for intelligence', and from there reading lots and lots of blogs by all sorts of people about knowledge and memory.

TR: *Memorising facts and learning by rote can be really unfashionable within schools and often discussions about the importance of knowledge can elicit negative reactions and language such as 'regurgitating facts' or 'stuffing knowledge down kids' throats'. Why do you think we have got to this point with the perception of knowledge in the curriculum and how have you gone about changing this in your school?*

CS: Like most teachers, I had a knee-jerk reaction to the new national curriculum's emphasis to be more knowledge based – especially since Michael Gove was the education minister at the time and he seemed to delight in upsetting teachers. Alongside this, I shared the profession-wide revulsion to the thought of teaching children something that they might not understand – rote learning – where they might be able to do a procedure, but not understand why it works. However, during some maths training, someone pointed out that while of course we need both procedural and conceptual understanding, it does not really matter if one comes slightly before the other, as long as in the end we acquire both. The example they gave was parents teaching their toddlers to count by chanting numbers as they climbed the stairs. The toddler at that point would have no conception of what this meant; but as soon as they started understanding the concept of numbers, the fact that they already knew the order that the numbers came in would be really helpful. I remember this as a real turning point in my thinking. Before that, I really thought that learning a procedure before you understood it was inherently damaging. Now, I realise that was completely daft and there are all sorts of things that we learn procedurally first and then come to understand a bit later, and vice versa. The important thing is that the two sides of the coin marry up at some point in the not-too-distant future.

We had a major focus on maths a few months after Ofsted. Our new programme was very strong on conceptual understanding through the 'concrete, pictorial, abstract' approach, but also championed children knowing not only their times tables, but also all their number bonds within 20 – not just ones where the answer was 10 or 20, but, for example, 7+8. It soon became really clear to us that what was holding back most of the children who struggled with maths was their inability to add two two-digit numbers automatically and having to resort to fingers. It wasn't that they didn't understand how to use vertical addition with regrouping, for example. It was rather that by the time they had laboriously worked out what 9+6 was, they had lost their place in the algorithm. At the time, I was not really aware of working memory or cognitive load; but I did realise that we had overemphasised conceptual understanding so much that we had neglected to give enough emphasis to the procedural side or to knowing certain things off by heart automatically, so we started to focus a lot more on that. It wasn't something I had to convince staff about at all; we could all see that this lack of knowledge was getting in the way of them being able to put conceptual understanding into practice. We had a similar epiphany about spelling and introduced a daily spelling programme at Key Stage 2 when it became clear that, however much phonics we did in Early Years and Key Stage 1, many children had forgotten much of this in terms of spelling as early as Year 3.

TR: I'm particularly interested in your example here about number bonds within 20, Clare; I have personal painful experience as a Year 6 teacher of children coming up without this fluency which meant that they would never be able to carry out a written subtraction method. How did you go from this point to developing the use of research further, both personally and across your school?

CS: At this point I was learning lots about knowledge and memory from reading blogs, but my own understanding was still a bit hazy and I wasn't sharing it yet. I was excited by the possibility of teachers learning from research, though, so we took part in a two-year EEF project on having research leaders in schools. In the first year, I and two other senior leaders took part and we did a whole school project on growth mindset, looking at the work of Carol Dweck. This led us to abandon ability grouping in maths. The project involved interviewing children and teaching assistants and sharing our results with staff at an Inset day. Everyone was shocked by the children's views about ability groups, so it was an easy 'sell' to move away from ability grouping and adopt an approach where children could choose their level of challenge for themselves. As well as looking at an area of research in detail, the project shared research about how to secure buy-in to change with lots of 'theory of change' stuff, which was really useful. I tend towards top-down models of change, then sometimes wonder why things don't take off like I'd hoped; so having models that mixed bottom-up and top-down approaches was really useful.

For the second year of the project, I therefore involved two middle leaders rather than senior leaders and we used the theory of change approach from the start. During this year, we extended the work on growth mindset to explore our deployment and practice of teaching assistants. Did we in practice have a fixed mindset towards children with SEN? The EEF had produced guidance to schools to alert them to the pitfalls of poor teaching assistant deployment, following on from the Deployment and Impact of Support Staff project – which had fairly damning evidence that deployment of teaching assistants resulted in worse pupil outcomes – and the follow-up Effective Deployment of Teaching Assistants project and the Maximising the Impact of Teaching Assistants initiative and book. The book was so good and accessible that we bought a copy for every teaching assistant and class teacher and used it throughout the year to great effect – practice was transformed.

I had also managed to persuade five teachers to join me at ResearchEd that year. One of them properly caught the research bug – although unfortunately for me, she left the next year. While the other teachers did not become full-on research enthusiasts, they certainly now understand that it has an important place in our thinking and that someone – just not necessarily them – should be reading a lot and informing the thinking of the rest of the team.

TR: I'm glad you make the point that not every teacher needs to be a research enthusiast, Clare; I agree that the most important thing is that everyone understands that someone does need to engage properly with what's written and that approaches should be adapted accordingly. What can leaders and teachers read in order to develop a more informed approach – are blogs, books and establishments such as the EEF better than one another, or is it a combination of all of these things?

CS: The point that I started to write my own blog was a real game changer for me – about a year and a half after I'd started on Twitter. At this point, I started reading a lot written by other teachers and my knowledge grew exponentially. I quickly realised that if you are going to publish something, you had better be as well informed as possible! I read a lot about knowledge organisers and multiple-choice quizzes, so introduced them to the staff in September 2017. To be honest, I reverted a bit to type and forgot the theory of change stuff, so it was a top-down initiative; but the time was right. We needed to look at how and what we taught in history, geography, science and RE, and how on earth you assessed it; so the knowledge organiser plus quiz approach fitted right in with that.

Over the past couple of years – starting with maths facts and spelling, but then moving on from there – we'd lost our horror of getting children to remember stuff. I know this feeling is still prevalent in some schools and advice on how to help people move on might be welcome, but it just sort of evaporated. It helped that children enjoyed doing the end-of-unit quizzes and almost all children did really well in them, scoring around about 100% – including children with SEN. All the negative rhetoric about 'stuffing things down children's throat' and 'regurgitating facts' just didn't hold true to what we experienced. The children enjoyed learning and took pride in their recall.

At some point, I started reading actual books rather than just blogs about books. Daisy Christodoulou's *Making Good Progress?*[25] helped me to firm up a lot of the thoughts I'd had about assessment. In particular, concerns about teacher workload were everywhere. The EEF produced a report and I realised from reading this that the evidence base for marking – which I had been led to believe was solid – was shown as wanting. Ironically, it was the EEF that was partly to blame for that misapprehension, as its promotion of feedback as a research-evidenced effective strategy went rogue. The profession as a whole, egged on by Ofsted, misinterpreted 'feedback' as marking and the rest is history. I have mixed feelings about the EEF. I've mentioned it a lot and it's been a useful starting point; but the trouble is that because the profession was so ignorant about research, we adopted its simplistic approach uncritically. My hope is that because there are now so many teachers who, through Twitter, read either actual research or blogs by people who have read the research, this won't happen again in quite the same way.

I know that the percentage of teachers on Twitter is tiny; but compared with, say, five years ago, the profession is so much better informed now. I think we really need to encourage teachers to at least know something about what research is saying. I've insisted that all our teachers read Willingham's *Why Don't Students Like School?*[26] and at least some of *What Every Teacher Needs to Know About Psychology*[27] by David Didau and

---

25. Christodoulou, C *Making Good Progress?: The future of Assessment for Learning* (Oxford University Press, 2017).
26. Willingham, D, *Why Don't Students Like School?* (Jossey Bass, 2010).
27. Didau, D and Rose, N, *What Every Teacher Needs to Know About Psychology* (John Catt Educational, 2016).

Nick Rose. Some have also chosen to read Daisy Christodoulou's book themselves. Our staff handbook references good blogs to read and people to follow on Twitter. I don't expect everyone to spend anywhere near as much time on this as I do – I accept in part that it has become a hobby – but if teachers don't want to be led down the garden path again by misinterpreted research, they need to take some responsibility for, at the very least, asking questions about the research. Ideally, every school should have at least a couple of people who read lots – preferably one of them being someone not on the SLT.

TR: Clare, it's been brilliant to talk to you about how your engagement with research has affected the reality of practice in your school and I look forward to following your journey further in the future. If there was one thing among all this that you would say has had the most impact on your school, what would it be?

CS: Of all the things I've read, the research from cognitive science is by far the most important and far reaching. I mentioned Kris Boulton and his excitement about 'discovering the cheat codes of intelligence' earlier, but it took me a lot of reading and time before I really got what he meant and how vital it is that teachers know about this. We need to teach for long-term learning, and that means actively planning to go back and revisit material regularly because initial instruction will never be enough for most children. The research from cognitive science about memory and the importance of things such as retrieval practice and spaced practice is really robust and longstanding; it's not just another flash in the pan.

People sometimes confuse cognitive science (about how people learn in practice) with neuroscience (about how learning happens at the level of structures within the brain). Neuroscience is exciting, but of little direct use to teachers – how does knowing where exactly in the brain something happens actually help us to teach better? It is also a relatively new science, so what seems to be true today may be disproved tomorrow. Cognitive science, on the other hand, is much older and therefore has a more solid evidence base to draw from. It is also much more directly applicable in actual classrooms.

It is of the utmost importance that, whether or not teachers choose to read research, they learn how memory works as part of their professional training. Not only is this important for our students, but so many of the things that the profession is rightly concerned about are the result of not knowing enough about how learning happens. Using lesson observations as a way of judging teacher quality is one thing that just doesn't hold up once you realise that there is a lot more to learning something than simply teaching children about it; this raises questions about the validity of performance-related pay. Marking is also thrown into question as an effective strategy to secure long-term learning, and it makes us consider that assessment must move away from crude reliance on data into something much more nuanced and intelligent. Our curricula need revising to ensure not only that they teach the knowledge and vocabulary that children need to become the creative, critical thinkers we want them to be, but also that regular repetition is built into them to reinforce key concepts in subsequent years, so that remembering them becomes inevitable.

ENGAGING WITH EDUCATIONAL RESEARCH

To help start or further develop your own engagement with educational research, here are seven things you can do:

1. **Start reading:** As a starting point, simply reading more around education using books, journals, blogs and Twitter is a great way to become more familiar with the issues. Once you have started to get a feel for some of the key debates, you can start to become more critical about what you read, spotting which views are informed and which are opinion or journalistic. You can then become more selective about which blogs are most useful from a research perspective.

2. **Become aware of your bias:** Different types of cognitive bias are prevalent in lots of our thinking and decision-making. Confirmation bias, where we tend to interpret data or information in a way that confirms our existing beliefs or theories, is familiar in schools and can cloud decision-making. The Dunning-Kruger effect, which describes a tendency for experts to underestimate their own ability and novices to overestimate theirs, is another common form of cognitive bias.

3. **Consider both sides:** Make sure to read around an issue, exploring the different arguments and counter-arguments. 'Holding your ideas lightly' is a good approach to adopt when doing this, so as not to let your inevitable bias sway your opinion.

4. **Connect with others:** The education research community is growing and through establishments such as the EEF, along with organisations such as ResearchEd and the Chartered College, you can start to build networks, join mailing lists and attend events. In my experience,

people within the research community are keen to connect and to debate and share ideas.

5. **Visit other schools:** Although reading theory, summaries and reports is useful, it is incredibly valuable to see different approaches with your own eyes and understand the context better. It is particularly important to be able to plan implementation, as often school improvement work fails not because the main concept was flawed, but because the implementation plan was poorly executed.

6. **Ask better questions:** What is the evidence that taking this course of action will be of benefit? What specific benefit is that likely to be? What are the unintended consequences that we should try to predict and mitigate against? Rather than asking whether something works, ask why or why not it works.

7. **Make more informed decisions:** As a result of reading more, you will be able to present different views and arguments when discussing school improvement plans. The likelihood is that the more you read, the less certain you will be about anything. This can slow down decision-making, which can be helpful at times – often no decision is better than the wrong decision.

FINDING A STRATEGIC MINDSET

Distancing yourself from the fray

Ronald Heifetz[28] describes the need to find space for strategic thinking through the metaphor of observing a dancefloor from a balcony:

> Let's say you are dancing in a big ballroom... Most of your attention focuses on your dance partner, and you reserve whatever is left to make sure you don't collide with dancers close by... When someone asks you later about the dance, you exclaim, "The band played great, and the place surged with dancers."

> But, if you had gone up to the balcony and looked down on the dance floor, you might have seen a very different picture. You would have noticed all sorts of patterns... that when slow music played, only some people danced; when the tempo increased, others stepped onto the floor; and some people never seemed to dance at all. You might have reported that participation was sporadic, the band played too loud, and you only danced to fast music.

---

28. Heifetz, R and Linsky, M, *Leadership on the Line: Staying Alive Through the Dangers of Leading* (Harvard Business School Press, 2002).

The only way you can gain both a clearer view of reality and some perspective on the bigger picture is by distancing yourself from the fray...

If you want to affect what is happening, you must return to the dance floor...

A man who does not think and plan long ahead will find trouble right at his door.

Confucius

Often, when I am on the gate in the morning saying hello to parents, I get into conversations about what different mums and dads do with their days. I find it really interesting to learn what parents get up to once they have dropped off their children. These conversations often remind me how preoccupied we become in schools with the here and now at the expense of strategic planning. One mum, for example, is a successful chef for a multinational company. When she says she is 'crazy busy' around Christmas, I assume it's because of the number of Christmas parties that she is catering for; but she corrects me that it's because she has deadlines to meet for the design of the spring and summer menus. Another dad works as a buyer for a local fashion retailer. When he is running off to catch the train to London in the summer, I ask whether he will be buying more stock for the holiday season. He laughs and says it's too late for that, and tells me of the number of coats he has just ordered for the winter. In schools, it is easy to become consumed by the number of urgent and important things that come up in any one day, at the expense of planning properly for the months and years ahead.

It's easily done, of course: there are hundreds of things we can get involved in at any one time in a school. There's also the nice, warm feeling of being helpful and needed; and of course, it is important to spend some time each day being present in the issues. But to fall into the habit of dealing only with daily operational matters and troubleshooting urgent issues is to neglect our responsibility to think strategically. This is where we must make sure we spend time off the dancefloor – perhaps off site to think and plan carefully and strategically about our next school improvement moves.

IN SUMMARY – SCHOOL IMPROVEMENT STRATEGY AND RESEARCH

- Using the four stages of school improvement, can you recognise where your school is on this journey: Stabilise, Repair, Improve or Sustain?

- What is the health of the vital organs of school improvement (safety, behaviour, curriculum, inclusion and teaching) in your school? Do any organs need specific care and attention? Are there any peripheral issues or 'cosmetic surgery' that you are distracted by that could be avoided?

- Is a clear structure established to ensure that these vital organs remain in good health, such as the 'engine room of school improvement' model? Are regular meetings held with the right teams to review, evaluate and plan action? Does effective follow-up and follow-through take place?

- How well do you use research in your work and how well informed are the many different approaches across school? Is engagement with research carried out critically or can you see where literature is cherry-picked simply to support an existing view or preferred approach?

- Are you finding enough time to think and work strategically within the school week? Booking some time away from the front line in a quiet space or even working off site is important in order to 'distance yourself from the fray'.

FIVE FIVES GRID FOR PLANNING

FIVE MINUTES: What immediate first steps can you take?

FIVE DAYS: What short-term actions can you take in the next week to kick start or plan change?

FIVE WEEKS: What actions or follow-up meetings/discussions can you plan for in the next half-term?

FIVE MONTHS: What follow-up and follow-through activities do you need to plan to ensure that the change is not just a flash in the pan?

FIVE YEARS: What might your change look like in five years? What structures, systems and processes will you need to amend to ensure that your change becomes embedded in the fabric of your school and is not a passing fad?

Healthy accountabilty

7

CHAPTER PREVIEW

But accountability has gone wrong in our system: processes are often clumsy and the stakes are too high. Rather than a 'healthy pressure' that keeps schools on their toes and increases motivation, the system is full of fear and discussion about 'what Ofsted is looking for'.

Any attempts to improve processes such as lesson observations or appraisal meetings are undermined in a culture built on fear, coercion or transactional 'carrot and stick' consequences.

A combination of high expectation for performance and improvement within a supportive and professional environment is the winning formula that takes the fear out of the challenge.

Being released from the shackles of grading lessons is empowering for both teachers and leaders, and this type of process can switch the focus from one of 'judging' to one of supporting improvement.

AND ONE FROM THE INTERVIEW INSIDE

Keep talk of accountability in the context of the pupil. I've never yet met a professional working in a school who doesn't have the best interests of their pupils at heart. By keeping the group of pupils concerned at the centre of discussions, we can mitigate some of the problems that lead to such fear and distrust.

Interview with Michael Tidd

HEALTHY ACCOUNTABILITY

> **"**
> God grant me the serenity to accept the things I cannot change; courage to change the things I can; and wisdom to know the difference.
>
> Reinhold Niebuhr

Dad

Like most sons, I have spent many hours of my life arguing with my dad about a great number of things.

Dad was a secondary music teacher in comprehensive schools for 42 years and saw a lot of change over this time. From his early pre-national curriculum days of cane-wielding housemasters, spectacular school musicals and annual trips to France conducting his 40-piece orchestra, he has spent the last 15 years fighting against the slide of music to the sidelines of the curriculum and continually dodging Ofsted and accountability bullets. Dad was, and still is, a brilliant teacher – primarily due to his love for music.

We argue about different things. Dad will say that the introduction of the national curriculum was where everything started to go wrong, and that it was so much better in the days when people who really knew their subjects could decide what to teach and when; I will argue that without some kind of agreed body of knowledge, the 'what' of education would be left to the whims and fancies of each teacher. He will argue that Ofsted is the disease of education and responsible for stifling teachers across the country; I will counter by pointing out that without the checks and balances of a regulatory body, some schools would slip into lazy practices and let down generations of kids, including his grandchildren. Dad will say something about the England team not having enough Spurs players; I will remind him that he knows nothing about football.

Our conversations often play out like this:

Me: Alright, Dad?

Dad: Hi, Tom.

Me: How's your day?

Dad: Kids were fine – it's the other stuff. More pointless meetings about data and marking policies. Learning walks happening later this week from middle managers – they've gone back to calling them 'teaching leaders' again now, rather than 'learning leaders'. Apparently we're not all writing our objectives on the board, so we've got to make sure that everyone's got them up as part of our consistency policy.

Me: (*Instinctively defensive of the middle managers who have tried to get my Dad to write a WILF on his board*) But surely you see that there's some sense in all that, Dad? I mean, trying to make sure that everyone's clear about what they are teaching isn't a bad thing, is it?

Dad: It might be right in maths or English, Tom; but they want to see me doing it in bloody music! I'm supposed to get the kids to write in books in music just so I can show that I'm doing some marking. I even staged a quiz this week rather than working on composition, just so there could be something in the books for a scrutiny that's coming up.

Me: OK, I agree that's total nonsense. But you do have to have some systems in place that people stick to. It can't just be a free-for-all, right? People need to check that teachers are doing the things they should.

Dad: It's rubbish, Tom, and everyone knows it. They should abolish Ofsted and the government, and just let good teachers get on with it. And while we're at it, they should dissolve the monarchy too.

Me: Drink?

And so the conversations continue: Dad wishing for freedom just to get on and teach, and lambasting any form of standardisation or accountability; and me standing up for (often questionable) managerial processes that might keep the occasional mediocre teacher in line.

Dad retired from his position as assistant head of a large comprehensive secondary school ten years ago to return to his first love of teaching music. When I watch him conduct orchestras and choirs across the county with his boundless energy, and I meet many of the adults who still play in his groups perhaps 25 years after they left school, it reminds me of the bigger picture that his life as a 'teacher' has played in the world. And it makes me cross to think of him spending hours after school and at lunchtimes wrapped up in meetings about data or learning walk feedback when he could have been running choirs or rehearsing soloists for shows. It makes me sad that he spends Sunday mornings writing lesson plans that no one (including him) will ever read.

It makes me both laugh and despair at the stories of how little time he would spend on national curriculum level assessments at Key Stage 3 – his logic was that whatever he put down, the data manager would soon come down and tell him what to change it to anyway.

Dad was right: the unintended consequences of accountability have spread like a disease across our schools.

Does it have to be this way?

ACCOUNTABILITY

I should start by saying that I believe it is important that schools and teachers are properly held to account for our role in education. Children only get one chance to go to school and the quality of their education has an impact on the rest of their lives. I don't think anyone would dispute that we must have high expectations and standards of what takes place in the classroom every day. Although teachers are mostly well-motivated people who want to do the best job they can, teaching is no different from any other walk of life in that, without regular and effective monitoring, things can slide and people can stop doing some of the things that they are supposed to do. It is important that we have checks and balances in the system, and I have always been happy to be held to account in a thorough and systematic way for my work.

But accountability has gone wrong in our system: processes are often clumsy and the stakes are too high. Rather than a 'healthy pressure' that keeps schools on their toes and increases motivation, the system is full of fear and discussion about 'what Ofsted is looking for'. This has led to the introduction of clunky processes, primarily as evidence-gathering exercises for external accountability, which take up precious resources that would be better directed in the classroom. A thirst for evidence of improvement rather than actual improvement has added to workload pressures and disillusioned many; this in turn has added to the recruitment and retention challenges across our schools. But it doesn't have to be this way.

Much time and energy are spent discussing where the problems of accountability come from and who is to blame, so I won't labour this further here. Instead, I will focus on what we can do as school leaders to improve things and the responsibility we have not to simply replicate crude and unhealthy external processes in our own settings.

AN INTERVIEW WITH MICHAEL TIDD

For some more thoughts on developing healthier approaches to accountability in schools, I spoke with head teacher Michael Tidd, who is well known for his expert views on primary curriculum and assessment.

TR: Accountability is such a big issue in our schools, and is often cited as a driver of stress and the reason that teachers leave the profession. Where do you think it goes wrong?

MT: I have never yet met a school leader or teacher who wants to be rid of accountability altogether. The issue always seems to be about the ways and means that we use to hold people accountable. Often, this seems to be a matter of priorities. Teachers are often driven by a moral purpose that underpins their work; when the accountability system seems to cut across that – or sometimes even plain contradicts it – there are inevitably clashes and pressures. The tools that we use for accountability purposes are necessarily broad and blunt. So often, we rely on data that requires careful and thoughtful interpretation; the system can too easily break down when that is forgotten – or when teachers feel that it has been forgotten.

TR: Key Stage 2 assessment is a subject that I know is dear to your heart. There has been such upheaval in recent years, and many see national tests as the reason why the curriculum often gets squeezed and teachers often report there is too much 'teaching to the test'. Are SATs really the enemy of primary education?

MT: I was a pupil in the pre-SATs era and it only needs one glance at the work I produced in Year 6 to realise that things have improved substantially in schools in the intervening period. You won't hear me opposing SATs in their own right. That said, it's absolutely the case that the improvements in core subjects have come at the expense of some of the breadth I experienced at that age. 'Teaching to the test' always sounds awful, but it's worth looking at what we really mean by that. If teachers are spending weeks practising test papers in lieu of teaching, then I worry about that; but if 'teaching to the test' means more arithmetic practice in Year 6 until pupils are confident in the key areas, then I think I'm in favour of it. The key thing, then, is to ensure that the tests are really testing the things we want to focus our teaching on. And I'm not sure we've cracked that yet.

TR: The tone of Ofsted has changed significantly in recent years – certainly since I first became a head ten years ago, when I was told that my job was to be the 'lead inspector in my school' and I used to maintain a 50-page self-evaluation form. Over the years, we've seen many things go out of fashion, such as graded lessons, a need to see 'progress in 20 minutes' and inspectors looking for particular teaching styles. What do you see as Ofsted's main purpose in education?

MT: I've become increasingly positive about the role of Ofsted in the system. It has some heavy baggage to offload, but we have seen real significant moves in the right direction, in my opinion. I want to see it focus its intention on the 'intelligent human' role. Schools are filled with data these days; we have no shortage of 'dumb measures' that we can use to raise questions about schools. Ofsted now needs to be the intelligent response to all the data: the human that can go into a school and discuss the data with the people on the ground to find out what is really going on. Ofsted should be the vehicle by which we move accountability beyond the bald numerical measure. First, though, it has to shake off the legacy of being the policeman of the data. Often, the stresses that lead teachers and school leaders to leave the profession are about the fear that the data will take precedence over the children involved; Ofsted could be a real success if it can persuade schools that it is really interested in interpreting the story behind the data.

TR: Regardless of what happens above us with Ofsted and the government, as leaders we are responsible for striking a healthy balance in our schools of monitoring, development, challenge and support. Having recently started headship at a new school, how have you gone about the business of monitoring and evaluating in your first year?

MT: I've tried, as much as possible, to immerse myself in the life of the school. I do the usual work scrutinies and observations of lessons; but I also try to teach in every class, to talk to children about their learning, to discuss with teachers their teaching and curriculum. Perhaps being out of the classroom has made that connection easier – at least for me. I know that when talking about data with class teachers, it's not helpful to be talking about percentages; instead, we focus on the class list. If we're setting targets, we start by talking about the individual pupils: who is where? What support is needed? Who could achieve that bit more? It's not starting from a number and trying to make the pupils fit. I also recognise that the teachers know their pupils better than I ever could. I remember only too well being told to find one or two more pupils to achieve a level or cross a threshold, with an apparent disregard for who or how. I have to hope that I continue to remember that as memories of having my own full-time class become more distant.

TR: *I think that remembering the reality of being a full-time classroom teacher is one of the most useful things that those outside of the classroom can do and something I've had to 're-remember' as time goes by. Michael, it's been great to talk to you about this important issue. Finally, if you had just one piece of advice you could give to school leaders in an attempt to create more healthy accountability in their schools, what would it be?*

MT: I think everything I could say would end up coming back to the same thing: wherever possible, keep talk of accountability in the context of the pupil. I've never yet met a professional working in a school who doesn't have the best interests of the pupils at heart. By keeping the group of pupils concerned at the centre of discussions, we can mitigate some of the problems that lead to such fear and distrust. Schools have got better at this: the focus of observation has shifted to consider the experience of the pupils rather than the performance of the teacher. Likewise, wherever possible, talking about data needs to get back to the level of the pupil. Don't discuss the gap between disadvantaged pupils and their peers; instead, look at the pupils in the class or cohort and ask what is stopping those particular disadvantaged pupils from achieving as well as other pupils. There's always more to it than the fact that their parents once received income support. Great teachers know their pupils well and can use that knowledge to plan steps to close gaps and improve attainment. Talking about the 17% gap helps no one.

Even at whole-school level, even in a large school, leaders and others would do well to remember that each one of those individuals that underpin those headline figures is different. It's very hard to devise a strategy that will raise attainment for boys or for pupil premium pupils or high attainers. Instead, we need always to think of the individuals and how their teachers can support them.

Towards healthier accountability

Much time and energy are spent discussing where the problems of accountability come from and who is to blame, so I won't labour this further here. Instead, I will focus on what we can do as school leaders to improve things and the responsibility we have not to simply replicate crude and unhealthy external processes in our own settings.

At this stage, I would like to propose three important tasks for leaders to create healthier accountability schools in our schools:

1. Take the fear out of the challenge, creating the right conditions in our school for healthy accountability.

2. Develop effective processes for school improvement that are used consistently as part of an ongoing cycle.

3. Manage external accountability with confidence, staying in control of inspection.

TAKE THE FEAR OUT OF THE CHALLENGE

As with all of the elements within this section on developing the 'Head' of wholesome leaders, it is impossible to get the processes right unless the culture and ethos are right first. Any attempts to improve processes such as lesson observations or appraisal meetings are undermined in a culture built on fear, coercion or transactional 'carrot and stick' consequences.

Creating an optimum school culture is at the heart of Mary Myatt's book, *High Challenge, Low Threat*.[29] In this, she writes: 'Top leaders create the conditions where critical guidance is not only accepted, it is expected.' Accountability processes within a culture where the threat is removed from the challenge can be highly effective, creating the right sense of urgency among staff and helping to drive improvement within a school.

Built on this concept of 'high challenge, low threat', the model I have developed in Figure 14 demonstrates how this balance is important in creating a healthy accountability culture.

---

29. Myatt, M, *High Challenge, Low Threat: How the Best Leaders Find the Balance* (John Catt Educational, 2016).

Figure 14. High challenge, low threat

- **Lazy culture (low challenge/low threat):** In these schools, expectations and performance are not high enough, yet relationships may appear positive. Leaders are likely to be too familiar and friendly with staff, and find it difficult to see the need for any change. There may be some surface-level 'nice things' happening, but overall self-evaluation is likely to be over-generous and difficult decisions are avoided. There is unlikely to be much consistency of effective teaching approaches other than lip service. Standards and staff turnover are likely to be low.

- **Toxic culture (low challenge/high threat):** Here, leaders may be trying to bring about change or insisting on things happening, but there are no high professional expectations or clarity on what excellence looks like. Leaders probably don't walk the talk and instead use carrot and stick methods of management to try to motivate staff. Standards are likely to be low. Staff turnover may be high, but not necessarily, as sometimes people become 'normalised' to these conditions.

- **Anxiety culture (high challenge/high threat):** In these schools, a high demand for performance exists, but is driven through threats of Ofsted, accountability and carrot and stick approaches. Teamwork is unlikely to be strong and conflict is the norm, with individuals competing against each other in order to hit individual goals and targets. Improvements and standards in the school may improve, but are unlikely to lead to long-term success. Workload is often high. Staff turnover may be high as teachers stay for a few years and then cannot sustain this way of working, although many stay because it might be perceived as a 'good' school.

- **Improving culture (high challenge/low threat):** A combination of high expectation for performance and improvement within a supportive and professional environment is the winning formula that takes the fear out of the challenge. In these schools, staff don't 'settle' or rest on their laurels, and improvement happens in a collegiate manner. Accountability processes are transparent and this helps to motivate individuals. Staff turnover is likely to be average, as staff generally move on to promoted posts or to progress their careers.

Question: What is the level of challenge and threat in your school? What people or processes contribute to this? What small changes can you make to increase the challenge and reduce fear within your school?

DEVELOPING EFFECTIVE SCHOOL IMPROVEMENT PROCESSES

Having first focused on creating the conditions for healthy accountability, we will now look at specific school improvement processes, often known as monitoring and evaluation or accountability processes. There is a real variety in the ways that schools approach these, and I have taken part in a wide range of different activities with countless different forms and associated paperwork over the years.

School improvement processes may be categorised as follows:

- informal first;
- the school improvement schedule;
- learning walks;
- review mornings;
- class attainment and progress (CAP) meetings; and
- appraisals.

Informal first

As Michael Tidd mentioned in our earlier interview, a starting point for keeping our finger on the pulse of a school is to spend as much time as possible visiting classrooms. Don't get comfortable on a chair somewhere in an office; get out among the action. Visit lessons and walk the corridors, lunch halls and playgrounds to find out what's really going on. Teach, talk to parents on the gate, flick through the books of the children you meet on your travels and play with children in reception to gain a wider perspective of school life, which will help to inform better decisions about where improvement is needed. This informal approach has always been my favourite part of leadership and probably suits my naturally restless and impatient urge to walk around rather than sit still. More about this in Chapter 11; but now for some more structured approaches.

School improvement schedule

In order to ensure a structured and coordinated approach, most schools will have some kind of schedule such as that presented in Table 8, which lays out different activities such as assessment, monitoring and evaluation. This is important in giving clarity to staff and leaders as to when different activities are happening and to ensure that the different processes flow from one to another.

Table 8. School improvement schedule

Week in term	School improvement activities
1	Checking intervention and SEND provision
2	
3	Termly learning conferences (teachers, parents and children)
4	Review mornings
5	Review mornings
6	Evaluation and adapting provision for next half-term
	Half-term
7	Checking intervention and SEND provision
8	
9	Summative assessment week
10	Summative assessment week
11	Analysis of assessments and CAP meetings
12	Evaluation and adapting provision for next half-term

Learning walks

Learning walks are more focused than the kind of unplanned classroom visits described above, but should still have a relatively informal feel. They should have one or two areas of specific focus, such as classroom behaviour routines, quality of classroom discussion or effective direction of support staff. These could either be a follow-up from previous development work or be identified through other monitoring or data analysis.

- Identify your area of focus and communicate a few days in advance, either by email or at a briefing, that you will carry out a learning walk to focus on one or two specific areas.

- Don't intrude too much on the learning – try to be an invisible observer. When the situation allows it, engage in conversation with teachers and children to find out more about what is going on.

- Adopt a curious mindset and avoid jumping to hasty conclusions based on first impressions of what you see. Stay long enough in each area to get a good feel for things and don't rush it, even though you are likely to have time pressure to finish quickly.

- If you are working alongside someone else, make sure you spend time looking from different angles and in different places, and then comparing what you noticed – it is interesting how similar and different two opinions can be.

- Recognise any of your biases that might have crept in. Are some of the things you notice 'pet peeves' or 'the way you would have done it', rather than things that evidence suggests are the most important to focus on?

- Follow-up with whole-school feedback, sharing successful things you saw and any areas you need to follow up on.

- Follow-up individually with any support or coaching conversations where help might be needed, but keep it light. If learning walks become perceived as being 'on show', you will stop seeing what is typical in a classroom and only get polished versions instead.

Learning Walks

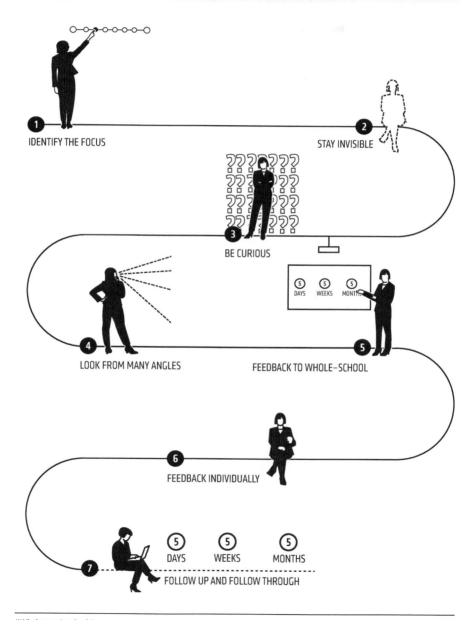

1 IDENTIFY THE FOCUS

2 STAY INVISIBLE

3 BE CURIOUS

4 LOOK FROM MANY ANGLES

5 DAYS 5 WEEKS 5 MONTHS

5 FEEDBACK TO WHOLE-SCHOOL

6 FEEDBACK INDIVIDUALLY

5 DAYS 5 WEEKS 5 MONTHS

7 FOLLOW UP AND FOLLOW THROUGH

Review mornings

Over the last three years, we have developed termly review mornings as a way of taking a more in-depth look at the learning taking place across a year group. Rather than a series of individual observations or occasional book looks, we tend to spend most of a morning in a single year group observing, reflecting and exploring the issues. Being released from the shackles of grading lessons is empowering for both teachers and leaders, and this type of process can switch the focus from one of 'judging' to one of supporting improvement.

- A couple of weeks before the review morning, send around a short survey asking staff for their opinions on what is working well in the year group at the moment, any areas that they feel might be weaker and any specific challenges or children that they would welcome support with.

- Read the feedback and do your homework on the issues or children that have been flagged up. If concerns were raised about the behaviour of individuals, do some background checks on them. If a particular subject was flagged as a weakness, talk to the subject leader about any involvement they have had. Analyse what any available data says about this issue too.

- Try to put people at ease. A morning can feel like a long time for staff to have leaders snooping in and around their classrooms, so it is important to try to make it feel more like a joint process of investigation rather than being judged.

- Have access to pupil data during the morning. It is really useful to be able to check out assessment information around groups or individuals that you might notice while in the classroom.

- Give some short general feedback to all staff involved (including support staff) at the end of the morning and then follow up with teachers individually that evening if possible. Do not give Ofsted-style grades as part of this feedback; it should focus only on helpful developmental advice and a 'next steps' discussion.

Review Mornings

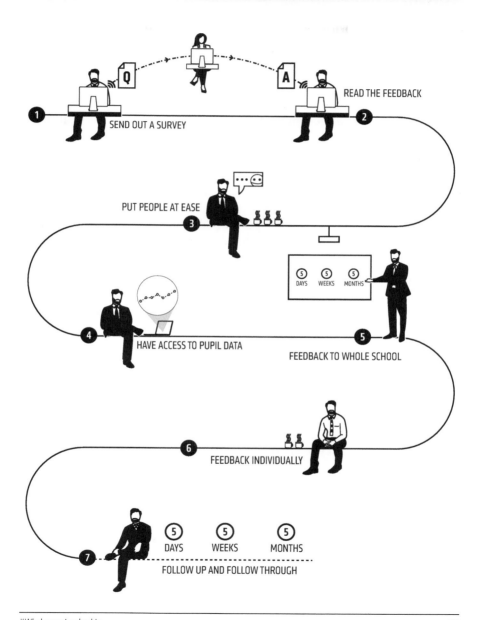

1 SEND OUT A SURVEY

READ THE FEEDBACK **2**

3 PUT PEOPLE AT EASE

4 HAVE ACCESS TO PUPIL DATA

5 DAYS 5 WEEKS 5 MONTHS

FEEDBACK TO WHOLE SCHOOL **5**

6 FEEDBACK INDIVIDUALLY

5 DAYS 5 WEEKS 5 MONTHS

7 FOLLOW UP AND FOLLOW THROUGH

CAP meetings

Class Attainment & Progress (CAP) meetings are carried out with each class teacher and relevant leaders shortly after each summative assessment point. Their purpose is for everyone to reflect on the current challenges and priorities within a class or year group. A range of sources, including assessment data, is evaluated to inform adaptations to the provision, curriculum or targeted support for the next term. Leaders can often interpret data in different ways from class teachers, so it is really useful to have this joined-up discussion once a term. It helps to hold teachers to account for provision and for children's development, and allows leaders to see where any additional support or intervention is needed.

- Organise CAP meetings to take place at the end of each term after a summative assessment point.

- Analysis should be carried out before the meeting and agreed documentation should be completed which identifies the strengths and areas of focus for the next period. Good teachers are constantly evaluating children's progress and adapting provision throughout the term, and this just formalises their thinking.

- The meeting should be a professional discussion that focuses on classes, groups and individual children and what can be done to address their needs, rather than crude percentages or which borderline children might get 'over the line'.

- The main discussion should centre on how teaching approaches and the curriculum can be adapted within the next term to address any areas of concern.

- Try to avoid the temptation to steer the discussion onto solutions to do with teaching assistant intervention and parental engagement. These may be useful things, but the 27.5 hours of curriculum and teacher time afford the greatest opportunity to make an impact.

- Use research to support your decision-making. If suggestions focus on specific interventions or organisation such streaming or reducing class sizes, look at what the EEF may have already evaluated in this area.

- Agree what the actions are going forward for the next period and make a shared record of these. Start each meeting with a review of the previous agreed actions. Did everyone do what they said they would? What impact did these actions have? What are the next steps?

CAP Meetings

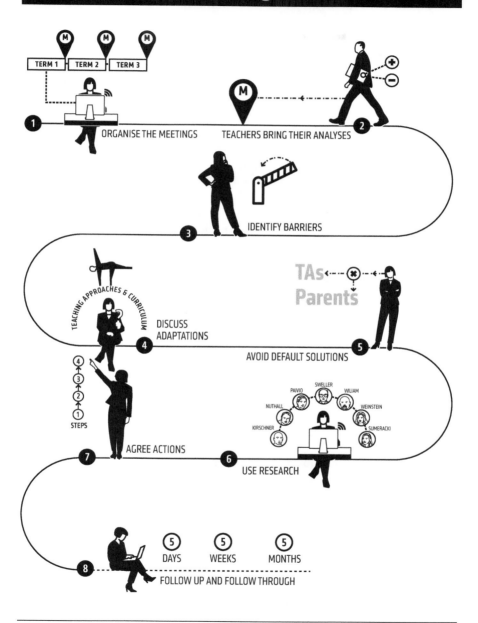

TERM 1 | TERM 2 | TERM 3

1 ORGANISE THE MEETINGS

2 TEACHERS BRING THEIR ANALYSES

3 IDENTIFY BARRIERS

TEACHING APPROACHES & CURRICULUM

4 DISCUSS ADAPTATIONS

TAs
Parents

5 AVOID DEFAULT SOLUTIONS

4
3
2
1
STEPS

PAIVIO
SWELLER
WILIAM
NUTHALL
WEINSTEIN
KIRSCHNER
SUMERACKI

7 AGREE ACTIONS

6 USE RESEARCH

5 DAYS | 5 WEEKS | 5 MONTHS

8 FOLLOW UP AND FOLLOW THROUGH

Appraisals

An annual appraisal should be a great opportunity to have a meaningful one-to-one with members of staff to thank them for their contribution to the school in the last year and to think about how they can develop in the future. Quality reflective time with staff is a rare commodity and the 40 minutes or hour that you spend with them in appraisals is precious. If this opportunity is not grasped, these useful discussions can be lost in meetings that race through the process, ticking the boxes but missing the point.

In recent years, the quality of appraisals has been limited due to a demand that they become a process where a judgement is made on performance-related pay. Since evidence now shows that the impact of performance-related pay is negligible[30], we should make sure that appraisals are used more effectively as developmental and motivational tools for our staff.

■ Be prepared for the meeting – make sure that you have all the documentation you need from the previous year and that the appraisee is prepared to talk through their objectives with supporting evidence. If either side is not properly prepared, stop the meeting and arrange a time to do it again; otherwise, it undermines the process.

■ Talk through the objectives set for last year and allow time for reflection and discussion on these points. Avoid simply focusing on the success criteria and whether a target has been 'met'.

■ Celebrate successes and take time to appreciate and thank people.

■ Include a discussion on wellbeing as part of the appraisal discussion and, if the appraisee would like to, write down some commitments that you will both make to support their wellbeing for the year ahead.

■ Avoid making the meeting a drawn-out game of cat and mouse which focuses on whether to give someone a pay rise. In my view, unless someone has not met the Teachers' Standards consistently throughout the year (in which case some kind of managed support process is warranted), they should automatically make progress on the pay scale (upper pay scale is a separate discussion).

■ Set challenges and targets that stretch and excite you both within a 'high challenge/low threat' discussion. Remind your appraisee that no one gets sacked for being ambitious and doing a good job.

---

30. EEF Toolkit – research into performance-related pay: educationendowmentfoundation.org.uk/evidence-summaries/teaching-learning-toolkit/performance-pay/.

Appraisal

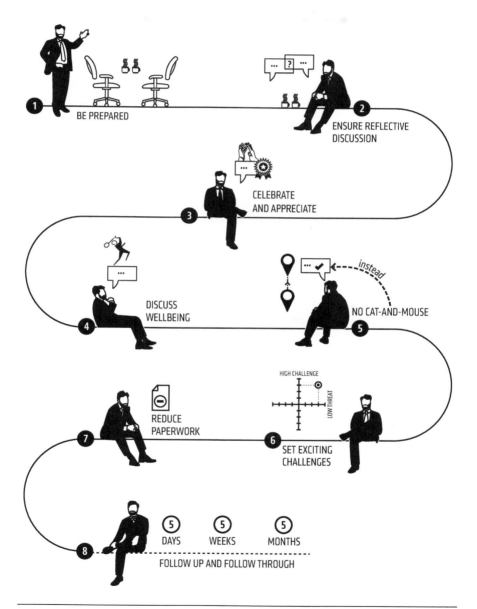

1. BE PREPARED
2. ENSURE REFLECTIVE DISCUSSION
3. CELEBRATE AND APPRECIATE
4. DISCUSS WELLBEING
5. NO CAT-AND-MOUSE — *instead*
6. SET EXCITING CHALLENGES — HIGH CHALLENGE / LOW THREAT
7. REDUCE PAPERWORK
8. FOLLOW UP AND FOLLOW THROUGH — 5 DAYS   5 WEEKS   5 MONTHS

■ Reduce the amount of written paperwork that accompanies appraisal. There is no need for pages of written comments on these documents. Every box you create on a form must be completed multiple times.

It ain't what you do, it's the way that you do it...
Whatever school improvement processes we use, it's the way we do them that matters most.

Here are ten considerations for school improvement activities:

1. **First, do no harm:** Keep in mind the unintended consequences on workload, motivation and wellbeing that monitoring and evaluation processes can cause. Plan and execute them carefully to avoid any counterproductive effect.

2. **Plan and communicate well:** Logistics are always a challenge for monitoring processes, as there are often several people who need to be involved and cover implications. Let everyone know what is happening in good time so that they can plan around it. Last-minute arrangements can cause frustration and add unnecessary stress to the process. If staff need to share planning or children's books, or present data, make sure the details of this are clarified in good time.

3. **Execute well:** Whether it's a learning walk, book look or classroom observation, carry out the process carefully and diligently, ensuring that your 'bedside manner' keeps people at ease. Make arrangements for others to be free to pick up any other urgent issues in school so you don't get distracted or pulled away; it is frustrating for teachers who will have put in a lot of preparation if those carrying out the monitoring get distracted by other issues.

4. **Do 'with', not 'to':** Avoid falling into the trap of acting like an inspector and involve teachers and children in whatever process you are carrying out, where possible. A book look is far more effective when talking to children and teachers about what you see on the pages and a planning scrutiny is almost pointless unless it is part of a conversation with the teachers who have written it. Try to capture the staff and student voice within any monitoring processes.

5. **Avoid judging:** In my experience, a lot of the discussion that takes place on these processes still relates to Ofsted grades, with people keen to hang their hat on a particular peg such as 'Requires Improvement' or 'Outstanding'. This type of discussion is pointless and avoids the more difficult thinking process of identifying the most useful types of development.

6. **Give good feedback:** Give kind, specific and useful oral feedback immediately after the activity and provide written notes within a week (more about feedback in Chapter 9). This feedback should identify time-bound actions using the 'Five Fives' approach, so it is clear which are urgent issues and which are more medium term. The feedback should also identify a time and date to meet again to review.

7. **Follow-up and follow-through:** This is an essential part of the process, but one which is often neglected due to time pressures and leaders being distracted by other challenges. If actions have been agreed, they must be executed, and it is the job of leaders to follow up the conversations and next steps. Never assume that anything has changed unless you have seen it with your own eyes. It's not enough to think that something has been done; we have to know it has been done.

8. **Keep workload lean:** Avoid the temptation to create lengthy documentation from different monitoring activities to try to prove that leadership happened. It is a common trap to spend your days monitoring and then evenings and weekends typing up wordy documentation to capture it all. Keep follow-up documents short and focus on clarity rather than an exhaustive list of everything you found out; otherwise, the main messages get lost in the waffle. If you feel that you are writing documentation for Ofsted or governors, remember that the only real evidence that matters is whether improvement happens in the classroom. Schools don't get better when leaders are writing documents.

9. **Evaluate properly:** This part of the process is another that is often missed, but is incredibly important. There is no point finding out information from across a school unless you then sit down and reflect strategically on what it means. Once the processes are over, put a bit of space between them and then sit down and ask some good evaluative questions. What were the main messages from this monitoring? What patterns can you notice? Do the things that need improving relate to people or processes? What is the next move?

10. **Repeat:** Once you have processes established, keep repeating the cycles to get improvement and avoid tinkering with them too much. Once embedded, they cause less stress for everyone.

MANAGE EXTERNAL INSPECTIONS WITH CONFIDENCE

It can be tempting to spend our lives complaining about those who hold us to account, but I believe that this mindset is unhelpful and unhealthy for both ourselves and the staff we lead. Ofsted scare stories are widespread in schools and unnecessary fear can cause poor decision-making, which often results in increased workload without any real benefit to learning. I think the experience I look back on and cringe about the most about is when I was told on a course that Ofsted expected all teachers to have their own personal professional development plans. With a 'Requires Improvement' re-inspection due, we cancelled the staff meeting that night and everyone wrote their own individual plan for professional development. Not my finest hour.

Marketing efforts take advantage of this fear – just ask any head teacher to search for 'Ofsted' in their junk mail and see what companies have been touting in pursuit of compliance or a better inspection grade. Too often in their language, leaders, trainers and consultants are guilty of using my most despised phrase, 'What Ofsted is looking for…'. It might be easy for them to say, but it's usually untrue – a lazy way of trying to get people to do what they want without convincing them of the benefits.

Resisting the temptation to dance to Ofsted's tune is easier said than done; I recognise that stomach-churning feeling when you are sitting in a briefing making anxious notes of all the things that you suddenly want to rush back and do, just in case 'someone wants to see them'. But spending our lives in a perpetual state of Ofsted readiness is a mug's game.

Leading through inspection
Whether it's an Ofsted inspection, trust review or local authority audit, this is a key time for leaders to provide calmness and certainty, to help everyone else keep perspective and to avoid the process being unduly stressful. Here are eight tips to help with this:

1. **Know the rules:** Whatever external review you are facing, make sure that you know the process well. All inspections and audits have detailed processes written around them with evaluation frameworks or rubrics; make sure that you have read all the information carefully and have spoken to others about their experiences.

2. **Prepare well:** Once you have an understanding of the framework within which you will be audited or judged, invest a limited amount of time in preparing so that you can have key documents or reports ready to go. This is not a green light to spend every waking hour getting 'Ofsted ready'; but it would be silly not to be prepared to show your school in the best possible light when the stakes are so high.

3. **Keep it normal:** Ideally, the best way to approach any inspection or audit is to keep it simple without trying anything new and avoiding bells, whistles and jazz hands. Often within classroom observations, you can see learning being made over-complicated in an attempt to impress an external audience. The best way to impress is through the best version of 'business as usual'.

4. **Create good first impressions:** There is a lot of evidence around the importance of first impressions and how these initial moments are significant in the judgements that people form of each other. Being personable yet professional at key times such as the initial phone call and the first handshake of an inspection can pay dividends, as first impressions are hard to shake off. These early moments really matter.

5. **Don't panic:** In almost every audit or inspection that I have been a part of, there was a stage where it felt like things were going badly – even for just a few minutes. It might be that a few lessons go wrong, someone gives a bad interview or you are unable to find an important document or piece of evidence somewhere. Try to remember that this is normal and hold your nerve when the early signs of panic creep in.

6. **Question the inspector:** Don't be afraid to question or challenge the views or opinions that you are uncomfortable with. In my experience, it is almost impossible to define summary opinions from the very limited amount of time that inspectors spend in the classroom; yet all kinds of things get written into schools' reports with varying degrees of accuracy.

7. **Detach ego from any judgement:** In many cases, I feel that school leaders attach their self-perception to the outcome of their latest inspection. While of course we should feel responsible for a school doing well in any external audit, if the inspection becomes 'about us' rather than the school, things have gone wrong. Personalising inspections can also drive us towards defensive positions where we become stuck arguing our corner rather than being open to learning from the process.

8. **Focus on the staff:** Try to do everything to minimise the stress of external accountability on staff, whether through offering reassurance, buying food or cancelling staff meetings for the few days afterwards. An intense few days around a visit from Ofsted can often take their toll on the team and lead to a 'slump' after the process. Remember that you need your staff fit and well for the rest of the term and try to lower the stakes for them wherever possible.

A changing Ofsted?

It's easy to blame everything on Ofsted. After all, it was an inspector who sat in my office and told me that we couldn't be outstanding unless Reading, Writing and Maths progress was 3.7 APS or above in every Key Stage 2 class. It was an inspector who sat in my office and told me what 'they' were looking for in terms of marking: unmarked books was inadequate, marked books was 'requires improvement', marked books with next step comments was 'good' and outstanding could only be achieved if children were then obviously responding to the marked comments. It was also an Ofsted inspector who led my round my own school asking me to make judgements of individual lessons based on 10 minutes of being in a lesson and then fed back to me as to whether I was right or wrong.

But while Ofsted has clearly been a central part of the accountability problem in our system, I think it is important to acknowledge a change in tone and approach in recent years.

Campaigns led by good people at the top of the organisation, such as Amanda Spielman and Sean Harford, are focused on important issues such as tackling teachers' workload and challenging myths that exist in the system. Ofsted is also so accessible these days – it's incredible how easy it is to tweet, email or talk to senior colleagues quite freely, and get answers to queries or concerns that might otherwise trouble us.

On one occasion I was working alongside a school which was about to join a new trust and where staff were absolutely petrified of a re-inspection which would almost certainly put them into special measures. A new head was in post and dealing with many difficult challenges during the day, but then spending her weekends and evenings trying to write a self-evaluation form and pull together a school improvement plan to try to be Ofsted ready. She knew that the school was in a mess and had a grip of the key issues; she just needed time to sort things out. One stressful afternoon, we decided to contact Ofsted directly to try to find out whether it was likely to inspect. A handful of tweets and a couple of emails later and we had clarified the inspection window arrangements, which meant that the school would not have a visit until well after the conversion in about two and a half years' time.

But while it does feel like those at the top of Ofsted understand the issues that inspections cause, there is still a gap between the rhetoric and the reality of what gets said on the front line by its inspectors. The challenge for Ofsted remains in gaining more consistency over time if the demons of the past are to be truly banished along with the old messages that still prevail. I remain cautiously optimistic about the role of Ofsted in the years ahead. And in case anyone is listening, here are three things that I would like to see it do.

Audit safeguarding in every school every year: At the time of writing, over 2,800 schools in England have not been inspected in the last five years and almost 100 have not been inspected since 2006. With so many schools not having faced external inspection for so long, it is completely unacceptable that their safeguarding processes have not undergone external audit or inspection during this time. In the same way that a school's finances are externally audited annually, so too should their safeguarding processes. The current safeguarding audits that take place in schools on a short inspection (Section 8) are a good basis for an annual 'MOT' that should happen in every school, regardless of its grading. The current regulatory arrangements suggest a system that values a school's finances as more important than keeping children safe.

Depersonalise school reports: While information on how well schools are performing should, of course, be in the public domain, the current process of written reports describing school leaders who can be identified either by name or by description places unnecessary pressure on individuals. This is often cited as a reason for people avoiding taking the next steps into leadership posts. I have no problem with leaders being held to account for improving their schools, but I don't see why public and personal descriptions of leaders (positive or negative) must be a part of the process.

If a school drops to 'Requires Improvement', why can't there be a period 'behind closed doors' when Ofsted, the local authority or trust and governors work intensively to address any issues? Only if they are not rectified should the report then be made public. Transparency of data and any gradings is fine; it is the 'damning reports' that follow that often make it untenable for school leaders to stay in post.

Positive reports can be just as problematic, with glowing letters posted publicly attributing the school's success to its 'uncompromising' or 'inspirational' head teacher. Whether or not these statements are true, they feed the 'hero head' narrative which is counterproductive to authentic and wholesome school improvement.

Remove the 'Outstanding' label and simplify the Ofsted categories: Switching to the alternative gradings set out in Table 9 would allow schools to focus on continuous and sustainable improvements, rather than trying to jump through arbitrary hoops. The 'Outstanding' tag has become such a distraction for schools, which spend their time obsessed about achieving this status rather than just getting better. It also often drives insular behaviour from those schools with the top grade, which are protective of their status and are therefore reluctant to play their part in supporting other schools and the wider system. Worse still, it is widely acknowledged that the pursuit of 'Outstanding' leads to narrowing of the curriculum, back-door exclusions and off-rolling to try to keep a school at the top of the league table.

Recent research has shown that schools in disadvantaged areas are ten times less likely to become 'Outstanding' than those in more affluent areas,[31] which makes a mockery of the top judgement. The banners and signs that are splattered around schools in leafy villages and well-heeled parts of the country are more a reflection of their intake and funding rather than any 'secret sauce' that can be replicated elsewhere. In my experience, the pursuit of 'Outstanding' is more of a hindrance than a help in improving overall standards across schools, and I would be pleased to see the back of it.

31. Education Policy Institute, 'School Inspection in England: Is there room to improve?', November 2016, epi.org.uk/wp-content/uploads/2018/01/school-inspection-in-england-web.pdf

Table 9. Alternative Ofsted grades

Grade A: Good and Improving

'Good and improving' is what all schools should aspire to and currently represents around 90% of the schools in the UK ('Good' and 'Outstanding'). Clearly, there is a wide range of both contexts and academic outcomes across these schools, and they will also differ significantly in their ethos and approaches. Ultimately, children will achieve good educational outcomes in relation to their starting points, behave well, be safe and leave these schools with well-rounded experiences across the curriculum which will help to develop them as individuals.

'Good and Improving' schools offer children a good deal and the taxpayer good value for money. Leaders of 'Good and Improving' schools will base their priorities on both maintaining and improving their own schools and playing a proactive part in system-wide school improvement, collaborating and supporting others within a trust, geographical cluster or local authority.

Grade B: Requires Improvement

The school is not yet good. The teaching at the school is not consistently good, and educational outcomes and behaviour are not as good as they should be.

Grade C: Inadequate

As above, plus either the leadership of the school does not have the capacity to improve the situation quickly or children are unsafe.

IN SUMMARY – HEALTHY ACCOUNTABILITY

■ What is the culture of accountability like in your school? Is there a healthy balance of high challenge and low fear which creates the right conditions for healthy accountability?

■ How often do you hear leaders use Ofsted as a reason to do things in your school? Even if leaders claim they do not do things for Ofsted, can you still hear it in the language of staff if you listen carefully enough?

■ Which school improvement processes are used for monitoring and evaluation in your school? Do these focus on improvement or evidence gathering? How can they be improved?

■ How effectively are school improvement processes used throughout the year? Are they planned and delivered well?

■ Is the workload considered around accountability to avoid unnecessary paperwork and lengthy documentation from leaders?

■ How effective is the follow-up and follow-through on issues that are picked up in the school?

■ How well do leaders manage external inspection or audits so that these processes become the best version of 'business as usual' and do not detract from the continued work to improve the school?

FIVE FIVES GRID FOR PLANNING

FIVE MINUTES: What immediate first steps can you take?

FIVE DAYS: What short-term actions can you take in the next week to kick start or plan change?

FIVE WEEKS: What actions or follow-up meetings/discussions can you plan for in the next half-term?

FIVE MONTHS: What follow-up and follow-through activities do you need to plan to ensure that the change is not just a flash in the pan?

FIVE YEARS: What might your change look like in five years? What structures, systems and processes will you need to amend to ensure that your change becomes embedded in the fabric of your school and is not a passing fad?

Assessing like a consultant doctor

CHAPTER PREVIEW

8

Assessment has become the primary culprit in the ongoing challenges to teacher wellbeing, recruitment and retention. Workload in this area has spiralled out of control – particularly in areas such as marking and data inputting.

Assessment should be about understanding children's grasp of specific aspects of the curriculum rather than assigning them with generic levels or labels.

Testing can often get a bad press in schools – largely due to the high-profile and public accountability of SATs and GCSEs. But tests in themselves are no bad thing and become helpful tools when used well.

One of the perks of having a child with a disability and a complicated medical history is that you get to see the expertise of consultant doctors up close.

Unless provision and interventions are adapted as a result of summative assessment, there is little point in doing it.

I think one good thing senior leaders can do is to 'time-cost' marking policies – work out exactly how long it would realistically take for a teacher on a normal timetable to fulfil every aspect of the marking policy. Often when you do this, you realise it is completely unworkable!

Interview with Daisy Christodoulou

ASSESSING LIKE A CONSULTANT DOCTOR

> **"**
>
> When a measure becomes a target, it ceases to become a good measure.
>
> Goodhart's Law

Consultant doctor or GP?

One of the perks of having a child with a disability and a complicated medical history is that you get to see the expertise of consultant doctors up close. I have immense respect for everyone in the medical profession, but some of the specialists who have worked with Freddie have been class acts. One of the things that strikes me about these doctors is how they look beyond the obvious and avoid drawing quick conclusions. Rather than making decisions based on limited information, the most skilled and experienced doctors will examine a range of information about a patient as part of their assessment, including blood tests, scans, examinations in clinic, patient history and referrals from other medical professionals. Similarly, the most effective teachers and leaders understand the limitations of any particular test or assessment and can use their experience and expertise to interpret them wisely. And just as careful and intelligent consideration of patient information can lead to an accurate diagnosis and the prescription of helpful treatment, meaningful assessment can lead to greater understanding of gaps in learning and effective tailored teaching and intervention.

Another attribute of these consultants is expert knowledge in their field. When Freddie suffered from a rare form of childhood epilepsy, we were prepared to travel the world to be seen by a paediatric neurologist with experience of this condition in babies with Down's syndrome. Armed with experience and well read in the research on this specific condition, Doctor Jay could offer more answers than the GP or even the majority of neurologists – prescribing specific treatment with a knowledge of the risks, side effects and chances of success.

Just as someone's health cannot be expressed in a simple number, learning cannot be captured in a single measure or grade. Like many aspects of education, answers to questions around assessment are very much dependent on the subject area and age range. The methods and interpretation of Early Years development are completely different beasts from Key Stage 2 writing; GCSE music assessment is an entirely different game from maths. With this in mind, we should become comfortable that assessment will look very different across different subjects and phases.

Allowing well-trained subject experts to adapt practices around their subject areas or age range is likely to be more fruitful than a leader insisting on consistency and implementing a one-size-fits-all approach to assessment. But accepting assessment as a subject-specific process raises further challenges for those of us in primary schools where teachers primarily operate more like GPs, with a working knowledge of many curriculum areas, rather than the greater subject expertise of their secondary school colleagues.

Assessment has undergone dramatic change in recent years and is a complex issue. 'Assessing like a consultant doctor' has become a useful analogy for me as we become more familiar with this world without levels.

SORTING OUT ASSESSMENT

Assessment is a key issue to sort out in any school and there is a significant opportunity to improve schools if we get it right. The implications of any decisions on assessment are significant and reach into many different places, including the following:

- classroom practice;

- marking and feedback;

- accountability and performance management/appraisal;

- school reports;

- the language of teachers when describing learning; and
- the language of parents and children and perceptions/comparisons of children as learners.

Assessment has become the primary culprit in the ongoing challenges to teacher wellbeing, recruitment and retention. Workload in this area has spiralled out of control – particularly in areas such as marking and data inputting. Alongside this, a lack of clarity around national assessment since the removal of levels and increased accountability pressure on schools to achieve in performance tables have combined to create the perfect storm.

It is fair to say that we haven't got assessment right yet. Two important challenges exist for school leaders:

1. How do we make assessment more meaningful?

2. How do we make assessment more manageable?

A LIFE BEYOND LEVELS

In 2014, following an expert review on assessment, the government removed national curriculum levels. For around 15 years prior to this, levels were the bedrock of assessment systems in English schools – a shared language used by millions of teachers, parents and pupils across the country in an attempt to quantify learning.

For many of us, levels offered indicators of children's achievements and became the basis for important conversations around progress and accountability. With hindsight, however, this was more of an illusion than reality. In its final report published in September 2015, the Commission on Assessment Without Levels said the following:

> *Despite being intended only for use in statutory national assessments, too frequently levels also came to be used for in-school assessment between key stages in order to monitor whether pupils were on track to achieve expected levels at the end of key stages. This distorted the purpose of in-school assessment, particularly day-to-day formative assessment. The Commission believes that this has had a profoundly negative impact on teaching.*[32]

This report also highlighted a number of reasons for the removal of levels:

- Too often, levels became viewed as thresholds and teaching became focused on getting pupils across the next threshold instead of

---

32. www.gov.uk/government/publications/commission-on-assessment-without-levels-final-report

ensuring that they were secure in the knowledge and understanding defined in the programmes of study.

- Levels used a 'best fit' model, which meant that pupils could have serious gaps in their knowledge and understanding, but still be placed within the level.

- Pupils could have more in common with those assessed at a different level than those at the same level. The difference between pupils on either side of a boundary might have been very slight, while the difference between pupils within the same level might have been considerable.

- Levels did not lend themselves to assessing the underpinning knowledge and understanding of a concept.

- Although levels were intended to define common standards of attainment, the level descriptors were open to interpretation. Different teachers could make different judgements.

- Too often, levels dominated lesson planning. Teachers planned lessons which would allow pupils to learn or demonstrate the requirements for specific levels.

- Levels were often the main focus of conversations with pupils and their parents or carers. Pupils compared themselves to others and often labelled themselves according to the level they were at.

There are many benefits to a world without levels that I think we are still yet to realise. It is proving a difficult shift for the system to come to terms with assessment as understanding children's grasp of specific aspects of the curriculum, rather than assigning them with generic levels or labels.

Since the removal of levels, many different approaches have been adopted in schools, with varying degrees of success. On the one hand, some have simply reinvented levels under different guises or have fallen into a black hole without any useful assessment data at all. On the other, some have really grasped the opportunity to gain more meaningful information about specific and important aspects of learning, which they can then use to tailor their teaching and make better strategic decisions.

AN INTERVIEW WITH DAISY CHRISTODOULOU

For some help with this challenge, I spoke to renowned assessment expert Daisy Christodoulou, author of *Making Good Progress?*, former head of assessment at Ark Academies and now a director of No More Marking.

TR: We have lived a 'life beyond levels' for almost four years now. It's been a turbulent time – particularly for those of us in primary schools where there are still lots of question marks about writing assessment, progress measures and a planned new Early Years Foundation Stage baseline. What do you think we have learned over this period and what are the big issues that still need solving?

DC: I think the good news is that teachers and schools are thinking a lot more about assessment: they realise how important it is and the importance of training. The bad news is that in the rush to put something in place when levels went, too many schools ended up creating a system that was levels under another name. In particular, I think that too many schools are too dependent on prose descriptors for both formative and summative assessment. RAG-rating pupils against statements such as 'I can infer insightfully' does not give us accurate summative information or helpful next steps.

TR: The first challenge I presented at the beginning of this chapter is how to make assessment data more meaningful to teachers – something that I work on every day with staff across our trust. So much anxiety and confusion around assessment still exists. What can we do?

DC: I think part of the issue has to be around better training – both at initial teacher training (ITT) and for CPD. The Carter Review of Initial Teacher Training in 2015 found that many vital assessment concepts were just not being taught in ITT. For example, validity, reliability, norm-referencing, criterion-referencing – these are really important concepts that lend themselves well to being taught in a training course. Evidence Based Education is currently doing some really good work in this area with its assessment academy.

I think that an understanding of these key issues would ease some of the anxiety that teachers can feel about assessment. In particular, it's important to understand about reliability, which is a measure of consistency. No assessment is perfectly reliable. A pupil's mark can fluctuate depending on how they felt on the day of the test, the exact pattern of questions that appeared on the test paper and whether the marker sees that particular test paper just after a set of really good or bad papers. There will always be error in assessment – but that doesn't mean it's worthless! Understanding and quantifying the reliability can help us understand the weight we can and can't place on the results. Validity is an equally important concept. Broadly speaking, this tells us whether the assessment is telling us what we want it to. If we are looking at the results of a pupil's maths test, we expect the test to tell us something about that pupil's performance at maths. If it turns out that the test had so many word problems that you would need to be very good at reading to understand it, then we have a problem with the validity.

TR: *This leads us on to the second challenge that I posed at the beginning of this chapter: how do we make assessment more manageable?*

DC: I think the confusion around assessment is definitely leading to workload problems. Again, I think a lot of the issue comes down to misplaced faith in prose descriptors – teachers are often writing lengthy written statements taken from the interim frameworks or mark schemes at the bottom of a piece of work. This is incredibly time consuming and isn't that helpful for pupils either! I think that one good thing that senior leaders could do is to 'time cost' marking policies: work out exactly how long it would realistically take for a teacher on a normal timetable to fulfil every aspect of the marking policy. Often when you do this you realise it is completely unworkable! That's the first step to realising something has to change; then you can think about using short answer questions, whole-class feedback, comparative judgement and other time-saving tools.

TR: *We've focused mainly on summative assessment here so far, but none of this makes learning any better unless teachers can use this information to inform and adapt their teaching as a result. What approaches would you suggest schools use to turn summative assessment into information that can drive more responsive teaching?*

DC: I think you can get some formative information from summative tasks. For example, whole-class feedback sheets, which are really popular at the moment, allow teachers to read a set of summative essays and then respond to the whole class in the next lesson with a series of activities based on their misconceptions. But I also feel that you need some different tasks. Some of the best formative tasks are quite precise and short, so you can't use them to get a summative grade.

TR: In recent years, you've developed comparative judgement as an alternative approach to teacher assessment. We've seen some real potential here in our schools – particularly in how writing can be assessed with more accuracy and with less workload. Do you think this approach could replace national assessments in writing?

DC: I think that comparative judgement is already providing more reliable and helpful data than the national writing assessments – and in a fraction of the time! We've also designed the judging process in such a way that it's very hard to manipulate – teachers compare their own pupils with their own pupils, and other pupils with other pupils, but they never compare their own pupils with other pupils, meaning that they can't be biased in favour of them. However, we are still at an early stage, and we know that there can be lots of unintended consequences of statutory assessments. So I think for the time being, comparative judgement is something that schools can use to inform and support national assessments.

TR: Thanks, Daisy – it's been great talking with you. If you had to give school leaders three pieces of advice when they are trying to set up meaningful and manageable assessment processes in their school, what would they be?

DC:

1. Time cost your marking policy!

2. Distinguish clearly between the different purposes of all your assessments – are they to help pupils learn? Or are they to arrive at a reliable and consistent grade?

3. Think about how often you want summative data. We are in the mindset of thinking that we need it six-plus times a year – but I don't think we need it more than twice!

SEPARATING SUMMATIVE AND FORMATIVE ASSESSMENT

Lots of discussion around assessment gets confused because it includes both formative and summative aspects. While there are inevitable links across all types of assessment, it is helpful for us to create clarity in school around three distinct forms of assessment and their separate functions. These are presented in Figure 15.

Figure 15. Formative and summative assessment

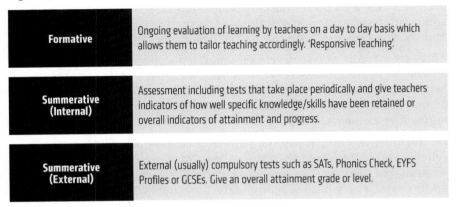

Formative	Ongoing evaluation of learning by teachers on a day to day basis which allows them to tailor teaching accordingly. 'Responsive Teaching'.
Summerative (Internal)	Assessment including tests that take place periodically and give teachers indicators of how well specific knowledge/skills have been retained or overall indicators of attainment and progress.
Summerative (External)	External (usually) compulsory tests such as SATs, Phonics Check, EYFS Profiles or GCSEs. Give an overall attainment grade or level.

Dylan Wiliam, who is largely responsible for making the phrase 'formative assessment' commonplace in education, has more recently suggested 'responsive teaching' as a better description. This shifts us to considering activities such as feedback and marking more in the category of 'teaching' rather than 'assessment'.

Example of really big mistake: calling formative assessment formative assessment rather than something like 'responsive teaching'.

Dylan William

TEN STEPS TOWARDS BETTER SUMMATIVE ASSESSMENT

It would have been far more helpful if the DfE had held on until Daisy Christodoulou had written *Making Good Progress?* before it removed levels, but now finally the fog is lifting. Having spent a number of years working hard on primary assessment, here are ten things I think are important to improve summative assessment in a school:

1. Choose what to assess and why.

2. Decide when to assess.

3. Beware the rubrics.

4. Use tests well.

5. Avoid the ghost of levels.

6. Read the data well.

7. Respond to assessment.

8. Communicate to parents.

9. Make it manageable.

10. Repeat and tinker with care.

1. Choose what to assess and why

It sounds obvious, but it is important for leaders to think hard about what assessments are being carried out in their schools and why. The prize of more meaningful assessment is significant, but comes at a high cost of thinking and planning time – something easily overlooked due to the feeling of urgency just to have something in place. Keeping in mind the ideal of teachers as consultant doctors and the range of different assessment information that is useful to have, we have chosen to build our summative assessment processes around the following information across our MAT:

- Prior academic attainment.

- Contextual information.

- Current and previous standardised test scores in maths and reading (reading ages and standardised scores) (three times per year).

- Attitudes to school and self (Pupil Attitudes to Self and School survey).

- Cognitive ability testing (CATs).

- Teacher assessment of specific curriculum knowledge and concepts.

While most schools are in the process of working out similar lists of summative assessments to provide consistent and reliable grades, it is the last point which is both the most challenging and the most important. Working out which specific concepts should be assessed shifts a discussion around assessment to one about the curriculum. What specifically are those fewer things that should be studied in greater depth and what is the best way of assessing how well children have grasped them? This is the important and difficult work that still remains for many and will require changes to a school's curriculum in order for it to be successful.

2. Decide when to assess

I made the point in the previous chapter that it is important for schools to have a well-established school improvement calendar, so that summative assessment points fit into the rhythm of the school year. It is also worth considering the timing of different assessments carefully.

Some lend themselves to being carried out twice or three times a year; others annually; and some, such as CATs assessments, might be carried out at a single point.

There is definitely an opportunity for many schools to benefit here by reducing the frequency of testing and summative assessment – particularly those with four, five or six assessment points a year. Spacing out assessment points frees up precious curriculum time for more teaching to take place and progress to be made between these points; it can also reduce workload significantly. In our earlier conversation, Daisy Christodoulou advocated just two formal assessment points a year; we have chosen to use three across our primary schools. Either way, there is a lot to be gained by reducing the frequency of summative assessment.

Unfortunately, many schools that I speak to insist on retaining six assessment points due to external accountability pressures from their trust, their local authority or Ofsted, and a perceived need to track progress more regularly. This concept that more regular summative assessment equates to more rigorous and effective leadership is flawed and takes up valuable teaching time. The worst version of this is the spreadsheet where every national curriculum subject gets a summative teacher assessment every half-term; I can think of few less reliable or valid pieces of data.

As well as fixed points in the assessment calendar, it is important that teachers still feel both the responsibility and freedom to carry out summative assessment at different points within their teaching sequence. The assessment calendar does not have a monopoly on summative assessment and teachers should still be building in opportunities to understand how well children have acquired and retained different knowledge and concepts using tools such as quizzes, observations and specific short tasks. A key point here is to consider the space between teaching concepts and assessing them – if summative assessments come at the end of a unit of work (often termed 'warm tasks'), children are much more likely to do well than if they come a month or so later. Spacing assessments to see what has been retained can potentially offer much more useful information than 'warm tasks' which might show an artificially positive picture.

3. Beware the rubrics
One of the most common tools used in assessment is the 'rubric' – or prose descriptor – such as the new primary Interim Assessment Frameworks. Daisy Christodoulou referred earlier to an over-reliance

on these within schools when assessing and there are three potential problems we should consider.

The first is one of reliability, as the written statements are often non-precise and leave themselves open to interpretation. Take, for example, the following statement from the Key Stage 2 Writing Assessment Framework:

■ *in narratives, describe settings, characters and atmosphere.*

This statement invites many questions from anyone attempting to decide whether it has been achieved. How well are the characters, settings and atmosphere described? What language should we consider to be effective description at this age? How often must the pupils do this to be sure they have learned it? In a room of ten people, you are likely to get several different answers.

While no one would dispute that it is desirable for children at the end of primary education to use description well within narrative writing, a statement that can be interpreted so differently is unlikely to be a reliable assessment. Attaching high-stakes accountability around statements such as this distorts their use further as teachers with a vested interest become prone to cognitive bias.

The second problem is to do with validity, as the descriptors often get broken down into a series of statements which can be seen within writing. The reality of this practice is that 'teaching to the rubric' takes place, with features such as 'use of a semi-colon' or 'use of fronted adverbial phrases' becoming objectives which teachers then focus on in order to ensure that they can be successful in an assessment. Taking the use of a semi-colon as an example, it may be that reliability is higher as a number of different teachers are more likely to be able to agree that semi-colons are being used. But the usefulness of this is questionable if it leads to children scattering semi-colons throughout work that is no better overall.

The third problem around rubrics is the workload that is driven by 'evidence gathering' to prove that individuals have met different aspects. Schools have invested countless hours into building banks of evidence to show that individuals have met different points on rubrics. This has developed into a culture of classroom practitioners spending less time teaching and more time gathering a comfort blanket of evidence. It is an example of where creating an illusion of effective teaching has overtaken the business of effective teaching itself.

For these three reasons, we should carefully consider the use of written rubrics in summative assessments. While they can still play their part as diagnostic tools and identify strengths and weaknesses in the development of individuals, groups and classes, they offer too little reliability and validity for the high workload they demand.

4. Use tests well

Testing can often get a bad press in schools – largely due to the high-profile and public accountability of SATs and GCSEs. But tests in themselves are no bad thing and become helpful tools when used well.

Using well-established standardised tests offers greater reliability and validity than a summative teacher assessment grade or level. Standardised testing also allows comparisons to a national benchmark and a more accurate prediction of children's end of key stage performance. Of course, no assessment is perfect and all have different flaws. Understanding the nuances and limitations of any test or assessment is important – not because it makes it worthless, but because it helps us to understand how and where they can be used and what level of confidence we can have in the inferences we draw from them.

As well as standardised tests at set points throughout an academic year, low-stakes testing or 'quizzing' is a simple and powerful tool which can be used within the curriculum with two key benefits. First, it can provide feedback to pupils and teachers of retention of knowledge and concepts, and therefore serve as a starting point for more precise teaching around misconceptions. Second, it is known that regular retrieval of information helps with the retention of knowledge, and that regular testing and feedback can be an effective way of committing curriculum knowledge to long-term memory. This theory, known as the 'testing effect', is considered most effective when carried out in a low-stakes environment, where the focus is on learning from misconceptions rather than comparisons of scores or grades.

Overall, the use of testing can be a positive and helpful part of any summative assessment system, providing more efficient and reliable ways of understanding children's achievements.

5. Avoid the ghost of levels

Although we might not call them levels any more, many schools' assessment systems have replicated old approaches that we had with levels. It is an easy trap to fall into – particularly when feeling under pressure to provide external bodies or governors with indicators of how well the school is performing.

Consider the following points to avoid the problems with levels creeping back in:

■ Where results from standardised tests exist, analyse the data from these tests itself, rather than attempting to convert it into a category or label. Standardised testing information is useful in its own right – labels less so.

■ Identify the specific curriculum knowledge or skills to be learned in each phase of school and focus on how these are checked. Steer assessment conversations away from talk of children working at generic labels (eg, EXS or GDS) and on to discussions about which key aspects of the curriculum have been secured.

■ Avoid placing accountability targets that relate to any invented labels, numbers or grades. Reporting to governors that X% of children are at B3 may feel satisfying, but is unlikely to be reliable and simply creates the illusion of attainment or progress.

■ Accept that in years with external statutory testing, it's OK to prepare children to do well in a test (without losing the richness of the curriculum). In other years, the focus should be on creating better readers, writers and mathematicians rather than boosting children over a particular arbitrary line.

6. Read the data well

Something we could become much better at in schools is interpreting assessment data more intelligently. It is too easy to draw simple inferences and conclusions from data without thinking hard enough about the real underlying cause. There are also many biases at work as we choose either to ignore or to engage with the question of how effective our individual practice may be.

In order to get to the root of issues, it is helpful to be able to understand both correlation and causation between input and outcomes – correlation being where we can see a connection between two pieces of data and causation being the understanding of which one caused the other.

One example of this could be a link that we notice between low attainment and poor attendance. It is easy then to draw a quick inference that the poor attendance is the cause of the low attainment. This may of course be true, as a child not at school is unlikely to learn; but it might be that the low attainment and an associated dislike of being in the lesson are leading to the absence. In this case we know that there is a correlation (a connection between both attendance and attainment), but we cannot be sure of the causation (which – if either – caused the other).

In many cases, the truth is that we don't really know, and it would be better to admit this and then carry out further investigation rather than jumping to the simplest conclusion.

In a response to some of the frustrations of levels, many recent attempts at assessment have become oversimplified, trying to give quick and convenient labels, levels or colours to individuals, groups and classes as a way of creating 'idiot-proof' data analysis. Rather than trying to simplify assessment, we would do better to accept its complexity and put our focus into trying to better understand what it tells us.

> *For every complex problem there is an answer that is clear,*
> *simple, and wrong.*
>
> **HL Mencken**

7. Respond to assessment

One major frustration with summative assessment is where nothing changes in teaching provision as a result of the time and energy invested in tests, teacher assessments and data. Unless provision and interventions are adapted as a result of summative assessment, there is little point in doing it.

Just as a doctor focuses on both diagnosis and treatment, we need not only to interpret data well, but also to become proficient at what we 'prescribe' following assessment cycles. In Chapter 7 I introduced CAP meetings as part of the school improvement cycle, with the main purpose of ensuring that adaptations to teaching approaches are agreed and implemented. There are many different types of 'treatment' that we can consider, including timetable adaptations, intervention groups, changes to seating plans, engagement with parents of individuals and pastoral/behavioural support. These types of prescription may be effective, but can often be too generic – focusing more on resource and logistics rather than identifying the specific parts of the curriculum that need investigation.

Just as it is often easier to take a tablet for an ailment rather than making a more difficult lifestyle change, in schools the easy option can often be to prescribe a generic or third-party intervention rather than addressing the fundamental issue within our own classrooms and curriculum. For example, if summative assessments shows that children find long multiplication tricky, rather than simply assigning more practice or creating an intervention group, we would do better by focusing on this specific area within the curriculum, learning more about why children are finding it difficult, whether they have secure number facts, whether the method is being taught correctly or whether they just need more regular practice. Ensuring that teachers feel they have 'permission' to adapt their curriculum around what they have learned through assessments is also important.

8. Communicate with parents

One of the initial reasons cited for the removal of levels was that they were unclear to parents; yet many of the new systems that have sprung up in place have caused much greater confusion. New labels, points and descriptors now exist that have not only changed, but are inconsistent across different schools. As part of any new assessment system, we should consider how we can communicate to parents in a way that gives them clarity and the best possible opportunity to give support at home.

One point to consider is the timing of reports and parent consultation meetings that are held throughout the year, to ensure that they are organised well so that the information from assessments can flow into the reports that parents receive before consultation meetings. Traditional primary school end-of-year reports are a major commitment, but offer little value to learning as they are written at the end of the year, with no chance for the report's contents to be worked on before children move on. Instead, it is worth considering using shorter reports earlier in the year which flag up areas to focus on so that parents and teachers can work together while there is still time in that school year.

Another point to consider is the content of reports – the most important being the inclusion of specific curriculum content that children need to work on to improve. Just like good feedback to children, sharing precise next steps with parents – such as knowing that a child needs to learn all the subtraction bonds within 20 – is more helpful than a generic statement such as 'improving recall of number facts'. Information such as reading ages and standardised scores over time are also more likely to be meaningful to parents, rather than vague language such as 'emerging', 'exceeding', 'mastery' or 'deep'.

Parents should also have some kind of clear explanation of where their child is performing in relation to national expectations. For all the problems with target grades and reporting levels and language, parents need to understand where their child's academic performance sits and what their end of key stage achievements might be. This sounds obvious, but can get missed: I have seen parents' evenings where parents come and go, have an enjoyable and personal exchange about their child and then leave none the wiser as to whether that child is a high flyer or struggling to keep up with curriculum expectations.

9. Make it manageable
Assessment has become a source of huge workload and school leaders – myself included – have been guilty in the past of implementing policies and procedures which have generated unnecessary work for teachers. Much of this workload is 'invisible': it's the stuff that happens late at night or over weekends and half-term holidays, so we don't necessarily see the true extent of the time and effort required to complete it. If we had to pay overtime for the additional hours that each new process 'cost', it would undoubtedly make us think more carefully about the value we get back in return.

Here are some examples of places where we can trim the assessment workload:

- Have you revisited marking expectations with staff? This is 'low-hanging fruit' for most schools in terms of trying to free up time to work on more important things. I have included a blog post later in this chapter on how we managed this in my school.

- Do you capture information from teachers on how many hours it takes them to complete assessment tasks such as data entry, school reports or marking assessments? Consider using this as a starting point to identify where to invest efforts to save more time.

- Are the processes for data collection slick and time efficient? A common concern from teaching staff is time-consuming processes including 'double data entry', where the same information must be entered into different spreadsheets or systems. Could these processes be made leaner for staff?

- Have you revisited the formats for children's end-of-year reports? These are an incredibly time-consuming element of workload for teachers, yet there is no correlation anywhere between more detailed reports and higher achievement in schools. Parents do appreciate a personal comment, so focus on this and make sure they are done well. I would avoid having senior leaders or the head making comments too, as a significant opportunity cost comes from the time invested in this process – usually at a really busy time of the year.

■ Are all the different layers of assessment necessary? Do you learn anything more about what to do as a next step with a class, group or individual as a result? It may be that you already know that inference is a real weakness for a specific reading group or that your pupils don't have secure number bonds and multiplication facts, which is the cause of their poor written methods. In these cases, what is the point in carrying out a wealth of further question level analysis tasks or highlighting diagnostic sheets when you could spend more time simply getting on and teaching the misconceptions? Not every patient with a headache needs an MRI.

10. Repeat and tinker with care

Summative assessment processes are more valuable when repeated over a number of years so that teachers and leaders can make comparisons with different cohorts and analyse patterns and trends. After several cycles, quirks of different tests become familiar and it is easier to be diagnostic and draw more helpful inferences and conclusions as a result. For these reasons, keeping summative assessment activities consistent is advantageous – it is unhelpful if leaders are constantly chopping and changing assessments because they have found something that looks better or cheaper.

Of course, a counter-argument to this is that in the current climate, change will inevitably be needed. The market is still responding to new national assessment guidance, so we have to accept that it will take time to settle down. We have also seen many schools which have simply reinvented levels in different guises; in these situations, another change (assuming that it's done well) is likely to be a better option than burying heads in the sand.

Overall, the principle of making careful choices and then sticking with them to get the benefits of repeat cycles is important.

FEEDBACK, NOT MARKING

Marking policies have become totally out of control across our schools during the last ten years – so much so that they were identified as the single biggest contributor to unsustainable workload in the DfE's 2014 Workload Challenge.[33]

---

33. DfE, 'Reducing Teacher Workload', www.gov.uk/government/publications/reducing-teachers-workload/reducing-teachers-workload

Marking has always been part and parcel of life as a teacher. As a child, I remember many evenings watching my mum ticking piles of books on the living room floor. But approaches have changed dramatically in recent years, becoming incredibly time consuming and burdensome. New language became commonplace in schools, such as 'depth marking', 'triple marking' and 'conversational marking'. Regular and lengthy written comments from teachers with expectations of children responding in writing have become the norm.

The important point to make here is that there is little evidence to suggest that 'depth marking' is effective and makes for better learning. It is therefore possibly the costliest example of where high-stakes accountability based on 'easy measurables' or 'proxies for learning', rather than real learning itself, has become a practice that is often unwieldy and ineffective.

Thankfully, pretty much everyone – including the DfE, Ofsted and teacher unions – has now made public that they do not support marking approaches that include lengthy written comments, and schools are changing their practices accordingly. Ofsted, in particular, has been proactive in making clear that it does not expect a specific type or frequency of marking, with the following statement:

> Ofsted recognises that marking and feedback to pupils, both written and oral, are important aspects of assessment. However, Ofsted does not expect to see any specific frequency, type or volume of marking and feedback; these are for the school to decide through its assessment policy. Marking and feedback should be consistent with that policy, which may cater for different subjects and different age groups of pupils in different ways, in order to be effective and efficient in promoting learning.[34]

The opportunity cost of marking policies in schools is significant and we should embrace this chance for change with enthusiasm. As an ex-Year 6 teacher who has spent thousands of hours of my life marking hundreds of children's books (many before the days of PPA time), this development is both liberating and wildly frustrating. Why did it take so long to come to this conclusion? What could I have done instead with all those hours of my life? And why, as a leader, did I not become wiser to this sooner, so that I could have saved my staff all these hours and let them focus on things that matter more?

---

34. Ofsted, 'Ofsted inspections: myths' (April 2018), www.gov.uk/government/publications/school-inspection-handbook-from-september-2015/ofsted-inspections-mythbusting.

Along the way, several mistakes have been made around the understanding of marking, including the following:

- 'Feedback' has been misinterpreted to mean 'marking'. This has been a major misconception, as there has been such a keen focus on feedback due the significant effect size on learning that researchers such as John Hattie have demonstrated. You can see how a train of thought following the research trail can take you to this point: the EEF says that feedback offers 'high impact for very low cost', so therefore we have focused on our marking approaches. What has become clear is that feedback is a lot more nuanced and we need to look more closely at the specific types of feedback that are effective.

- 'Children responding to marking' has been misinterpreted to mean 'children writing written responses to marking'. This is perhaps the key misconception which has driven the workload, as there is now an obsession with schools creating visible ways of proving that somehow learning is happening because a process is happening.

Ultimately, marking has got out of hand because it is visible and therefore something that is easy to monitor or use as an evidence base for purposes such as inspection. It is another example of where we have created a proxy for learning because the learning itself is so hard to see.

It is interesting to look back at how we might have got wrapped up with this obsession about time-heavy marking – not in the interests of apportioning blame, but so that we can prevent other initiatives from spiralling out of control in the future.

Although Ofsted would like to absolve itself of responsibility through its recent myth-busting campaign, the truth is that the biggest driver of these policies has been a fear of Ofsted and advice from inspectors. I sat in a review many years ago and was told by an Ofsted inspector that to become 'Outstanding', we needed to get children responding to marking. His explanation of how marking related to becoming outstanding was as follows:

Inadequate marking is where books aren't being marked.

RI marking is where books are marked, but without good next step comments.

Good marking is where teachers are writing good next step comments.

Outstanding marking is where children are writing comments back to the teacher in response to their feedback.

Clearly, this is nonsense; but you can see why it is alluring, with its neat fit into four categories. It is these conversations that create 'myths', and we need to become stronger in standing our ground and challenging such potentially damaging feedback. In fairness, it is exactly this type of advice from inspectors that Ofsted has tried hard to stop through its myth-busting campaign and more recently as its national director provided further clarification to inspectors in November 2016: 'I remain concerned that we continue to see some inspection reporting which gives the impression that more detailed or more elaborate marking is required, or indeed that it is effective in promoting pupils' achievement.'[35]

What can we do?

It is crucial to address the issue of marking in schools: if we haven't already revisited this issue, it is an easy way to cut some faff out of teachers' lives and help to create genuinely better learning.

> *Marking practice that does not have the desired impact on pupil outcomes is a time-wasting burden for teachers that has to stop.*

Dawn Copping, chair of the DfE Marking Policy Review Group

At Simon de Senlis, the tipping point for me was when one of my staff walked past me in the corridor looking exhausted just before 6:00pm on a Friday, wheeling books on one of those trolleys that you should only see in airports, but that have crept into our schools over the years. I awkwardly made a comment about hoping that she wouldn't have to work too much over the weekend; she smiled politely and said that perhaps she would get a marking fairy for Christmas.

The following is a blog post that I wrote detailing the process of how we went about changing from a marking to a feedback policy.

For the last six months, like many schools, we have been reviewing our approaches to feedback and marking and this September we'll be starting term with a revised approach. We hope that this will have a positive impact on learning whilst reducing the workload of teachers in the school.

Having been through this process, here are 10 things I know or think about marking and feedback in no particular order:

---

35. Sean Harford, 'School Inspection Update', November 2016, www.gov.uk/government/uploads/system/uploads/attachment_data/file/595745/School_inspection_update_November_2016__1_.pdf

1. *Although it is widely talked about that feedback has the biggest effect size on children's learning, in 38% of cases feedback has shown to have a negative effect on learning (Kluger & Denisi, 1996[36]). Therefore, we should be really thoughtful in the future about the models of feedback we use in school.*

2. *Feedback can be more effective when it's used sparingly rather than children being overloaded with feedback.*

3. *Unless children are given time and an opportunity to respond to feedback, it's pointless.*

4. *Misconceptions and careless errors are separate things and should be marked or fed back on using different strategies.*

5. *There is much that is known about marking and feedback that we probably don't know enough about in schools. Documents such as those from the EEF and Teacher Workload 'Marking Policy Review Group' are really important but, due to time pressures, many teaching staff are unlikely to have read them.*

6. *Despite what I've said in point 5, there is not enough evidence around the effectiveness of marking to be sure of much really and so we should hold our ideas and beliefs lightly as more research takes place into this.*

7. *When you talk to teachers or read what they write on Twitter, they generally say that they predominately mark for book scrutinies and Ofsted rather than for any real effect on learning.*

8. *There are crystal clear messages from Ofsted that there is no requirement for any specific type or frequency of marking and we do not need to spend time creating evidence of verbal feedback which is simply a part of teaching and can be seen in almost any lesson.*

9. *There are more effective ways of giving feedback to children than through written comments such as verbal feedback or responsive teaching.*

10. *It is still impossible to write a feedback or marking policy without quoting Dylan Wiliam.*

---

36. www.researchgate.net/publication/232458848_The_Effects_of_Feedback_Interventions_ on_Performance_A_Historical_Review_a_Meta-Analysis_and_a_Preliminary_Feedback_ Intervention_Theory

If there's a single principle teachers need to digest about classroom feedback, it's this: The only thing that matters is what students do with it. No matter how well the feedback is designed, if students do not use the feedback to move their own learning forward, it's a waste of time.

Dylan Wiliam

How did we get into this mess?

Throughout the last six months, I've reflected a lot on how we have got to this point on marking nationally, not for the purposes of attributing blame but through genuine interest into how a mix of bright ideas, poor evidence and the pressure of accountability can quickly become runaway trains like marking approaches have become across the country or 'hornets' (to quote Joe Kirby's excellent blog[37]).

I think there are two key misunderstandings we have made as a profession:

- 'Feedback' has been interpreted to mean 'marking'.

- 'Responding to marking' has been interpreted to mean 'children writing comments in response to marking' rather than children putting the feedback they receive into practice in their future work.

At the heart of all this lies one of the biggest problems for all of us involved in education: **we can't see learning**. Because we can't see learning happening, we often focus on the visible things that we associate with good learning or 'proxies for learning'. Focusing on the visible and the 'easy measurables' makes the job of monitoring easy but potentially means we value the wrong things; I think marking falls into this category. Far more valuable than marking is the verbal feedback that takes place in every lesson up and down the country every day but will never be seen in a book scrutiny. The irony is that although marking is a visible end-product, the process of marking is often invisible with teachers spending hours, often at home, in the evening wading through piles of books.

The opportunity cost of marking policies in schools is huge and we should embrace the current opportunity for change with both hands.

---

37. pragmaticreform.wordpress.com/2015/10/31/marking-is-a-hornet/

I'll duly hold my hand up and say that our staff have been marking too much in recent years. Although we felt we had a workload-friendly approach (teachers were not expected to provide written feedback in core subjects more than once a week), the reality was that the staff were doing much more and there are far more useful things they can be doing with their valuable time.

The process of changing marking approaches...

Marking is an ingrained habit for teachers and so we have taken time and been cautious with this change not to throw out processes that, on reflection, we still feel are valuable and important. The following process was led brilliantly by one of our Assistant Heads and I take no credit for it.

Reading and Research – At this stage, a handful of us were reading about different approaches to marking and finding out what the approach of other schools is and how they are (or aren't) changing these. As part of this process, a survey was also carried out with teachers in our school to find out how much time they were spending on marking and also to understand their perceptions of what was more and less useful. It's great to be able to read about other schools' experiences as they've changed their processes and learn from them.

Working Group Trials and Pilots – A working group was set up consisting of six teaching staff who met and trialled different approaches including whole-class feedback, marking crib-sheets keeping tabs on how long processes were taking and what effect they felt this was having on learning.

Presenting Ideas to Staff – At a staff meeting, the rationale for change was made alongside some suggested practices for staff to use. This was a really important point for me – you can't pull the carpet from under people's feet unless you can offer answers to what should happen in its place.

Whole Staff Road Test – At this stage, we had outlines for practices which had been tested in some classes and in other schools and staff were told that there was no expectation for more than one written comment in children's books throughout the half-term. We collected feedback at staff meetings throughout these seven weeks and staff were great at emailing round their thoughts – it was helpful to hear how much time they'd saved and also how they felt they were able to spend more time planning responsive teaching rather than working through the process of documenting it in individual books.

Feedback – At the end of the Summer Term, we spent a staff meeting with staff feeding back on how the process had been and what their thoughts were about how we should adapt the process further for September. My Assistant Head then did the policy work which we will present back to staff at the beginning of term.

Implementation – We already know that staff have found it hard to kick the habit and that feelings of guilt still exist because they are not spending time every evening putting written comments in books. Like all habits, it will take time and so we will keep working on this to make sure that teachers can adapt to the change.

Our revised Feedback Policy

Some key points from our revised approach are as follows:

- Our policy is for Feedback rather than Marking and pays attention to the important business of verbal feedback to children and responsive teaching first and foremost.

- There is no requirement for staff to evidence 'verbal feedback'. Verbal feedback is an integral part of teaching and learning which can be observed taking place in almost every lesson.

- Marking crib sheets such as the one below are now commonly used to support whole-class-feedback and inform 'responsive teaching'. The one below is from Mr Thornton's blog[38] – we have adapted similar versions which staff can use either as paper copies or more often using online versions in our OneNote planning documents.

Things I think are still worth thinking about with marking and feedback...

The differences in successful marking approaches between different subjects or age ranges are significant and therefore a blanket approach clearly isn't appropriate. Even the subtle differences between year groups are worth discussing and being specific on – the difference between the ability of children in Year 1 and 2 for example to respond to written feedback is considerable.

---

38. MrThorntonTeach blog on crib sheets as an alternative to marking, mrthorntonteach. com/2016/04/08/marking-crib-sheet/

Where we hear about 'no more marking' approaches, I hope this isn't interpreted as 'no more looking at children's work on a daily basis'. My teachers know their children inside out – partly due to the attention they pay to reading their work. Although I understand that at a secondary level, there may be challenges over reading through the books of the hundreds of different children a teacher sees each fortnight, this is not the case in primary and it's reasonable to think that primary teachers will still read through children's work throughout each week.

No more marking?

As the system starts to kick back against marking processes, some schools are now implementing 'no marking' policies in their schools. While clearly this may sound very appealing – particularly from a workload perspective – I think we should be cautious around this, as there are still aspects of marking which may well be useful. As unhelpful as blanket approaches to lengthy marking may have been, blanket bans on marking may turn out to be misguided, rather than allowing well-trained teachers to decide when and how marking is most appropriate.

While writing lengthy comments may well not be time efficient, reading children's work carefully certainly is. Michael Tidd explains this well using the law of diminishing returns:

> I'd argue that in the first few moments of looking at a piece of work, a good teacher can take in a fantastic amount of knowledge and understanding about how a child has understood a given taught concept. In the next few moments of reading or reviewing in greater depth, they gather much more. By the time they come to write the comment, they have probably exhausted the task's usefulness to the teacher, so the only further impact to be made is on the pupil.[39]

---

39. Michael Tidd, 'Why we've got planning and marking all wrong', michaelt1979.wordpress.com/2015/11/05/why-weve-got-planning-and-marking-all-wrong-part-1/

Figure 16. The law of diminishing returns in marking

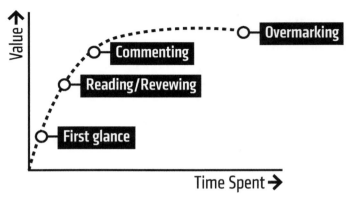

Source: Michael Tidd

IN SUMMARY – ASSESSING LIKE A CONSULTANT DOCTOR

■ What is the link between assessment and accountability in your school? Is your assessment system designed to offer genuine diagnostic opportunities or is it driven primarily around accountability?

■ How well trained are teachers in the use of assessment? Do teachers use assessment like consultant doctors, GPs or online symptom checkers? How accurate are their assessments and do they lead to effective 'diagnosis and treatment'?

■ Is your school living a life without levels or do the same problems that we had with levels still exist as 'ghost levels' within your new approach?

■ Is there a clear separation between summative and formative assessment in your approach? Does feedback form a fluid part of responsive teaching and learning, or is it stifled by structured visible processes that are easy to monitor?

■ Are your assessment processes manageable for staff? Have you 'time-costed' each part of the assessment process and considered whether the information it gives you is value for money?

FIVE FIVES GRID FOR PLANNING

FIVE MINUTES: What immediate first steps can you take?

FIVE DAYS: What short-term actions can you take in the next week to kick start or plan change?

FIVE WEEKS: What actions or follow-up meetings/discussions can you plan for in the next half-term?

FIVE MONTHS: What follow-up and follow-through activities do you need to plan to ensure that the change is not just a flash in the pan?

FIVE YEARS: What might your change look like in five years? What structures, systems and processes will you need to amend to ensure that your change becomes embedded in the fabric of your school and is not a passing fad?

Section 4

Leading with your Hands

Be visible and 'hands-on', walking the talk of your leadership. Be relentless in the development of staff and manage people well.

Chapters

#WholesomeLeadership

Training and development

A SELECTION OF QUOTES FROM THE CHAPTER

#WholesomeLeadership

This responsibility for growing future teachers and leaders reaches beyond our own schools and further into the future than the current three-year plan or next inspection.

Developing the ability to give and receive useful feedback is one of the most powerful investments we can make when developing ourselves and others.

Becoming comfortable as both coach and mentor is an important part of our leadership toolkit, as we are required to play both roles at different times and in different situations.

When planning training and development opportunities, it is important to consider the level of expertise and self-awareness of colleagues. Understanding their 'consciousness of competence' for different skills is important, as it helps to identify the right strategies and approaches to support them.

AND ONE FROM THE INTERVIEW INSIDE

We take the approach that if we focus on great training and development and colleagues want to aim for promotions, we may lose them to other schools; but this is nonetheless great for the system and hopefully good for us as former colleagues become advocates for our approach – **Stuart Lock**

I do encourage people to take risks to develop their ideas and confidence further, but often with a safety net below – **Jill Ramshaw**

Interview with Jill Ramshaw and Stuart Lock

TRAINING AND DEVELOPMENT

> **"**
> Every teacher needs to improve, not because they are not
> good enough, but because they can be even better.
>
> Dylan Wiliam

Several years ago, Adele and I were on a humid and sweaty temple
tour in central Bangkok. She was pregnant, uncomfortable but
patient as I took enthusiastic pictures of temples and statues. While
photographing a particularly impressive golden Buddha, a tour guide
appeared next to me, having noticed my interest. He told me that the
statue dated back to around the 13th century and was made of solid
gold worth over £250 million today.

According to the guide, the Buddha was moved to the Siamese
kingdom of Ayutthaya, a large and wealthy city of the time,
hundreds of years ago. Due to the threat of invasion from the
Burmese armies, it was covered in clay in order to hide the gold and
make it appear less precious. Invasion came and the statue sat in
an outbuilding before being moved to Bangkok to become part of
a collection. For centuries, the statue sat in the temple, disguised
by its modest exterior. As the generations passed, tales of a golden
Buddha slipped into folklore. Although hundreds of people saw it
every day, no one knew the precious interior that lay beneath the
surface.

After the Second World War, the statue was being transported to
a new part of the temple when one of the ropes snapped as it was
moved into its final position. As it fell, the clay coating became
cracked, revealing its gold interior. Immediately, the work was
stopped and a team of people carefully chipped and peeled away at
the outer layers, revealing its true identity and restoring the golden
Buddha from legend to reality. For hundreds of years, something

priceless and precious had lain trapped behind modest and earthy external layers.

I framed the picture I took of the golden Buddha and it lives in my office at school. It challenges me not to give up on people too easily – to remember that everyone's true value can be worth far more than is appreciated at first glance. All of us have layers of external 'clay' masking the gold within.

In the first two sections of this book, through the Heart and Head of wholesome leadership, I have emphasised how important it is first to create the right professional culture in a school and then to introduce effective structures and systems for staff to work within. These next two chapters focus on developing and managing people – the 'Hands' of the organisation.

One of our most important responsibilities as leaders is to develop the people around us. This responsibility for growing future teachers and leaders reaches beyond our own schools and further into the future than the current three-year plan or next inspection. The education system itself depends on us investing in good professional development. If one measure of successful leadership is that the school continues to thrive when the current leaders step away, another is how many of its staff go on to become leaders themselves in the future.

FIRST WHO?

In *Good to Great*, Jim Collins places emphasis on the importance of people. 'First who, then what', is the sentiment behind one of his most famous quotes: 'Get the right people on the bus, the wrong people off the bus, and the right people in the right seats.'

Recruiting well and dealing with underperformance are clearly vital to the success of any organisation, and being 'on or off the bus' is now a common term in the vocabulary of many school leaders. However, I worry whether this quote captures a simplistic view of staff performance (those who are simply up to the job or not) and therefore encourages a school improvement approach that is ultimately centred around 'hiring and firing'.

But what if leadership is more than a simple binary choice between the 'right' people and the 'wrong' people? What if there are also underdeveloped people, poorly managed people and demotivated people with the potential to be the right people in the right conditions?

In Chapter 6, within the vital organs of school improvement model, I argued that we have a responsibility as leaders to ensure that things such as behaviour, curriculum and inclusion are well established in a school before making career-altering decisions about whether staff are capable. In my experience of underperforming schools, it is almost always the case that poor leadership or professional development has led to weak classroom practice and an overall lack of performance. In these cases, staff who have spent five years teaching may only have the equivalent of one year of developmental experience, in effect having repeated the same year five times.

Focusing on the potential of people alongside their current performance can often reveal more of the 'right people' than at first glance.

Working with the wood
A leadership model focused primarily around 'moving on' staff who don't fit to make way for others is also practically flawed, without a national pipeline of highly capable replacements waiting in the wings.

Unless a head teacher is fortunate to have opened a new school and therefore has personally recruited the entire staff, the likelihood is that any team will consist of a mixed bag of experience, skills and attitudes. In the same way that a skilled carpenter will 'work with the wood', learning how to deal with the knots, kinks and imperfections in timber, a trait of effective leaders is how well they can motivate and develop the skills of a diverse team, warts and all.

A recruitment crisis
Challenges around recruitment have reached crisis point in the system, with the National Audit Office including the following points in its gloomy 2017 report:[40]

- Teachers are increasingly leaving state-funded schools before they reach retirement.

- Workload is a significant barrier to teacher retention.

- Schools are finding it increasingly difficult to fill posts with the quality of teachers they need, which may have implications for the quality of education.

---

40. National Audit Office, 'Retaining and Developing the Teaching Workforce,' 12 September 2017, www.nao.org.uk/press-release/retaining-and-developing-the-teaching-workforce/

- There are local variations in teacher supply, and the DfE and schools do not have mechanisms to make sure that teachers are available where they are most needed.

- Schools filled only 50% of their teaching vacancies with candidates with the required experience and expertise, and in around 10% of cases schools did not fill the vacancy at all.

In response to these challenges, schools are now working much harder at their recruitment processes: hiring earlier, using professional companies and investing more resource into marketing their profiles. But simply becoming savvier at marketing and capturing the best teachers does not help the system unless there are enough teachers to go around. Of real concern is the increased competition between schools over a dwindling pool of teachers. This inevitably leads to schools in more deprived contexts losing out again, while at the same time sucking money out of the system and into recruitment and supply agencies.

RECRUIT, RETAIN AND TRAIN

Increased effort to attract new staff into a school is of little benefit unless we also focus on the other end of the pipeline and think seriously as to how we can stop losing so many teachers from the profession before retirement.

In the five-year period from 2011 to 2016, the number of teachers in English schools over the age of 50 reduced by almost 25%, now representing just 17.7% of the workforce.[41] According to the Organisation for Economic Cooperation and Development (OECD), teachers in the UK are among the youngest in the world, with 27% of primary school teachers under 30 – double the OECD average of 13%.[42] At secondary level, the proportion of teachers aged 50 or older has seen the largest decrease in any OECD country since 2005.

A focal point of the conversation around retention, rightly, is the wellbeing of school staff across the country – something in pretty poor health. This is why the Heart of wholesome leadership is so important and why Chapters 12 and 13 are dedicated to self-preservation and staff wellbeing respectively.

However, professional development has an equal role to play in the challenge to keep more teachers in the profession. I believe that training

---

41. DfE census data (2011–2016).
42. OECD, 'Education at a Glance 2016', www.oecd-ilibrary.org/education/education-at-a-glance-2016_eag-2016-en

is the often-forgotten poor relation in the holy trinity of 'recruit, retain and train'. Improving both the quantity and quality of professional development for all school-based staff should be at the top of every school leader's agenda.

Table 10 sets out some suggestions for the role of training and development at different career stages.

Table 10. The importance of career-long development

Career stage	Importance of training and development
Pre-service and induction Pre to +1 year, including ITT and NQT	Through stronger ITT, we can ensure that young teachers are better placed to meet the demands of life in the classroom. Delivering highly positive NQT years and induction programmes with meticulous rigour is essential to ensure success at this early stage.
Early career Post NQT 2-5 years	Building more robust professional development for young teachers post NQT can support important building of confidence and competency at this stage. Although the stabilisers of NQT support have been removed, this phase of development still requires a high level of support. The role of mentoring is important at this stage, as there is still a lot to be shown, explained and modelled. This is a critical stage if we are to change the current pattern where 30% of teachers leave the profession within an initial five-year period.[*]
Established career Approximately 5 years+ Stability Consolidation Fresh challenges To avoid frustration and disillusionment	Establishing a developmental culture and high-quality training opportunities allows for professional engagement and growth and helps to avoid the frustration and disillusionment that can be a feature of this stage. For some, career progression at this stage may be through leadership responsibility, but leadership roles outside of the classroom should not be the only career route. More opportunities to develop subject expertise or to carry out additional professional study with academic qualifications, for example, should be made available. While stability and consolidation are features of this career stage, training and development can energise staff. Sometimes career changes can come within a school: perhaps a change of subject or phase or a role working across schools in a MAT can offer a new 'lease of life'. For many teachers, these years can coincide with part-time teaching or flexible working arrangements due to family circumstances. I think that we can get better at ensuring that part-time staff still feel that they are developing professionally, not missing out on training or developmental opportunities.

Twilight of career (wind-down and exit) Final 5 years	In the twilight of people's careers, good training and development can help to motivate and re-energise colleagues. In my experience, there is a wealth of individuals with the expertise to make a contribution within schools who have either retired or found alternative employment. Alongside designing better training aimed at the 'twilighters', we can also improve our approach to more flexible and part-time working arrangements and help to avoid 'cliff-edge' career exits.

*Nick Gibb's response to 'Teachers: Labour Turnover: Written Question – 47083', www. parliament.uk/business/publications/written-questions-answers-statements/written-question/ Commons/2016–10–07/47083/.

AN INTERVIEW WITH JILL RAMSHAW

For some more thoughts on the importance and practicalities of developing the staff in our schools, I spoke with Jill Ramshaw – the hugely respected and successful head teacher of Weston Favell Primary School in Northampton. I have been fortunate to work alongside Jill in our trust in recent years and see her staff grow into different opportunities that have arisen over this time.

TR: One of the (many) things that you do so well as a head is developing the people around you. Is this something that you've always been good at or have you honed the skill during your career?

JR: It is definitely something that I have developed over the years. I think as a teacher I was always aware of the skills of the support staff I was fortunate to work with and tried to utilise those skills to support the children, while also trying to identify training for them to ensure that they developed all aspects of their role. I have always worked as part of a team of teachers and teaching assistants, and so I learned how to support and challenge others, as well as using their strengths to develop my own skills.

I worked for a variety of leaders in a range of schools and learned from the way they did things too – many good and others not so good. I was given lots opportunities to develop my skill set and made numerous mistakes along the way. It is important for all staff to feel that they and their ideas are valued. If they can articulate an idea and can explain the rationale behind it, I think it is often worth letting them try it out.

TR: You've seen many great teachers develop in your school and lots of leaders are now playing bigger roles as either heads or senior leaders across our trust. I'm interested in how you identify potential in future leaders: what are the key things you look for?

JR: Enthusiasm, positivity, the willingness to go that extra mile. The ability to cooperate, but also take responsibility when needed. The determination to be the best they can be. I also look out for people who take opportunities when they are offered and those who can identify the strengths in others and support them. I believe that showing people that you trust them to do a job enables people to have faith in themselves; giving people time to discuss ideas is key.

TR: Good-quality professional development is something that I know you really value and work hard at. What are the key things to get right when planning and organising training and development in your school?

JR: I lead very little training in my school – our middle and senior leaders do most of this. They have been encouraged and enabled to develop their skills and knowledge in certain areas; this could be through external training or working in partnership with other schools and staff to develop an idea further. Each teacher leads an area of the curriculum or school life, identifying an aspect of this that the whole staff would benefit from being trained in, and we allocate a training session for them. The session is discussed with a member of the SLT prior to it taking place, to ensure it meets the needs of the staff. We provide a termly staff training overview so that everyone knows what is happening and can prepare appropriately for it.

For external CPD, we investigate the trainer and the content prior to booking anything, to ensure it will meet our needs, and try to encourage staff to discuss their training with others to share the knowledge gained. Nowadays, we try to send two members of staff on any training, to ensure that key messages are brought back and implemented into school.

TR: In order for leaders to learn, they need to make mistakes along the way. How do you become comfortable with balancing the need for learning through mistakes alongside the pressure to remain a high-performing school?

JR: I do encourage people to take risks to develop their ideas and confidence further, but often with a safety net below. Plenty of support and close monitoring are needed to ensure that the quality of provision is being maintained and that the new idea is achieving its purpose.

We also really value consistency and therefore no one person can develop a new idea and embed it within the school practice – it must be a team effort. Staff need to be convinced or willing to give it a go before they invest any time in implementing a new idea. The leader of any new initiative must be able to engender enthusiasm for the idea before it can be implemented successfully. As everyone has the opportunity to introduce ideas, everyone is willing to give new ideas a go as they realise it could be their idea next.

Professional dialogue is key – we can discuss what went well and what didn't go so well with colleagues and learn from each other.

I think the central thing is not to allow any new idea or initiative to develop without it being monitored, as this can lead to us investing heavily in something which has minimal impact on children's learning experiences.

TR: It's been great to discuss this with you, Jill; it's important to prioritise the development of staff in our schools. What three things could leaders do to create better development opportunities for staff in their schools?

JR:

1. Keep looking outwards that so you can see what others are doing and encourage staff to be 'outward facing' too.

2. Work with other likeminded schools to develop opportunities for professional dialogue for the staff.

3. Encourage competent people to take calculated risks while making sure that a safety net is in place.

PLANNING FOR BETTER TRAINING AND DEVELOPMENT IN SCHOOL

Despite its paramount importance, the quality of CPD for school staff is often hit and miss, varying significantly from school to school. Ask any group of teachers to describe their training experiences and this often becomes clear.

It is not easy to develop good training programmes in schools; typically, the person responsible is far too busy to do it well and there are many conflicting pressures for the limited time available. In particular, the following issues are commonplace:

■ Training days and staff meetings become focused on administration or general message sharing rather than structured professional developments.

- Training opportunities can be invested in short-term initiatives which add no long-term improvement to teaching or different fads – such as learning styles, personalised learning or Brain Gym – which are quickly superseded.

- Training can often be piecemeal, with different people 'booked' to deliver occasional staff meetings without any structured programme of development.

- There may be a lack of expertise within the staff to deliver high-quality training across all priority areas.

- Budget pressures have made it more difficult to fund cover for staff to attend training and to bring in external expertise to the school.

- The promise of system-wide improved school support through teaching schools is yet to be realised across the country.

Perceived risks of delegation can also prevent professional growth when schools are under pressure to improve results quickly. Universities are finding it more difficult to get schools to agree to placements for students; teachers' presence in the classroom is often too precious to allow them out on training; and leaders are notoriously bad at prioritising their own professional development. But a feeling of saving in the here and now is a false economy if it denies developmental opportunities that could help us with retention or recruitment in the future.

Training opportunities are limited in schools. Typically, there are just five training days a year which, along with an hour and a half or so after school each week, make up the only dedicated time for professional development beyond the teaching day. In total, this adds up to less than 100 hours a year (39 weeks x 1.5 hours of meetings = 58.5 hours, 5 x 8 hour training days = 40 hours, total = 98.5 hours). This is just 5% of the 1,928 hours that teachers are reported to work each year[43] and only slightly more than the 91 hours a year that men are reported to spend on the toilet (according to various tabloid sources). Just let that sink in.

With this in mind, it is critical that we make the most of these limited opportunities and plan them with thought and care, ensuring that they are aligned with our key priorities and challenges.

---

43. EPI, 'Teacher workload and professional development in England's secondary schools', (October 2016) epi.org.uk/wp-content/uploads/2018/01/TeacherWorkload_EPI.pdf

A standard for professional development

One DfE document that I have found particularly useful is the 'Standard for Teachers' Professional Development'[44], written in 2016 by an expert group tasked by the government with creating a standard alongside guidance to schools. Generally speaking, publications by the DfE and Teachers' Standards documents aren't the first place we might look for inspiration to improve training and development in schools, but I thought this was well worth a few hours of my life.

The 'non-statutory' standard identified the following five 'shoulds' for professional development in schools:

1. Professional development should have a focus on improving and evaluating pupil outcomes.

2. Professional development should be underpinned by robust evidence and expertise.

3. Professional development should include collaboration and expert challenge.

4. Professional development programmes should be sustained over time.

5. Professional development should be prioritised by school leadership.

As a leadership team, we sat down with this document and looked at our current practices through the lens of these five points. We discussed the following four key themes:

■ We considered the difference between direct professional development (activities that impact specifically on practice in the classroom) and indirect professional development (activities such as statutory safeguarding, first aid and training in IT systems or administrative issues). We analysed the hours spent on both and reflected that indirect professional development was probably taking too much time within our staff development programme. As a result, we rebalanced the schedule, ensuring that the overwhelming amount of time was allocated to development that would impact directly on classroom practice.

■ We reviewed several of the larger school improvement initiatives we had implemented over the previous four years and discussed how many of the five 'shoulds' within the standard had been present.

44. DfE, 'Standard for Teachers' Professional Development' (July 2016), www.gov.uk/government/publications/standard-for-teachers-professional-development

Typically, we felt we were pretty strong on the first two, but the remainder were less consistent; we lacked expert challenge at times and initiatives were not always sustained due to conflicting priorities.

■ We discussed 'expert challenge' not only in terms of initial training, but also within follow-up and follow-through activities. Almost all new initiatives have a positive impact in the first six to 12 months – it is almost impossible for a whole-school focus not to raise standards at least superficially in a specific area. It is in the transfer from current priority to embedded practice that the real challenge lies and at this point where further expert challenge is really necessary. We felt that we needed to involve external expertise more regularly at the follow-up and follow-through stage of implementation

■ We reflected on the difference between 'activities' and 'programmes'. At times, we recognised that our professional development calendars sometimes felt a bit piecemeal in school. At its worst, there were times when I felt like air traffic control, simply coordinating the different consultants coming in and out of school and sorting cover for teachers to take part in training opportunities without it being joined up as part of an ongoing programme. We decided that we would limit the focus of CPD and ensure that more energy went into the implementation of existing priorities rather than constantly looking for new ideas.

Towards unconscious competence

When planning training and development opportunities, it is important to consider the level of expertise and self-awareness of colleagues. Understanding their 'consciousness of competence' for different skills is important, as it helps to identify the right strategies and approaches to support them. The model presented in Figure 17 is based on the 'Four Stages for Learning a New Skill' model, attributed to Noel Burch.[45]

---

45. en.wikipedia.org/wiki/Four_stages_of_competence

Figure 17. The conscious competence matrix

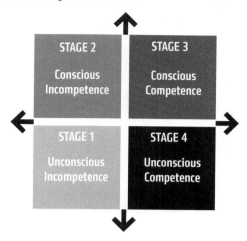

Stage 1 – unconscious incompetence (unaware): At this first stage, we are unable to do something, but don't yet recognise the deficit ourselves: we are unaware of our incompetence. It may be that this is a new skill we have been introduced to; or perhaps we have developed a 'blind spot' over time. This could be anything from the need to sharpen up behaviour in our class to realising that our marking is ineffective or that our subject knowledge in a particular area is weak. Often in schools where training and development is not effective, some staff will be in this stage.

For people who are unaware of a weakness, the challenge is to carefully shift their self-awareness so that they can see where improvements can be made. This can be a bit like taking the stabilisers off a bicycle. Until this point, the child can be very confident, pedalling around in blissful ignorance; it is not until the stabilisers come off that it quickly becomes apparent that a skill needs developing. Although sometimes uncomfortable, making someone aware of an area of deficit is often the first and most important step in a learning process.

It is impossible for a man to learn what he thinks he already knows.

Epictetus

Stage 2 – conscious incompetence (awareness): Once we have become aware of something which we need to improve, we are more likely to be open to training, advice and learning. This is where it can be really useful to attend training and spend time in others' schools and classes as we deliberately work on an area to develop. Making mistakes at this point is normal and can be helpful.

NQTs or teachers new to a school often jump straight into this category, as they are keen to learn and take on ideas from others. This is why it is so important to get things such as induction and training for new staff right, to make sure you can embed important and consistent practices upfront.

While it is much easier to train people on a topic when they know this is something they would like to improve, it is important to handle people with care through this stage, as being aware of a weakness can bring a feeling of vulnerability. Taking our bicycle example, this might mean falling off a few times and can cause people to back away unless they keep getting 'back in the saddle'. Lots of regular guidance and support are useful at this stage.

Stage 3 – conscious competence (learning): At this point, a skill or process may be learned, but it is not yet automatic or mastered, so still requires a lot of conscious effort, time and reminders for it to be performed. It might be, for example, that we can teach certain aspects of maths as long as we have written planning next to us or have worked the examples through ourselves before the lesson. Or perhaps when spelling a particular word, we have to keep reminding ourselves of the mnemonic (eg, there's 'a rat' in 'separate'). Generally, it may appear that we can hold our own, but the amount of effort required is still high.

This is like riding a bicycle without stabilisers, but still having the occasional wobble and having to spend a lot of time concentrating on not falling off. It would not be wise to go out riding in a peloton at this stage or to try to navigate at the same time. When working with staff at this stage, skills may be acquired, but not embedded, so it is important to keep planning follow-up and follow-through activities to help make it become second nature.

Stage 4 – unconscious competence (skilled/automatic): At this final stage, skills, actions or routines have become second nature as a result of considerable practice. They can be performed with an automaticity or fluency that requires minimal effort or attention, so it becomes possible to multi-task or to focus our attention on other areas.

Here, we become better able to teach these skills to others and better placed to adapt our practice as we go, relying less on set plans, scripts and structures. Returning to the bicycle example, this is now the competent cyclist who can navigate and ride safely as part of a group while holding a conversation.

Gaining this conscious competence across different facets of teaching is important, so that our attention can be freed up to become mindful of what is actually going in the classroom, developing the 'sixth sense' that the best teachers seem to have which leads to the informed responsive teaching that we strive for.

Coaching and mentoring
Coaching and mentoring are two essential approaches used as part of professional and personal development relationships, with subtle but important differences.

Mentoring is the process of offering help, guidance and advice to others who need it. This is particularly useful for inexperienced staff or those new to a role who do not yet have the knowledge or skills they need either to carry out tasks or to make decisions. Assigning a mentor is common practice for roles such as NQTs, but there are many other times in our careers when we benefit from having someone who can act as a mentor.

Coaching, in contrast, is more of a facilitative process where, through asking the right questions at the right times, a coach can help others to think through challenges themselves, being clearer about what they want from a situation and considering their best options to get there. One widely used coaching model is 'TGROW'[46], which provides a structure for coaching conversations to take place; I have adapted it in Table 11.

---

46. TGROW is a coaching model attributed to Myles Downey from his book, *Effective Coaching*, Texere Publishing 2003. TGROW is a variation of the GROW model to which there are many claims of authorship: en.wikipedia.org/wiki/GROW_model

Table 11. TGROW coaching model

	Stage	Coaching questions
T	Topic	What is the specific topic that you want to talk about? Why this issue and not another – is it the one that will make the most impact? Can you tell me briefly about this issue?
G	Goals	What is it that you want the future to look like? Describe your 'utopia'. How will you know when you achieve this goal? What will be different? How will it look, sound, feel? If you were to achieve this goal, what would be the benefits?
R	Reality	What is the reality of the situation now? What specific things are happening that make you think this? What is your analysis of why this reality exists? How sure are you of your analysis/reading of the situation?
O	Options & Obstacles	What are your options moving forward? What are the benefits and risk of each of these? Have you thought about...? What would happen if you did nothing? What are the barriers to success? What are the reasons this option might fail?
W	Wrap-up	Which option will you choose? What support do you need and where can we get it? What is your next move?

Becoming comfortable as both coach and mentor is an important part of our leadership toolkit, as we are required to play both roles at different times and in different situations. While wise mentors are often valued for their reassurance and for providing clarity and direction, the danger of always providing all the answers is that others do not learn to think for themselves and can become too dependent on leaders to do the thinking for them. Equally, skilled coaches can elicit extraordinary personal growth in their coachees through patient and probing questions; but this approach is frustrating and counterproductive if used in a situation where a member of staff simply does not have the requisite knowledge and instead needs showing, telling or demonstrating what needs to be done. Revisiting the conscious competence matrix is a good starting point to help identify which type of approach and relationship is required.

We may also have a predominant style that we tend to default to. In my case, I know that I am prone to talking too much and offering the answers – more of a natural mentor than coach. To counter this, I've often written 'TGROW' on the board in my office so that when people come in, it prompts me to use this approach rather than trying to solve every problem that comes my way. Retraining myself to use lines such as 'What are your options?' rather than jumping in with my solutions all the time is an ongoing challenge for me; I have remained at the stage of conscious competence for a long time!

GIVING, RECEIVING AND PLANNING FOR BETTER FEEDBACK

At the heart of all professional development lies a lot of professional feedback that we share with each other. In successful schools and organisations, this often happens freely and effectively – partly due to the culture established, but also as a result of a deliberate focus on personal improvement. Although lots can be learned informally from each other, the value of feedback and critique in development is too important to be left to chance. Developing the ability to give and receive useful feedback is one of the most powerful investments we can make when developing ourselves and others. The following ideas around feedback are developed from work I was first introduced to by Peter Ford and Ewan McIntosh of NoTosh some years ago.[47]

Giving feedback

Whether informally or as part of more formal processes, such as observations and performance reviews, feedback should always be kind, specific and useful:

- **Kind:** I will offer feedback in a personable and considerate way. Although the message might feel uncomfortable to give or receive, I am doing this with good intentions and believe that others can learn and develop as a result.

- **Specific:** I will give specific examples of what I am talking about, rather than generalisations. I will limit any development points to two or three, and then be clear about what specific actions we can both take to implement them.

- **Useful:** I will make sure that developmental feedback is relevant and will be of practical use in improving performance. I will agree timescales for any actions and follow-up so that we can revisit the situation again soon.

Applying the principles of kind, specific and useful feedback, consider using the five-point plan set out in Table 12 for giving feedback after monitoring activities, if you find yourself searching for some structure. Of course, giving feedback is a personal thing and everyone will find their own voice when delivering it.

47. www.notosh.com

Table 12. Five-point plan for giving feedback

	1. Create a safe and relaxed environment to offer feedback. Give feedback as quickly as possible after the lesson or monitoring.	1. 'Hi Tom, is this a good time to offer you some feedback on the lesson? Great – let's grab a drink and discuss how it went.'
	2. Identify the positives seen within the practice through a number of WWWs ('What's Working Well'). Avoid 'judging' a lesson and using Ofsted language within this.	2. 'I really enjoyed being in your classroom today, Tom. Thanks for being so welcoming. I thought the relationship you have with the group was great – they really enjoyed learning and were so enthusiastic throughout. I thought you were firm but fair when needed, making sure you had 100% attention before starting any explanation was good to see. I particularly liked your initial explanation about the different use of commas and your worked examples. Your confidence of subject knowledge shines through and making those deliberate mistakes when modelling was a really effective strategy. That really had the class eating out of the palm of your hand at that stage and reinforced the common misconceptions you want to see them avoid.'
	3. Offer a maximum of two EBIs ('Even Better Ifs'). Ensure these are about the practice, not the person.	3. 'Thinking of some EBIs, I know you flagged up a concern about this group who are finding grammar and punctuation tricky last week and you were worried about your delivery. I thought your teaching input was strong, but the group who are still confused with commas to demarcate clauses may have benefited from some more worked examples and focused practice before moving on to applying in writing. They got a bit lost trying to apply the rules of commas and I think just need more practice. Perhaps that's something you could build into some daily practice as a focus for them? 'I also noticed that Alex, Matthew and Lauren are still holding their pencils with those unhelpful grips. I know in your handwriting sessions their grip is fine and they were able to tell me how to do it when I told them to check. They will need some extra reminders and practice to help them embed that as a new habit.'

4. Agree what help can be put in place to support any change, such as visits to other classrooms, reading, team teaching opportunities etc.	4. 'Regarding the pencil grips, I think that's an easier one as just one of those things to have a bit of a focus on and give plenty of reminders. I'll also make a point when I pop in to remind them. Regular reminders as they are writing throughout the day will help it to become habitual. 'On punctuation, it would be great for that focus group to really secure their accurate use of commas, so this is probably worth thinking about a bit more. I was in Greenhouse Lane Primary last week and spoke to Sue in Year 4 there who was facing similar punctuation challenges with her class. She's developed a 'cracking commas' campaign with her class. There's a display and it's a real focus – the children are really enjoying it. They do a daily 'cracking commas' exercise each afternoon – it might be worth you either having a conversation on the phone or popping down and seeing it in action? 'Is there anything else that you would find useful moving forward?'
5. Clarify the agreed actions. Finish by repeating back what has been agreed as the next steps, paying particular attention to who owns the action and what specific timescales will be put in place using the 'Five Fives' model.	5. 'OK so, to clarify: in the next five days, I'll introduce you to Sue at Greenhouse Lane on email. Then, in the next five weeks, we'll make arrangements for you to visit Sue to see her approach. Also over the next five weeks, you'll give those regular reminders regarding pencil grip checks. Then at the end of this half-term, let's sit down with the books together and look at how both the handwriting and punctuation have developed with those groups. I'm happy for you to send and children down to see me with their work when they've made progress you're pleased with. Let's check in in a fortnight and see how we're getting on.'

Receiving feedback

Perhaps even more important to the improvement cycle than how effective feedback is delivered is how well it is received. Useful feedback can be offered in the most expert of ways, but if the recipient cannot take advice or critique, it falls on deaf ears. Equally, those who are resilient and open to receiving feedback can take on development points from both the clumsiest debrief and the most vociferous complaints. Feedback in all forms is a gift and we should try to allow ourselves to learn from all situations. But too often, feedback offered can be interpreted as personal criticism and the opportunities to learn can be lost. *It's not what you say – it's what people hear.*

Try this simple protocol for receiving feedback – planned or otherwise:

- **Listen** carefully when someone is offering you critique or feedback. Try to avoid talking; just listen to what is being said.

- **Be open** to receiving critique. Avoid defensive body language or facial expressions that might prevent people from offering you honest critique because they feel it is awkward. If you start to feel defensive, just notice this feeling and what it is making you do. Let it pass, trying to remain neutral and interested.

- **Write down** what is said in the words of the other person. This will be useful later, so that you can reflect on what was said rather than your memory of what was said, which may include emotion.

- **Thank** the person for the feedback and do nothing immediately.

- **Reflect** on what was said, tick the points you agree with and circle the points you find challenging. Try to avoid justification or defensiveness around these; instead spend some time processing what has been said. Return for clarification if you need to after you've slept on it.

Planning feedback

Despite its usefulness, feedback among colleagues is often avoided in schools, due to the potential for it to become awkward or emotive. It is therefore important to plan in lots of opportunities to give feedback across the hierarchy, so that it becomes normal and part of the culture. Leaders should develop this process consciously by building in routines to receive honest and constructive feedback in a low-stakes manner; it doesn't just happen by osmosis. Surveys, evaluation forms, debriefs, feedback loops and honest ongoing dialogue are all processes that we should be planning in throughout the weeks to nurture this culture of ongoing professional feedback and dialogue.

This culture was exemplified on my recent visit to Bedford Free School (BFS), where principal Stuart Lock was the most generous host – offering visitors the opportunity to see staff briefings, full access to lessons with coffee, lunch and copies of all documentation in exchange only for some honest feedback on how we thought they could improve before we left. Inviting professionals to give open feedback in this way encouraged those present to give thoughtful feedback which was accepted gratefully in a refreshingly open manner.

Another place to capture feedback is through exit interviews. When people are about to walk out the door, they are more likely to say the things that we need to hear rather than the things they think we want to hear. If we listen carefully to this, it can help us to reflect and evaluate more effectively.

At the insistence of a governor (and against my own inner resistance), I started to hold exit interviews with staff on their last day some years ago, asking them the following questions:

1. What do you think you will remember Simon de Senlis for?

2. What things were really effective in helping you to do your job as a teacher?

3. What didn't work so well and either was frustrating or got in the way of your job as a teacher? What are our 'Even Better Ifs'?

If people offer us honest feedback in these situations, it is a rare gift and we should avoid the natural urge to justify or discuss and simply thank them and take it away to reflect on.

AN INTERVIEW WITH STUART LOCK

For further thoughts on how we can implement better training and development in schools, I spoke with Stuart Lock, executive principal of BFS and the Advantage Schools Trust. Having visited BFS and been taken by the quality of teaching and learning on show, I was keen to learn more about the school's approaches to staff development.

TR: Stuart, with recruitment and retention being such a challenge for schools, how important is it for us to focus on the quality of training and development of teachers?

SL: I don't think anyone would argue that it's not important to focus on training and development. Recent moves to 'beef up' the standard for Qualified Teacher Status are welcome and in some respects, I wonder what position we would be in without Teach First attracting some top graduates who otherwise wouldn't be in teaching at all.

At the same time, it's important to recognise that schools have been somewhat inefficient for a while. Particularly in secondary schools, where there are substantial leadership teams, these cause their own worries; but they can also lead to a culture where each leader has to prove their necessity by leading an initiative or substantial aspect of school improvement, almost always causing workload issues and a lack of focus on the main aspects of schools.

Our focus at BFS is on implementation ahead of innovation. Our development plan for this year can be summarised as 'Do what we already do, but do it better'. In this respect, our training is both little and often – in bitesize chunks every staff briefing – and subject specific, with time scheduled for subject specialists to meet together. We don't try to do what others do better, so we send our colleagues on courses run by a fairly local large academy trust to focus on their subjects and curriculum. We also send many of our colleagues to other schools across the country where we think we can learn about implementing an approach that marries with our ethos.

This year our only whole-staff training has been led by three teachers who are all new to the school, including an NQT and a recently qualified teacher. They led these sessions after being trained by Doug Lemov in 'ratio' and we invited local schools to join us for no cost. There was great take-up.

We take the approach that if we focus on great training and development and colleagues want to aim for promotions, we may lose them to other schools; but this is nonetheless great for the system and hopefully good for us as former colleagues become advocates for our approach.

Great training and development isn't enough, though. Workload and behaviour are the two biggest issues that schools and the school system has to fix to sort out the recruitment and retention crisis.

TR: At BFS, you have some very consistent approaches to classroom management, including silent corridors, highly structured transitions and the use of some of the techniques featured in Doug Lemov's **Teach Like a Champion**.[48] *How do you go about deciding these 'signature' approaches and then ensuring that teachers are well trained and confident in each of them?*

SL: The school had an approach in the past of asking teachers to engage with *Teach Like a Champion* and select their own approaches. But our approach to culture has led to us needing to focus on some of them to run the school well and ensure that everyone can teach.

---

48. Lemov, D, *Teach Like a Champion* (Jossey Bass, 2010)

So we insist that all staff – including those who have the pupils eating out of their hands – use the language of '100%' and 'track the teacher'; and that if a class doesn't meet 100%, they 'do it again'. We do this as positively as possible, but very consistently, so that teachers gain compliance on their first day at BFS.

We chose these core techniques through assiduously debating which core techniques would allow us to structure our school day most appropriately so that our procedures were clear to pupils, parents and staff.

We are very routines and structures based. On the first day that anyone new starts at BFS, they get an extensive staff handbook. This contains 'microscripts' for things like start and end of lesson routines. This accompanies a whole day of internal training, observations and practice. If the colleague is starting in September, we only have Year 7 for a week while they also get used to our routines, so everything is practised by everyone in the school. New colleagues hence get to 'see one, do one, teach one' (a phrase I took from Martyn Oliver, CEO of Outwood Grange Academies Trust) before even meeting our existing pupils. We spend a lot of resources ensuring that more experienced staff can coach, support and feedback.

Once teachers have mastered these routines, the very secure and safe structure allows for incredible creativity and freedom.

TR: I'm interested in this point about creativity in the classroom. In schools where there are highly structured approaches, a common criticism is that it can inhibit teachers' freedom and restrict innovation. Do you see a risk that highly structured or scripted approaches can deskill teachers?

SL: Yes, this is a risk. It is particularly a risk if teachers are not curricular thinkers, involved in the subject communities debating the structure of their subject, the sequence of the curriculum and the content of what is taught.

But it is more of a risk if the generic consistent approach across the school impinges on the subject. As Christine Counsell says, the distinctiveness of our subjects is the beating heart of the school. So we encourage colleagues, above all, to break our routines rather than butcher their subject, and then seek 'forgiveness' and debate how we need to adjust our routines to allow for the full and rich experience of their subject to come through. I'm a maths teacher by training. It's not for me to insist on how languages or literature or art are taught. If a teacher is fully immersed in the curriculum and says, 'I don't think this works in my subject', they are more likely to be right than I would be if I argued with this. So we encourage this; it's unprofessional for colleagues not to challenge if our routines are butchering the subject.

At the same time, as I said before, routines and structure lead to teachers being free to teach properly and to develop their craft and skill – real creativity and innovation. I don't think innovation is trying something completely new – that's usually irresponsible in teaching – but rather doing something or building on something that has been done before to make it work more effectively and ensure that pupils know more.

TR: At BFS, I was particularly struck by the close attention that your leadership team pays to induction. Why is this such a focus for you?

SL: Working at BFS, our approach to systems and structures makes it vital that everyone sticks to these, or they collapse. They allow teachers to teach, but we have to ensure that they have the best chance of contributing to them. It can be bewildering to be faced with a whole load of new ways of doing things and not be able to actually follow them.

I would argue that most schools have their own ways of doing things. The issue is that without induction, new colleagues are faced with trying to work out the effective methods and routines via trial or discovery, and we leave to chance that the school will be consistent. We want to take away that chance and ensure that the 'BFS way' is one that we actually implement in practice, without leaving new colleagues to flounder while they work out what our way is.

Our routines are also an expression of our values and, as a values–driven organisation, I would always employ those closest to our values ahead of someone with more teaching skill.

TR: As well as consistent classroom approaches, a phrase I've heard you use is that you want your teachers to be 'curriculum thinkers'. How can teachers become more involved in thinking and developing the curriculum within their schools?

SL: Most secondary teachers love their subject and have spent at least three years studying it at university; asking them to love their subject is not the most onerous thing. So I think the first thing it requires is the bravery of school leaders. This means that school leaders have to embrace that they don't know everything about the best content and methods in each subject, at both primary and secondary; and they need to trust that our teachers – as members of the community of subject specialists – are best placed to develop the best curriculum.

And a curriculum is not deciding which pupils will enter 'the EBacc route'; or how many hours will be given to maths on the timetable; or whether you will deliver French or Spanish. It is the content and sequence at every level. To be the best teacher, one must be involved in developing the curriculum: breathing the curriculum, living the curriculum and challenging the curriculum in your subject via debate and argument, academic study and scholarship and, having taught it, the experience of transmission.

It is curricular thought that dictates what we think are the most important things pupils should know when they leave school. It is through this debate that we establish what they should experience, know and be exposed to in order to join the community of educated citizens; and it is through the curriculum that we hence express our values, our ambition and our position in the world.

It is, in summary, everything that is important about a school.

Like most things, I think this is the responsibility of senior leaders. If they have never asked why we teach a certain topic in Year 5 or Year 7, never talked about hierarchical subjects and cumulative subjects, treated subjects generically and imposed generic teaching and learning policies on all teachers regardless of subject or phase, or if they accept that the examination assessment dictates what should be taught, then there is probably not going to be the opportunity to develop the staff and school as a centre of curricular thought. Indeed, if every conversation starts with outcomes rather than content, if progression is referred to via numbers rather than the curricula models, then we're a long way from where we need to be and probably missing what is rich and valuable about our subjects and hence our schools.

I think schools probably talk too much about pedagogy and not enough about curriculum. In fact, pedagogy should be dictated by what is being taught. I recognise that this is so much more challenging in a primary school than a secondary school, and that most things are both phase specific and subject specific.

TR: Thank you, Stuart, for your insight. Finally, what three pieces of advice would you give to school leaders to help create better training and development in their schools for teachers?

SL:

1. Visit the best schools in the country and copy what they are doing.

2. Ensure that all teachers can teach via very strong routines and structures.

3. Having done that, prioritise the content of the curriculum ahead of everything else, in everything you do.

IN SUMMARY – TRAINING AND DEVELOPMENT

- Is the training and development calendar well planned and carefully scheduled to maximise this limited and precious time?

- Are appropriate approaches in place to support the development of colleagues across different career stages?

- When planning professional development, is there an understanding of the different levels of competence for specific areas? Could you use the conscious competence matrix to help tailor approaches rather than taking a one-size-fits-all approach?

- Is there a balance of coaching and development in the school and can you change approach depending on the circumstances?

- Have you read and taken on the points from the Standard for Teachers' Professional Development? Is your training plan focused mainly on standards (not admin or statutory training) and based on evidence, and does it include expert challenge and input?

- Is professional development planned to be sustained over time as a programme rather than a scattergun approach of different activities, and is there genuine leadership buy-in from the top – essential to make any initiative or focus work?

- Are opportunities for feedback planned into the school weeks and is the giving and receiving of feedback commonplace? Is feedback given effectively (consider the kind, specific and useful model)?

- Can people in the organisation receive and process feedback to use as part of their development, rather than being defensive?

FIVE FIVES GRID FOR PLANNING

FIVE MINUTES: What immediate first steps can you take?

FIVE DAYS: What short-term actions can you take in the next week to kick start or plan change?

FIVE WEEKS: What actions or follow-up meetings/discussions can you plan for in the next half-term?

FIVE MONTHS: What follow-up and follow-through activities do you need to plan to ensure that the change is not just a flash in the pan?

FIVE YEARS: What might your change look like in five years? What structures, systems and processes will you need to amend to ensure that your change becomes embedded in the fabric of your school and is not a passing fad?

People management

10
CHAPTER PREVIEW

Confrontation can be awkward but I always feel better after it's done and people have said what they need to. It's the anticipation I don't enjoy

In nearly all cases, I believe that the intentions of leaders are good. It's just that in many cases, messages can be delivered clumsily, defensively or without consideration of how they are received.

When we become mindful of our own ego states and those around us, we can have healthier exchanges and develop better relationships.

If leaders are not prepared to have awkward conversations and choose instead to walk past things that aren't good enough, mediocrity will quickly become the norm. You get what you tolerate.

Being 'upfront' does not imply that we have to become heavy handed or confrontational in our approach.

AND ONE FROM THE INTERVIEW INSIDE

Be authentic. A conversation that starts with 'Ofsted will expect...' is not the way to go.

Interview with Andy Buck

PEOPLE MANAGEMENT

> " I've learned that people will forget what you said, people will forget what you did, but people will never forget how you made them feel.
>
> Maya Angelou

People bring challenges and there is no getting around that. We are all subject to human behaviour, where the many threads of ego, relationships and ambition weave a complex and fragile web, which is easily tangled. Even in the best-run schools, it is inevitable that a lot of time is spent managing people. Just ask most school leaders whether it is dealing with children or adults that causes the most sleepless nights and see what they say.

Throughout my career, there are a few real stand-out moments where people have managed me both really well and really badly. I am sure that everyone has similar experiences that they can reflect on, where they were either totally inspired or deflated depending on how they were 'handled'. Here are two contrasting experiences of mine from opposite ends of this spectrum.

As a young teacher, I am full of energy and eager to be involved in everything. Sport, music or technology – I want to run any club and attend all competitions.

This particular lunchtime, having taught all morning, I perform my usual trick of simultaneously eating a stack of sandwiches while marking 30 books and then make for the ICT suite to run computer club. Anyone who has worked in a school knows how quickly time passes and, having got totally lost in a world of PowerPoint animations with Year 6, lunchtime is soon over and children are spilling into the corridors. I am panicking. We've been told in no uncertain terms that being in class when children return from lunch is non-negotiable and the head (John*) will probably be on the prowl. I quickly send the children off, dash to the toilet to avoid an irreversible bladder condition and sprint back to my class.

As I burst through the door, my class is silent. Too silent. All eyes are fixed firmly on the front, staring at John. With arms folded, John is staring at me. I know I'm in trouble – he has a reputation for being really strict with both children and staff. And it's a fair cop: he has made a point of letting us all know that it's important we're all in class on time and I've not managed it, even if my reasons are good.

But what I'm not prepared for is what follows, as John tears a strip off me in front of my class, reminding me clearly that I need to always be back ready to teach at the start of each lesson and not to let it happen again. Embarrassed, lost for words, I mumble apologies towards his back as he marches out of the door and then make for the stock cupboard to pretend I'm doing something important for a minute or so, to avoid having to make eye contact with the kids.

I get my head down and teach through the afternoon. A brilliant thing about teaching is that once you get your head into the lesson, it's almost impossible to think or worry about anything else. But after school, when the children have left, the situation is really bothering me. OK, I might have been late to a class; but I'd been working all lunchtime setting up a club that the school wanted me to run. And even if I was in the wrong, he could have raised it with me professionally after school – not in front of a class that I then had to teach for the afternoon.

I take a deep breath and head to John's office, apologise for being late but make it clear that I think it's unprofessional to talk to me like that in front of the kids. Confrontation can be awkward, but I always feel better after it's done and people have said what they need to – it's the anticipation I don't enjoy. He apologises, recognising that he overstepped the mark, but then has to have the last word, telling me not to be late again.

Although we both said our piece and went on to have a decent professional relationship, I was always disappointed with that experience. I was OK standing my ground and fighting my corner, but I knew there were others in the school who would have found John really intimidating and thought it was wrong to use his status in this way. It's OK to get things wrong in leadership, but some behaviours are difficult to recover from – even with an apology.

In contrast, I remember a time when I felt the leaders moved heaven and earth to help me out at a difficult time. It was one of those personal crisis situations where you really need people to be great. We were living in Dubai and our eldest, Freddie, was really poorly. Adele had flown home to see a consultant in the UK and I was staying out for the last few weeks of term before planning to fly home at Easter for the holiday. It was the most bizarre school day of my life

I teach a perfectly normal English lesson to Year 4 and walk them out for morning break. Being on playground duty in 28 degrees is no real hardship and I'm hiding behind my sunglasses enjoying the warmth when a message comes out. 'Tom – you'd better come quickly. Adele's on the phone.' I know this is going to be difficult if Adele has called the school landline directly. Sure enough, she tells me through tears that Freddie is really unwell. They're in Bradford Royal Infirmary and the doctors have decided that the next step is to put him on a ventilator. Before I have time to process what any of this really means, the head calls me into his office and says the following words, which I'll never forget: 'Tom, drive home and pack your bags. My driver will come and collect you from your apartment and take you to the airport. My PA is booking you a flight now.'

The deputy walks with me to my class, helps me to get my things and checks I am OK. She gives me a hug and wishes me all the best. The message is just what I need to hear – to go and put my family first, with no second thought about the logistics or implications which they will pick up later.

The next eight hours are a blur as I race back to our apartment, throw an unsatisfactory collection of things in a case and am chauffeured at speed to Dubai airport in time to catch the afternoon flight to Manchester. By 10:00pm I am in a Bradford hospital, about to start three of the hardest weeks of my life, living on a hospital floor praying that the seizures will stop and we can get our baby boy back.

We never went back to Dubai. It was a tough decision that made itself in the end; but throughout it, our friends and colleagues were amazing – they even packed up our apartment to be shipped home and sold our car! The leadership team was fully supportive, recognising the difficulty of the situation, and made it clear that I had done the right thing.

I have often wondered how long my class were left out on the playground, waiting for me to collect them.

This isn't a routine situation that happens every day. But there are things that crop up in any week that require us to apply perspective and to put our human interactions first. When they do, you really see what leaders are made of. Their body language; their eyes; moments of hesitation before they respond that give away the feelings behind their words.

These are high-stakes moments in leadership and we need to get them right.

*Not really John.

Handle with care...

Staff in schools care a lot about what they do. Many see their jobs as a vocation and invest a lot of time and energy in their profession – sometimes too much. This can make teachers sensitive to any perceived criticism and easily bruised as a result of interactions with leaders, inspectors or parents.

In nearly all cases, I believe that the intentions of leaders are good. It's just that in many cases, messages can be delivered clumsily, defensively or without consideration of how they are received.

AN INTERVIEW WITH ANDY BUCK

For some thoughts on how we can get people management right, I spoke with Andy Buck, former head teacher, MAT managing director and founder of Leadership Matters.

TR: You now work with thousands of leaders in schools all over the UK and internationally. How important are the 'people skills' of school leaders?

AB: Absolutely critical. In fact, you could argue it's one-third of the job! In his elegantly simple 'Future-Engage-Deliver' model, Steve Radcliffe reminds us that a key element of leadership is getting people bought into where you want to go. What we sometimes call 'people skills' are at the heart of being able to do this. This ability starts with self-awareness, is enabled by the ability to read the emotions of others and results in the ability to build and sustain great relationships, so others want to lead alongside you.

TR: Sometimes teachers who have been promoted to leadership roles can be great with the kids and effective at logistics, but find it difficult to step up to a position of authority among colleagues whom they have worked alongside 'in the trenches'. What advice do you have for those who find themselves in this situation?

AB: You are right. This can be really hard, especially for newly appointed middle leaders or those promoted to senior leadership who have risen up through the ranks in the same school. I guess my advice is to focus on what you want to achieve and think carefully about how you plan to manage the changes you want to make. If you use a good change process (eg, Kotter's model[49]), this can give you the confidence you need to proceed without worrying so much about what others may be thinking. Plus, obviously, you just need to manage those emotions that could hold you back, while remaining authentic and values driven in what you are doing.

*TR: In your book **Leadership Matters**[50], you talk about 'managing up' as a way of thinking about how we manage those people in positions of authority above us. This is something that many leaders are often doing: trying to influence their bosses for time, money or decisions. Can you explain a bit about how we can do this effectively, as it's obviously an area that can cause some anxiety and is potentially risky?*

AB: Most people tend to think of managing up as some rather Machiavellian activity, where you get your boss to do something you want them to without them even realising you've done it! My own view is that managing up is all about taking one's own share of responsibility for the quality of relationship that exists between you and your line manager. This is about being open and honest with them, helping them to understand the world from your perspective, as well as taking the time to try to see their perspective and understand the pressures they are facing. In other words, helping to work out how you can both support one another with each other's work. Clearly, building trust is at the heart of this, rooted in maintaining integrity and competence on both sides.

---

49. www.kotterinc.com/8-steps-process-for-leading-change/
50. Buck, A, *Leadership Matters: How Leaders at All Levels Can Create Great Schools* (John Catt Educational, 2016).

TR: Despite how well developed our people skills are, sometimes there comes a time when leaders have to grasp the nettle and have uncomfortable conversations. Occasionally, these will lead to people leaving the organisation. No one enjoys this part of the job, but they are important challenges that shouldn't be ducked. What advice would you give to leaders who are currently having that uncomfortable feeling in their stomach, knowing they have a situation like this to handle?

AB: First of all, have the conversation! It is too easy to keep on hoping something will improve. Second, be authentic. A conversation that starts with, 'Ofsted will expect...' is not the way to go about this. Finally, plan for the opener of the conversation carefully. In *Leadership Matters*, I write about NEFI ART, adapted from the work of Susan Scott, as a way of structuring the first 60 seconds of a conversation:

- **Name** the issue.

- Give an **example**.

- Say how it makes you **feel**.

- Explain why it's **important**.

- **Accept** what you might have done to contribute to the problem.

- Make it clear this needs to be **resolved**.

- Over to **them** – what do they think?

Trying to solve an issue before they have accepted it is an issue is usually pointless.

TR: Thanks, Andy – this is great advice on a potentially tricky subject. Finally, if you had to give us three things that you suggest all school leaders keep in mind when thinking about managing people, what would they be?

AB:

1. Develop the habit of asking first in any conversation. Asking great questions and listening carefully is a powerful way to build relationships.

2. Play back what others say. This builds rapport and confirms understanding.

3. While difficult conversations are sometimes necessary, try to keep things as positive as possible.

Tact is the ability to step on a man's toes without messing up the shine on his shoes.

Harry Truman

HUMAN BEHAVIOUR – TRANSACTIONAL ANALYSIS

One benefit of having a deputy head with a psychology degree in my first headship was that I learned a bit about what was going on with human behaviour that took place in different situations. This was the upside to the perpetual fear of being analysed by someone who knew about psychology as I responded to the rollercoaster of daily challenges with varying degrees of competence. In particular, I gained a little knowledge about transactional analysis, a psychology theory which helped me to understand more about different interactions that took place with staff.

Transactional analysis (a theory attributed to Eric Burne[51] which builds on many of the ideas of Sigmund Freud) suggests three 'ego states' in which we exist: parent, adult and child. These are outlined in Table 13.

Table 13. Three ego states

Parent ego state	In this state, we display thoughts, feelings and behaviours copied from our parents or other significant adults/others from earlier in our life. When operating in the parent state, we might find ourselves using 'nurturing parent' language such as 'Let me help you' or 'I understand – that must be really difficult'; whereas on other occasions, we find ourselves as the 'controlling/critical parent', using language such as 'I expect you to do this' or 'I'm disappointed that you haven't done this yet'.
Adult ego state	This is a state in which we make direct responses to the here and now and where we can deal with issues in a way that is not influenced in an unhealthy way by our past. When operating in the adult state, we might use language such as 'What are our options?' or 'I think/I believe...'. We tend to be more rational and in control of a situation when operating in an adult state and avoid forcing opinions on others.
Child ego state	In this state, we feel, think and behave in similar ways to when we were a child and are more likely to respond emotionally to a situation. When in the child state, we may display creative and playful behaviours, using language such as 'I've had a great idea' or 'Let me have a go' (free child). We may also display more insecure or rebellious behaviours, using language such as 'I don't care', 'It's always me' or 'You can't make me' (adapted child). These behaviours, thoughts and feelings are usually replayed from our childhood.

None of these states can be categorised as simply good or bad; each can play a useful part in the relationships and exchanges we have with others. Sometimes it can be good to play at being 'free child' when developing

---

51. www.ericberne.com/transactional-analysis/

ideas or to just openly express delight. At other times it is useful to support someone through difficult times as a 'nurturing parent'; and inevitably sometimes in leadership, we have to put our foot down and insist that something happens quickly in a controlling parent state.

Becoming able to use these different states is healthy in building effective relationships with others. It is easy, for example, for some managers to default to a controlling parent state which can then result in stifling the professional development of others who do as they are told and can potentially build resentment. Equally dangerous are managers who spend too much time as a child – perhaps fearful of being perceived as controlling – where no authority or clarity is felt.

Holding professional exchanges primarily in an adult/adult state is desirable, as this allows us to be rational and reasonable, and to solve problems without emotions getting in the way. One approach to remember is that to act in the adult state is more likely to elicit an adult response in return. This can be useful if staff (perhaps subconsciously) 'play child', as it can help you shift the dynamic back to an adult/adult exchange.

When we become mindful of our own ego states and those around us, we can have healthier exchanges and develop better relationships.

STRATEGIES FOR MANAGING PEOPLE

All strategies for managing people are unlikely to be successful if the soil of a school's ethos and culture is not healthy. Before reaching for any strategies, it is worth returning to the model for healthy relationships introduced in Chapter 4.

Figure 18. The components of healthy staff relationships

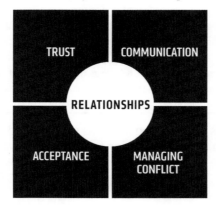

Built on a bedrock of positive professional culture and healthy relationships, here are five strategies to support effective people management.

1. The little things.

2. Clarity is everything.

3. Pulling rank and cutting slack.

4. Act in haste, repent at leisure.

5. Getting people 'off the bus'.

1. The little things

The most valuable types of interactions are the informal, everyday exchanges that happen when leaders are out and about in the school. This is why activities such as the Gemba walk and 'managing by walking around' (see Chapter 11) are such useful techniques, as they allow us to be around people.

Sometimes these types of interactions can be overlooked, but they are vital. They are what speaker and author Adrian Webster refers to as 'Tiny Noticeable Things' (TNTs)[52]:

> *In a world of emails and text messages a TNT is a handwritten note to say 'thank you', it's as small as a smile, it's remembering people's first names, making time for others, listening to people, remembering birthdays, going out of the way to praise staff, phoning back when you promised you would, surprising someone with a small gift of recognition – all the little things that put very big smiles on hard working faces, that show we care.*

Making small but regular investments in our relationships with people is essential – particularly as we never know when we might need to make a significant withdrawal. Often in a school, we might find ourselves needing to ask staff to go above and beyond the call of duty – perhaps covering additional classes, standing in at short notice or having to change rooms. Having some credit in the bank with them is always helpful.

If a meeting gets cancelled or we find ourselves with an hour to spare, there are few better things we can do than taking a trip around school to deposit some TNTs among staff to make people feel appreciated for what they do.

---

52. Webster, A, 'Grow Your People and Your Business with TNTs', www.adrianwebster.com/tnts-tiny-noticeable-things/

2. Clarity is everything

Many things go wrong in school simply because people are not clear enough about what it is they should do. Although leaders can often fall back on claims that an expectation is in a policy somewhere or that it was once covered at a staff meeting, the reality is that we should all probably work a lot harder at making sure people are clear about what is expected of them. Here are four things we can do to help increase clarity:

- **Do fewer things:** There are many different processes and expectations in most schools and if we listed all of them, we would probably realise that it is impossible for them all to be carried out well. Saying no to new ideas and ditching some things that we might think are important is difficult, but necessary. If there is one thing I would go back and do differently over the last ten years, it would be to make the whole thing a lot simpler for everyone.

- **Make fewer changes:** The amount of disruption that change brings to schools should never be underestimated. To avoid unwanted confusion, we should avoid tinkering unnecessarily with any system or expectation unless we are convinced that the effort of change will reap a reward. Using Stuart Lock's phrase of 'Implementation before innovation' from Chapter 9 is a good reminder to embed what we do before introducing more change.

- **Communicate better:** Every day, we speak or type thousands of words which can be read or heard by hundreds or even thousands of individuals. It is interesting to consider what proportion of these words offer clarity as opposed to those which invite further questions, inaccurate inferences or unhelpful rumours. Communication, ultimately, is not about what you say; it's what people hear. Daily briefings, emails, notes on staffroom whiteboards, meetings and one-to-ones: these are all examples of regular communication that takes place in schools. But often this can focus on the changes taking place or new things being implemented rather than revising and embedding the existing expectations. One of the most important things we can do is to keep 'over-communicating' about the existing expectations so that these become known and understood well across the staff. Staff handbooks, scripted example approaches and video examples can all be really useful in helping to make this clearer.

- **Improve induction:** In my experience, many schools do induction really badly – throwing staff in at the deep end without all the necessary information, training or guidance as to how they can be effective. This is in contrast to the most well-organised companies, which invest considerable time and resources in ensuring that new staff are inducted well and so are up to speed more quickly. Despite budget pressures and the challenge of covering staff from class, it is important that we see induction as an investment, not a cost. In recent years, I have visited some high-performing schools which have invested in detailed and rigorous induction programmes. These have included new staff spending the first few days (or even weeks) being taught new systems, observing them and then applying them with someone alongside them as 'co-pilot'.

3. Pulling rank and cutting slack

There are times when every leader will need to 'pull rank' and be firm about the decisions they make. While the coercive leadership style we observed in Chapter 3 was identified as less effective overall, inevitably there are times when we are 'telling, not asking'. Difficult conversations can be a cause of stress for everyone; but handled well (perhaps using the NEFI ART model described by Andy Buck), they can help to resolve things positively.

I used to get personally disappointed in people when they dropped a ball or let something important slide. Now I believe that even the highest-performing human beings need a nudge in the right direction on occasion. And if leaders are not prepared to have awkward conversations and choose instead to walk past things that aren't good enough, mediocrity will quickly become the norm. You get what you tolerate.

That said, leadership is a moral and human activity, and there will be times when we have to cut some slack to people for various reasons. Just as every rule is there to be broken, at some point individuals may need us to make exceptions for them. Schools are complex places and the reality is that not everything we want to happen is possible. Humans make errors; I have certainly made plenty.

Knowing where the line is and when to pull rank or cut slack is a skill of the most experienced leaders and we will inevitably get it wrong at times. Acting with compassion and honesty when we do can help our mistakes to be less damaging.

4. Act in haste, repent at leisure

Staff in schools often work at a furious pace and are prone to making mistakes as a result. One way we can get things wrong is by rushing into potentially tricky conversations without thinking through their implications. Trust and relationships can take a long time to build up, but just a moment to crash down when we get it wrong.

It is also easy to trip up when being put on the spot and responding too quickly without time to think things through. We did some work as a staff a few years ago looking at how to avoid the reptilian brain responses of fight, flight or fright, and how we can try to build in time to think before responding. From this training, I developed a simple tactic of listing seven different places I have visited on holiday when I feel myself getting hot under the collar and am about to make an instant (and potentially damaging) response.

Buying some time to allow the brain to reason rather than respond is wise, however busy we might feel. We need to find space to think through a response or it can end up costing us a lot more time in the long run cleaning up a mess.

5. Getting people 'off the bus'

Throughout this book, I have focused a lot on creating the right conditions for staff to thrive and the importance of healthy school improvement processes designed to motivate rather than destroy. I have also promoted my belief that teachers deserve the opportunity to be developed and teach in an environment where behaviour is sorted and curriculum and assessment are well organised before their teaching can be judged as failing.

But all this said, situations arise from time to time when we have to grasp the nettle and deal with underperformance – sometimes using formal HR processes. Where children are getting a bad deal, we can't afford to duck these difficult issues by hiding behind policy, being too concerned about the impact on other staff or interpreting HR advice in a way that makes it conveniently impossible to deal with.

Although dealing with these issues can be stressful, I have always found it easier to sleep at night knowing that I'm doing something about a difficult situation than when I know something isn't right, but isn't being tackled.

'Back me or sack me': In his first book, *What Makes a Great School,*[53] Andy Buck suggests how schools can effectively manage the process and avoid protracted periods of dissatisfaction on both sides:

---

53. Buck, A, *What Makes a Great School?: A Practical Formula for Success* (Leadership Matters, 2014).

What great schools will do is offer 100% support to a colleague in the first instance. Only if the required improvements fail to take place does it become necessary to consider the alternatives. This will involve working out an appropriate exit strategy and keeping to it. The best schools have real clarity about where they are in the process and avoid vacillating between trying to support and trying to move someone on. When all else has failed, they take decisive action and relentlessly pursue the goal to move someone on. This 'back me or sack me' approach sounds somewhat draconian, but it is seen as important to be clear about where a school is in tackling underperformance.

Although these processes can be challenging all round, they are a normal part of any industry and every organisation has to have a bottom line.

DEALING WITH PARENTS

One of the most important parts of school leadership, but one in which I have never received any formal training, is how to manage parents. It's crazy, really, given its importance and the potential operational, reputational and even legal risks if we get this wrong.

The power of a supportive and 'on-side' parent community cannot be overstated and should never be taken for granted. The debilitating effects of disenfranchised and dissatisfied parents are to be underestimated at our peril.

Parents play a crucial role in supporting their children's learning, and levels of parental engagement are consistently associated with children's academic outcomes.

Education Endowment Fund

There are many things we can do to try to build better engagement with parents in our schools, from formal opportunities such as parents' evenings, reports and productions to informal engagements such as assemblies, coffee mornings and conversations at the classroom door. Across all of these, we should always work hard at the quality of our engagements.

'UP' our approach to parental communication

The 'UP' approach to parental engagement set out in Table 14 focuses on six things we can do across all situations to interact with parents effectively.

Table 14. The 'UP' approach to parental engagement

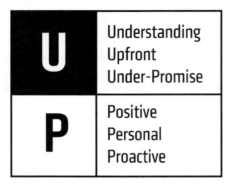

U	Understanding Upfront Under-Promise
P	Positive Personal Proactive

Understanding: Being a parent is the most difficult job I know and has helped me to understand the many complexities of family life that can underpin the behaviours of parents at school. Often, the specific issue we are dealing with or talking about is just the tip of the iceberg. The biggest mistakes I have ever made when dealing with parents came when I rushed to put across my point of view without giving them the time to simply talk. A good starting point with parents is just to listen well.

By listening with genuine interest and empathy, we not only are more likely to get an understanding of what the real issues might be, but also allow parents to feel that their opinions or concerns are taken seriously.

Allowing people to put their point of view across without interrupting or becoming defensive can help to build better relationships and defuse potential issues. And if we fail to listen, we can find ourselves in a position where parents are less likely to engage with us in the future. I would always rather that parents told me their frustrations directly instead of allowing them to develop into disgruntled playground gossip or become the topic of discussion on social media.

Under-promise: It can be tempting, in difficult meetings or conversations, to make promises to parents that can then be difficult to keep or maintain over time. This is particularly the case when concerns are raised and we feel under pressure to rectify things quickly.

For example, when dealing with a complaint about a lunchtime behaviour issue, if we say something like, 'I'll look into this issue first thing this morning and call you at lunchtime with an update', the danger is that something else important might crop up in the morning and we might not call them back in time. In this situation, we could then end up with a parent now unhappy about both the initial issue and our handling of it. Instead, we could manage parents' expectations by saying something like, 'I'll look into this issue as a priority tomorrow and will be in touch as soon as possible.'

By under-promising, we can then potentially exceed parents' expectations if we do call back by lunchtime the next day and this can then help to build confidence in our ability to respond to issues. To under-promise but over-deliver on actions with parents can help to build trust and better relationships in the long term.

Upfront: Being frank and open with parents is almost always the best approach in the long run, even if it can be a challenge at times to communicate difficult messages. If a child is not where they should be academically or there are some learning or behavioural challenges, it is far better for parents to know this early rather than finding it out later. Likewise, if there are issues in the school that need to be sorted, being upfront with parents and saying that you will address them is a better strategy than glossing over things and pretending that things are perfect.

Being upfront about the expectations of the school is also important, to avoid any dissatisfaction that the reality does not match parental expectations. Despite the financial pressures that drive the 'recruitment' to fill our places, it is still important to spell out the expectations of the school. Being clear about what parents can and can't expect when they join is a better strategy than promising the earth and ending up with disappointment down the line.

Personal: Being 'upfront' does not imply that we have to become heavy handed or confrontational in our approach. In contrast, we are much more likely to develop effective relationships if we develop personable approaches to parents. Making time for incidental conversation, listening with empathy to their challenges and generally becoming interested in their lives helps us to connect better with parents while also putting them at ease and opening up a more relaxed conversation.

Being called into school or receiving a phone call from a school leader can feel intimidating to parents – particularly if this builds on negative personal experiences from their own school days. Being mindful of the different states of transactional analysis can help us to keep our interactions at an adult/adult level and avoid the common trap of leaders defaulting to the state of 'critical parent', which is likely to result in confrontation or rebellious responses. Sometimes conversations can be difficult, but we can have these without relying on our 'teacher voices' with parents.

Proactive: Keeping on the front foot with communications is essential – both on a whole-school level, with things such as upcoming dates, events and changes to staffing; and on an individual level, feeding back any behaviour issues so that parents hear them from the teacher first rather than through gossip. Staying ahead of the game is vital.

- Advancements in technology now allow us to communicate instantly and widely, using social media, email and messages to keep parents up to date.

- It is also useful to stay highly visible and accessible to parents. Whenever possible, I still spend mornings or afternoons on the school gate, saying hello and enjoying chit-chat with parents as they drop off and pick up. This is one of the most important routines that SLT members can take part in, as it allows us to take the temperature of the parents' mood and acts as an early warning radar, enabling us to pick up anything we might need to address before it escalates. Ten minutes on the gate nipping an issue in the bud is a wise investment if it avoids the debilitating amount of time and effort of dealing with formal complaints.

- It is useful also to engage well in advance with parents when considering any specific changes that are likely to be controversial – particularly those which might affect a family's finances or shopping routines (I've learned this the hard way!). Changes to uniform, snacks and rules around lunchboxes are those which we might view as 'no-brainers', but can cause great commotion among parents if not handled well. Early consultation or 'offline' conversations around these can help us to understand the scale of any potential opposition to change.

Positive: Overall, we should always make sure that we keep the tone and spirit of our engagement with parents positive. A smile, a 'good morning', knowing the names of the younger siblings in the prams are all TNTs that can help to grow a positive parent community. Inviting parents into the school whenever possible also helps them to feel a genuine part of the community.

Celebrating and sharing children's successes – however small – with parents may at times feel routine for us; but positive comments, phone calls and notes from teachers mean an awful lot. If parents feel that we have their children's best interests at heart, they are much more likely to support us at times when we need them.

Thanking parents for their feedback or for taking the time to come and see us is a useful habit to get into and helps to promote an ongoing positive and solution-focused dialogue.

Difficult parent meetings

Sometimes there are situations that crop up with parents that can really set the cat among the pigeons and become challenging to manage. You can't win them all and sometimes the truth is that you end up getting a bit of a pasting. Handled well, these conversations can create greater trust and understanding between home and school; but poorly handled, they can quickly escalate into feelings of resentment, resulting in a state of longer-term vexation.

Over the years, I have gone from dreading and occasionally avoiding these conversations to quite enjoying them, as I see them as an opportunity to build a stronger relationship with parents. Our greatest advocates often start as our fiercest critics.

Leapfrog conversations: The 'leapfrog conversations' model presented in Figure 19 and Table 15 is one I have developed to use in difficult meetings when trying to reach an agreement or resolution – particularly if the other party is aggrieved or emotional about the situation. The purpose of the leapfrog structure is to allow the other person to 'get everything off their chest' and then leapfrog to the solutions by avoiding an argument which no one can win. While written here for parents, it is a tool that can easily be adapted for other scenarios and is structured into three stages.

Figure 19. The leapfrog conversations model

Table 15. The three stages of the leapfrog conversations model

Listen	
	■ Make the environment welcoming and as relaxed as possible.
	■ Welcome the other person warmly to the meeting, breaking the ice through normal introductions. Make sure they have a drink.
	■ Invite them to talk first and just listen to what is being said.
	■ Try to avoid butting in or justifying at this stage. If you do speak, try to use emphatic language of listening, such as 'I understand that must have made you feel angry' or 'Yes, I can see that from your perspective'.
	■ While listening, try to put yourself in the other person's shoes and empathise with that position.
	■ Be aware of your body language.
	■ When the other person has finished speaking, invite them to carry on and ask whether there is anything else they want to say.
Leapfrog	■ At the point where you feel that everything has been said, repeat back what you have heard and check that you have understood it correctly.
	■ Explain any points that you think are important, but avoid getting into an ongoing justification where things just get repeated back and forth.
	■ Don't be afraid to apologise on behalf of the school if this helps to move the conversation on.
	■ Agree some next steps and ways forward (be careful not to over-promise).
	■ Agree a timescale and date to review either in a meeting or on the phone.
	■ Avoid having to have the last word.
Learn	■ Take time to reflect on the conversation – perhaps talking it through with a colleague.
	■ Try to analyse what was said and why.
	– What can be learned from this issue?
	– Are there any processes or practices that could be changed in the future to avoid a similar situation?
	– Is there any communication that needs to take place to staff as a result – do class teachers or other adults need to be informed of what was agreed?
	■ By analysing the discussion in this way, it can help to avoid looking at the situation through an emotional or defensive lens.
	■ Don't take it personally.

IN SUMMARY – PEOPLE MANAGEMENT

- Building on the chapters that dealt with the 'Heart' of leadership, are the professional culture and ethos healthy in the school? Without these in place, any attempts to 'manage people' are likely to be problematic.

- Have you considered the different ego states that take place within your school using transactional analysis theory? Could you become more mindful of these as interactions take place across school? Can you consciously promote more adult/adult problem solving across the hierarchy?

- Do you have a range of strategies for managing people issues across the school? Is this consistent or do you find that staff can play one leader off against another?

- Are approaches to managing people underpinned by strong professional relationships and is there investment from senior staff in the people? Do they do the TNTs that matter?

- How good is the organisation at supporting staff through difficult times? Can you find the right balance, knowing when to cut people slack and when to pull rank?

- When it comes to the crunch, are leaders prepared to take strong decisions to deal with underperformance?

- How healthy is the relationship with parents across the school? Is there a balance of trust and useful feedback that avoids time-consuming and protracted complaints and grievances? Could the 'UP' model of parent communication help in developing this further?

FIVE FIVES GRID FOR PLANNING

FIVE MINUTES: What immediate first steps can you take?

FIVE DAYS: What short-term actions can you take in the next week to kick start or plan change?

FIVE WEEKS: What actions or follow-up meetings/discussions can you plan for in the next half-term?

FIVE MONTHS: What follow-up and follow-through activities do you need to plan to ensure that the change is not just a flash in the pan?

FIVE YEARS: What might your change look like in five years? What structures, systems and processes will you need to amend to ensure that your change becomes embedded in the fabric of your school and is not a passing fad?

A lean operation

11
CHAPTER PREVIEW

#WholesomeLeadership

This need for calm in the centre of a storm matters and requires leaders to 'think correctly under pressure' – one of Clive Woodward's coaching mantras as manager of the England World Cup rugby team in 2003.

All schools and classrooms operate on the basis of routines and processes, and teaching is far more effective when they run smoothly.

A big part of our role as leaders is to oil the wheels of the operation every day, to minimise the distractions and disruptions within the classrooms and problem solve when things go wrong.

A useful and simple process when trying to get to the root cause of a problem is the 'Five Whys' approach. It's simple and does what it says on the tin.

'Time costing' is a useful process for leadership teams to get into the habit of doing for any new policy or process that they are thinking of implementing.

AND ONE FROM THE INTERVIEW INSIDE

I found that those schools that felt well run and well organised were those that had seemingly ever-present senior staff.

Interview with Craig Jones

A LEAN OPERATION

> Action is the foundational key to all success.

Pablo Picasso

In Chapter 6, I introduced Ronald Heifetz's metaphor of the 'balcony perspective' of the dancefloor as a way of thinking about how strategic thinking and considered decision-making cannot happen when you are running around putting out fires, covering lessons or sorting everything from lost lunchboxes to irate parents. An important line that can be missed from Heifetz's quote, however, is the following, which should remind us that nothing changes in our school while we are in meetings, sending meetings or tied up in strategic planning or evaluation:

If you want to affect what is happening, you must return to the dance floor. The challenge is to move back and forth between the dance floor and the balcony, making interventions, observing their impact in real time, and then returning to the action.

Strategy is nothing without the operational. We can have a great vision, strategy and well-thought-through implementation plan; but unless everyone knows important things such as who is on playground duty and the plan for covering a staff member who has just gone home with a migraine, the whole place descends into chaos. In this final chapter on the Hands of wholesome leadership, we focus mainly on the unglamorous but essential operational aspects of running a school.

Between headships, I spent a year on secondment working in the education technology industry. Technology was being introduced *en masse* to schools in England at the time and I travelled the country working with local authorities, schools and teachers to help them get their heads around the change. It was an unusual arrangement: usually, secondments mean supporting in another school or working for the local authority rather than being part of a commercial environment. I learned an awful lot that year.

I learned to appreciate the tightrope that businesses walk due to unpredictable revenue and the added pressure that this places on staff. Whereas in a school, it is almost certain that the income set in the budget at the beginning of the year will arrive, the income of a business can often be volatile – relying on contracts being honoured, customers paying bills on time and new business being won. I saw how relatively secure and stable our jobs in schools are and realised that I had always taken this for granted.

I also learned how, through a constant obsession around efficiency, it is almost always possible to deliver the same or better results with less money or fewer staff. Despite what their marketing or mission statements might tell us, the main reason businesses exist is to turn a profit; otherwise, they would be charities. Therefore, every process or job that can be cut or carried out at reduced cost is essential to the mission. Increasing the head count of the team is often a last resort and I saw how people could deliver 'lean' projects or contracts, maintaining the quality of service without losing the confidence of customers. Having small budgets and teams also meant that technology was used efficiently and innovatively to automate various processes. This was in contrast with some of the laborious and inefficient processes that still exist in schools today.

Perhaps the most important lesson I learned that year was to appreciate the working conditions within a school. While I was happy to receive the remuneration of a commercial salary, it came at the expense of school holidays with my young family – something we found more difficult than expected. On Christmas Eve I found myself in a North London office working on presentations for a January trade show, waiting for the boss to give us the nod to 'go home early' at around lunchtime. This was a stark contrast to the Christmas Eves I was accustomed to – usually in the middle of a two-week break.

As the year progressed, despite the lure of the six-figure salary, I decided that my future lay back in a school.

It would be easy for me to claim that I chose a second headship purely for the love of working with children and the sense of service the job brings. But if I'm honest, with a young family missing their dad, the opportunity to spend ten weeks a year 'off the treadmill' was a big part of it too; and I was happy to exchange the motorway miles and weekday hotels for a 20-minute drive to Simon de Senlis and being home for bath time.

I returned to school with a greater appreciation of how 'family-friendly' life in a school is, alongside a better understanding of how we can get more done in an organisation through better systems and processes and without thinking that we always have to increase the headcount.

Although I do think that our education system is significantly underfunded, I think we could probably do more to run our schools with greater efficiency and make better use of our existing resources.

THE MACHINE

Using a factory as an analogy to describe schools can be unpopular, as it conjures up images of children as products on an assembly line. But I think we can learn a lot from the manufacturing industry – not by viewing children as products, but through considering the mechanics of school life and the way that classrooms run. All schools and classrooms operate on the basis of routines and processes, and teaching is far more effective when they run smoothly.

Just as factory machinery can stop for various reasons, such as incorrect servicing and excessive operational demand, learning in our classrooms often gets derailed. Sometimes, the causes are common and can be predicted, such as disruptive behaviour, staff absence and changes to timetables. Others are unpredictable, such as snow days, fire alarms and wasps in the classroom (a guarantee to wreck even the most well-prepared lesson!).

Even if the machinery isn't broken, an important focus is to keep it running for as many hours as possible each day. A school year is just 190 days in length and every minute of every day is a crucial learning opportunity that shouldn't be lost. One common frustration for teachers is the pressure to improve outcomes in such a short school day with many disruptions during term time. Special assemblies, rehearsals, sports days, collapsed curriculum days, trips and residentials all add up; and before you know it, there is a significant proportion of the 190 days when the planned curriculum might not happen. Behaviour, too, can be a major disruption. If five minutes are lost in every lesson, that's 25 minutes a day, just over two hours a week or 80 hours a year – the equivalent to 15 days of education. These lost learning opportunities are significant and are why I am a stickler for slick routines, as few term-time disruptions as possible and no wind-down at the end of a term.

A big part of our role as leaders is to oil the wheels of the operation every day, to minimise the distractions and disruptions within the classrooms and problem solve when things go wrong. But there is a lot more to getting the most out of the machine than simply keeping it running for longer.

THINKING LEAN

I first became interested in lean manufacturing through Matthew Orton, a friend who worked across various production companies helping them to add value through eliminating waste. What started as enthusiastic talk about the work he was doing in the production industry around lean culture spilled into my thoughts about how I could run my school better. Over the years, I have become more and more interested in how we transfer some of the lean concepts into a school context.

Lean methodology originated in production and manufacturing and is often attributed to Toyota[54] and the way it has developed its working practices, tools and philosophies over the last 60 years – hence the Japanese terminology. Today, it is used in businesses and organisations around the world. In this next section, we explore three lean principles of 'Gemba', 'Jidoka' and 'just in time', and see how they can be useful processes to develop in a school.

Figure 20. Three keys to a lean school operation

___

54. en.m.wikipedia.org/wiki/Toyota_Production_System

Gemba – 'the real place'

The Japanese word 'Gemba' is commonly used in lean methodology to refer to the factory floor or the point where the work is taking place; its translation is 'the real place'. In a lean environment, leaders and managers adopt a Gemba style, spending less time in their office or in meetings and more time out and about talking and listening with workers at the sharp end of the workplace. Whereas office-bound leaders must rely on third-party reports and data, the 'Gemba walk' enables leaders to see things with their own eyes, hear them with their own ears and understand the reality of the organisation. In a school environment, Gemba is the classroom: this is the only place that matters and everything else should be considered as a secondary process.

Gemba walks are the basis of the learning walks in Chapter 7 and are more effective when there is less structure, allowing leaders to move more freely around the school, following their noses rather than being constrained by a particular checklist or pressure to produce evidence of what they are doing. This shop-floor style of leadership is similar to the 'managing by wandering around' approach developed in the 1970s by Hewlett Packard. In this model, emphasis is placed on the word 'wandering', to encourage managers to spend time among workers on the front line in a non-structured way.

A good example of where I have seen this approach implemented well was in a school that was working hard to improve its phonics provision. With many children at low starting points, the school had introduced an effective but logistically challenging approach where many simultaneous groups were taught by a combination of adults. When evaluating its effectiveness, it became clear that one issue was the difference in quality of delivery across the 25 staff who were delivering groups. To address this, the school took one of their most skilled teachers out of teaching a group and instead timetabled her to work across all groups for the 30-minute session every day.

Using the principles of Gemba, this leader was briefed to be in and among the learning each morning, picking up and correcting any teaching issues at the point of delivery. She was trusted to move freely between the different groups, intervening as necessary in a low-stakes, supportive way. This had a dramatic impact and increased the quality of provision across the group far more effectively than a series of more formal processes. Although it initially felt counter-productive to have a highly skilled teacher not delivering a phonics group of her own, the impact that she made through this Gemba approach was overall far greater than what she would have achieved by teaching in a single classroom.

Leaders should spend as much of their non-teaching time in 'the real place', talking with teachers and children and seeing where they can make a difference with their own eyes and ears. It is easy to become a busy leader, getting tied up in meetings, fighting fires, becoming wrapped up in unnecessary bureaucracy and losing the daily connection and urgency of being in the thick of it; but being busy doesn't make us effective. There is always a gap between the rhetoric of the leaders when describing what takes place in classes and the reality of this from the perspective of teachers and children who spend their time there. To reduce this gap, we can employ the simple principle of spending as much time as possible in and around the front line in a Gemba style.

Jidoka (autonomation)

'Jidoka' is the word used to describe a particular process of detecting abnormalities and then correcting them as efficiently as possible. In production industries, this is critical: for every minute a production line is not running correctly, thousands of pounds can be lost, so early identification of problems and the ability to fix them quickly are essential. But Jidoka is much more than just focusing on quick fixes: it also encompasses the intelligent analysis of problems, focusing on root causes which can then lead to long-term fixes and the prevention of future problems. 'Jidoka' has no direct translation, but the word 'autonomation' (automation with a human touch) is used as an English alternative.

The autonomation process can be described in the following three stages:

1. Detecting problems early.

2. Stopping to fix the urgent problem.

3. Finding root causes and implementing long-term fixes.

A big part of operational school leadership is about solving problems, whether these are logistical challenges or 'firefighting'. Here are some ideas on how we can use the Jidoka process to help us do this more effectively.

Stage 1 – early detection of problems: Large sums of money are now invested in the refurbishment of lean factories and production environments, with a key principle of making potential problems highly visible. Bright, open areas and glass walls are common so that machinery and workers are visible and problems can be detected early. In a school environment, it can be difficult to see what the problems are as learning is happening in different rooms and when you visit, staff can often cover them up for fear of being seen as doing something wrong. This is another reason why the ethos and culture must be right first. Formal inspections often see everyone 'at their best', which may be good for morale, but creates a false sense of reality. More important is to understand the typicality of a classroom so that issues become visible and can be addressed.

Many different types of problem can crop up and throw a spanner in the works of the daily school operation, including the following:

- behaviour issues;
- cover for absent staff;
- technology fails;
- a parent 'issue' that needs investigation and time to resolve;
- a wasp entering the classroom; and
- snow.

These examples are all fairly visible and also relatively easy to solve – even if we make hard work of it in schools sometimes. They are also the types of problems which staff willingly report, as they can be attributed to external factors. More difficult to identify are the following less visible problems, which might be getting in the way of the learning process but which staff can be less willing to report, as they open up prickly issues:

- relationship issues between staff;
- lack of planning or preparation;
- weaknesses in subject knowledge;
- bullying issues among students; and
- anxiety or stress.

Over time, skilled leaders develop intuition for finding these 'hidden' problems, perhaps reading the body language of staff, seeing changes in behaviour of classes or noticing that expectations have slipped when looking in books. Spending time on the front line through the principle of Gemba is helpful in developing this radar for early detection of problems. Intervening proactively with teachers at the planning stage is also useful: it supports and influences teaching and learning before it takes place, as opposed to more reactive processes such as finding problems when looking at data or through book scrutinies when it is too late to change. Although it is less fashionable to look at teachers' planning these days, I think this is a much better point in the teaching cycle for leaders to get involved. It is also an easier way in to offer support with planning than having to sit down after some monitoring and try to offer retrospective advice.

Stage 2 – stopping to fix the urgent problem: Once problems are identified in production environments, they must be fixed. This typically involves the empowerment of the team member to 'stop the line, call for assistance and wait for support to arrive', and then take part in collaborative work to quickly resolve the problems and prevent reoccurrence. This is the same in a school environment, where every minute of every lesson counts; one of our most important operational responsibilities is to make sure that we iron out any disruptions and let teachers get on with the business of teaching.

It can be a stressful part of the job, lurching from problem to problem and trying to put out fires – often in public, where you are conscious of others judging your decision-making. In these highly charged moments, it is important for leaders to focus on de-escalation, rather than contributing to the escalation of the situation, which can then lead to a longer-term or bigger problem.

This need for calm in the centre of a storm matters and requires leaders to 'think correctly under pressure' – one of Clive Woodward's coaching mantras as manager of the England World Cup rugby team in 2003. When Jonny Wilkinson kicked the famous winning drop goal, the final passage of the game worked like clockwork as the team carried out their separate roles.

This mantra is useful when the pressure is on in school – don't rush decisions or allow emotion to play a part when you are trying to problem solve. Even when the pressure is on, give yourself some time and space to reason, and maybe talk it through with someone else. This time helps to engage the reasoning part of the brain (neocortex), rather than the 'fight or flight' limbic or reptilian brain. Thinking correctly under pressure can help you to make better calls in the thick of the action and avoid unhelpful emotions of guilt and blame becoming part of the situation.

As an example, take a situation where a child has momentarily become lost in school. This happens from time to time – perhaps at the end of the day when a parent has come to collect them and they have gone to a club or are in the toilet, or another parent has collected them and there has been a communication breakdown. Whatever the cause, there can be a handful of anxious minutes while people are searching, making phone calls and passing on messages to try to make sure the child is safe.

The process of solving this problem is hampered if we don't manage to keep calm under pressure, and the situation is made worse where emotion and blame creep in and the discussion becomes defensive. While the adults are all trying to cover their backs and attribute blame elsewhere, no one is thinking clearly about solving the immediate problem. As important as it is for leaders to become competent trouble-shooters, we need to do this in such a way that everyone can walk away from solving the problem without feeling blamed.

Stage 3 – finding root causes and implementing the long-term fix:
The intended effect of Jikoda is to find long-term fixes to problems to avoid them being repeated in the future. In lean workplaces, there is often talk of the '100-year fix' when implementing fixes that prevent similar mistakes in the future. Thinking this way is more than just fixing machines and hoping that people learn from their mistakes; it forces us to think about the processes and systems that need altering so these mistakes are eradicated.

The biggest barrier to finding the 100-year fix is often identifying the real root cause of the problem. Again, blame can get in the way when searching for explanations if people become preoccupied by finding fault with themselves or each other; this in turn can trigger defensive conversations where no one ever gets to the root cause. Most of us will recognise the post-mortem meetings after a poor set of results or a poorly handled situation where everything is being questioned, but we don't really get anywhere because people feel threatened by the enquiry and so self-protection kicks in. When things go wrong, it is an important opportunity for managers to lead with humility in a no-blame atmosphere, so that people can think analytically rather than defensively.

I take full responsibility for this situation, so please – there's no need to talk about whose fault it was. Let's work out the details of how it went wrong and find the root cause so that we can avoid it happening again.

A useful and simple process when trying to get to the root cause of a problem is the 'Five Whys' approach. It's simple and does what it says on the tin – keep asking 'why?' at least five times until you are satisfied that you have got to the bottom of an issue. Imagine, for example, sitting down at the end of the day after a really difficult afternoon trying to investigate why behaviour had gone so wrong in assembly:

1. **Why was behaviour such a challenge in assembly this afternoon?**

   It's hard to say. There were plenty of staff present, but the children didn't come in as well as they usually do and it wasn't great from then on. We had to stop twice and talk to the whole school.

2. **Why didn't the children come in properly?**

   The hall wasn't cleared properly after lunch and the chairs weren't set out in time. This caused some disruption and we had to get help from the caretaking team to sort it out at the last minute.

3. **Why wasn't the hall set up on time?**

   Steve (the deputy head teacher) is usually here before assembly starts and makes sure the caretaker has clear instructions on set-up. But he wasn't here today, so they were late and weren't sure what the set-up was.

4. **Why wasn't Steve there?**

   He was busy supporting a safeguarding issue in Year 4 that came up over lunch. Someone was covering his class, but they didn't know how to set up the projector.

5. **Why have we got a process that relies on Steve being present? Does the deputy head need to be there in person to get an assembly set up?**

   He doesn't need to be there – it's just the logistics of setting it up. He's always done it, but if the caretaker knew in advance, he could do it without Steve.

In this situation, unless we continue to ask 'why?', we could shrug this off as just one of those things that happens, as safeguarding incidents cannot be helped and have to take precedence. The focus of the discussion also goes beyond the children (first and second 'whys?') and adults (third and fourth 'whys?') to get to the process (fifth 'why?'). By doing this, we get to understand the real root cause – not that there is a problem with the children or Steve, but that there is a process that can change. Knowing that Steve as deputy head is often likely to be called on for safeguarding issues, arrangements for assembly should be a part of morning briefings on Fridays which the caretaker attends. This can be added to the weekly briefing sheet as a reminder so it won't happen again.

Notice that I haven't specified who is asking or answering the questions in this example. Although it is likely that leaders will often be asking the questions, a good technique when the culture is right is for leaders to ask others to lead the questioning, which further removes the issue of hierarchy and can encourage more transparent and honest analysis.

This example might seem like a trivial operational issue, but it is these things that get in the way of teachers doing their job and adding value in the classroom. It's important that we 'sweat the small stuff'.

Just in time

The final lean principle to explore here is 'just in time' – the second pillar of Toyota's philosophy. In manufacturing, 'just in time' is a philosophy around efficiency in which things are bought or produced just before they are needed, as opposed to building up large inventories of both products and materials. It is a key part of how lean businesses operate, reducing waste in areas such as materials, transport, storage and staffing. The basis for this philosophy is that too often, we build lazy systems and processes that rely on us having contingency of staff, stock or money to fill in when things go wrong. By removing the contingency, problems that would previously have been covered up become exposed and the systems themselves must be examined more closely. While this can be uncomfortable, it allows us to identify the root cause issues and then improve our systems and approaches so that we can cope without the contingency.

At a time when budgets are under intense pressure in schools, we are being forced to make cuts into areas we have relied on in the past, such as support staff, tiers of middle management and curriculum budgets. While this is initially challenging and unwelcome, it forces us to think harder about where our limited staffing and resources add the most value and which tasks and processes could be superfluous if we were more effective. This links back to the principle of a disciplined culture discussed in Chapter 4: a lean and effective disciplined staff avoids the time and expense of bureaucracy created to try to manage problems.

An optimistic take on the funding crisis in our schools is that it might force us to examine our approaches more carefully, cutting away some of the unnecessary things that have become part and parcel of teaching in recent years and leaving us with a simpler, more effective version of teaching. Our job as leaders is to be brave and thoughtful enough to preserve the things that matter and cut the things that don't, as opposed to taking easy options and just preserving the *status quo*.

Organisations which run on the principle of 'just in time' become agile in response to new demands and have operational flow – a sense that everything is done as it needs to be. It is this sense of flow that I think is important for us to focus on when developing a well-run school environment.

Here are five ways to create better flow in schools.

Flow of the school day: Does the school day have a flow to it and are the logistics well organised so that time is not wasted? At times when lessons change over or children get changed or have breaks, it is important to get the transitions really slick so that everyone is where they need to be, to ensure that a 60-minute lesson contains 60 minutes of learning. If staff are asked to complete something, they should be given all the documentation and instructions required to avoid time being wasted clarifying details. Do meetings start and finish on time and are they productive? Short stand-up meetings or 'huddles', where things get sorted out face to face to respond to different challenges, are a leaner way of keeping the flow in the day as needed.

Absence and cover: How efficient and effective are processes to manage staff sickness and planned cover? Are communication processes clear and is there a good plan for how to get the right people in the right places at the right times? In lean organisations, highly flexible working arrangements allow staff to be redirected depending on need rather than stuck in clunky fixed structures. Are there good induction and training processes so that the people who provide regular cover can do this effectively? In lean environments, the concept of 'drop down' is used in situations to cover staff absence, where senior staff drop down and fill in the gaps on the front line. This is because it is recognised that the most value in the organisation is created in 'the real place' – the principle of Gemba. If leaders can drop down to cover, the quality of teaching on the front line should remain high; they might also spend less time picking up behaviour and parent issues which can often arise when unsatisfactory cover arrangements are made.

Termly scheduling: Do the different parts of the school term naturally lead on from each other or do they feel disjointed? It is important in particular to join up the processes such as assessment points, CAP meetings, reports and parents' evenings so that there is a natural flow which enables us to make the biggest impact on learning. If everything comes at the same time, it is chaotic; if they are too far apart, the flow is lost and it takes too long to turn assessment and analytics into responsive action.

Schools with poor organisation or discipline can slip into the habit of setting artificial deadlines with buffers to allow for the fact that deadlines are not being met. In a disciplined culture with lean processes, the turnaround times can be reduced between reports being written and sent to parents, assessments being carried out and any intervention starting.

Recruitment: Schools have to work much harder these days on recruitment. Whereas I remember receiving 20 to 30 applications for class teacher positions in the past, today it is rare to get to double figures. I think we still miss a trick in schools when we recruit just to fill our structure rather than recruiting to fill the predictable gaps that will appear. When schools say they cannot afford the risk of over-staffing, they often forget both the financial and opportunity cost of recruitment and induction processes and the risks that mid-year recruitment brings. In a two-form entry school, it is probable that you will find yourself recruiting mid-year, so thinking more flexibly about doing this before September can then allow you to redeploy staff throughout the year 'just in time'. It can sound like a risk, but over time I believe that the risk of starting the year with no options up your sleeve is greater – once you share this risk across other schools or within a MAT, it soon becomes a no-brainer.

Technology: Is technology being used as an enabler of flow in school through effective communications and good diary organisation? When implementing technology, there is inevitably an adoption hump to get over – usually to do with practical things such as log-ins, training and new habits for staff. Once technology is established, though, it can enable free and timely communication and access to information and knowledge to enable better decision-making and flow in a school.

THE 'COST' OF TIME

Falling budgets force us to look harder at how we can generate both cost savings and additional funding in schools. These days, the £3,000 we might raise from a summer fair or even the odd £200 from a school disco are no longer nice extras to have, but necessary parts of the budget that often support essential resources. We have become very good at making do and mending, and suppliers into education have become used to working a lot harder for sales as we have all trimmed our spending in line with budget pressures. But the resources part of the overall budget is a relatively small amount: between 75% and 80% of our budgets is spent on salaries and another 10% on supplies and services, which means that the whole conversation around buying 'stuff' is about the remaining 10% of the overall pot. In a typical two-form entry primary school, for example, we might spend approximately £1.4 million on salaries, including on-costs, out of a total budget of £1.9 million. This is a lot of money; and even if we might be happy that the staff are all worth it and we think we have got the right people on the bus, it would be lazy for us to think that we can't help to make them more productive by thinking more carefully about the work we ask them to do.

Financial versus opportunity costs

There are two ways we can look at the value or cost of activities that we get our staff to do. The first is the financial cost: that is, the actual nominal cost of the time it takes to carry out an activity. To calculate this, it is good to have a general rule of thumb around the hourly rate of your teachers, leaders and support staff. Using this, you simply add up the different staff members participating in each activity and then add up their hourly rates (including all on-costs), and multiply by the length of the meeting.

For example, if you have ten teachers in your school with an average hourly rate of £35, it will cost £350 per hour every time you get them together or £700 for a two-hour meeting. Using this approach, we can create some rule of thumb nominal 'financial costs' of staff activities as follows:

- Staff meetings per week (one and a half hours – all teaching staff) – £1,500.

- Training days (one full day for all teaching and support staff) – £7,380.

- Planning meeting (two teachers for two hours) – £ 760.

- Leadership meeting (five SLT members for two hours) – £450.

- Trust heads meeting (ten heads for two hours) – £1,000.

This is partly a theoretical exercise because the money has already been committed to these salaries; it's not as though by cancelling a staff meeting you will get £1,500 back in your budget. Nevertheless, it is a useful measure of how much of your limited resources different meetings and processes 'cost'. For example, if we start to think of staff meetings as costing £1,500 a week or £19,500 per 13-week term, it might sharpen our approach to making sure that each of these sessions is better planned, delivered and evaluated.

The second way of looking at the value of what we do is the opportunity cost. This is where, instead of a monetary value, we look at what else could have been achieved in the same amount of time. So, for example, the financial cost of an SLT meeting for two hours after school could be valued at £450; but the opportunity cost is that these leaders could have spent those same two hours having developmental and supportive conversations with colleagues around planning, reading or researching, or following up on behaviour issues from the day with staff and parents.

Some other examples of opportunity cost are as follows:

■ The opportunity cost of ten hours of marking a week could be ten hours of additional planning or resourcing. Perhaps more preferably, it could be five additional hours of planning or resourcing and five fewer hours of work, giving time for staff to rest in the evenings so that they have more energy for teaching their class the next day. It could therefore be the opportunity cost of a teacher either having Sunday afternoon and evening with their family or not.

■ The opportunity cost of staff running after-school clubs for two hours a week every week could be the ability for the same teacher to spend those two hours planning or resourcing lessons more effectively.

■ The opportunity cost of teaching staff being on morning break duty is that they are unlikely to be as well prepared for their lesson after break as if they didn't have that duty. It could also be that they don't get a chance to have a drink or use the toilet.

■ The opportunity cost of the head teacher teaching daily booster classes in Year 6 could be that decisions about the budget are not made on time, or that communications around changes of arrangements or policies are not made as effectively as they should be.

'Time costing' is a useful process for leadership teams to get into the habit of doing for any new policy or process that they are thinking of implementing. Of course, I'm not suggesting that staff shouldn't run clubs or that every school shouldn't have teachers on playground duty; the point here is that we should be looking more closely at all the tasks and activities that staff do each week, scrutinising their importance and evaluating whether they are either necessary or worth their opportunity cost.

AN INTERVIEW WITH CRAIG JONES

For his thoughts on operational leadership, I spoke with head teacher Craig Jones. I first worked with Craig at an international school in Dubai some years ago. He was the type you knew would be a head one day, even though he had just passed his NQT year. Now in his second headship, Craig runs a recently opened free school in the South-west and keeps his attention firmly on the practical.

TR: One of the things I know that you pay a lot of attention to in your headship is the organisation and operational parts of your school. Before headship, what were your experiences of how well schools were organised and run?

CJ: I found that those schools that felt well run and well organised were those that had seemingly ever-present senior staff. But not just physically: senior teachers would have a view on all matters and pay close attention to detail; they would teach well and you heard and saw it; they sorted stuff out that affected the lives of many children and concerned themselves with small things/details. I feel, looking back, that it was the heads who fostered that behaviour and, in some cases, relied heavily on ever-present senior teachers to organise and run the school. I now draw upon those experiences and these leaders as to how I try to influence the school.

TR: I agree that sweating the small stuff really matters in a school, and things such as getting the cover diary sorted, rotas timetabled and rooms booked are important and can cause stress for staff if they're neglected. So as the head of a new school with a million different challenges around buildings, recruitment and communications, what routines and rituals do you carry out during the week to make sure that your school is a tight ship and that you remain 'ever present'?

CJ: Well, manning the school gate in the morning is the first on the list. This to me was as important when we had just 31 children walking through the gates as it is today. It's here that you meet and greet families, build a picture around the child, support school communication; and it keeps me in touch with the quality of parent and teacher/staff interactions. During the morning, I will usually walk around school at least once. With six classrooms in use, I like to see the learning in action. For me, it helps to see the front line and build evidence of daily teaching and learning. I pop into the staffroom to see if everyone's OK and I'll always be on duty at lunchtime; we have a small midday supervision team who welcome the senior support with behaviour management.

TR: What about the logistics of school life – the unglamorous but vital arrangements that help everything 'tick'. How do you go about this making sure you run a well-oiled machine?

CJ: I suppose if we take the well-oiled machine metaphor, we could look at both the people who run the machine (operators) and the people who design the machine (engineers).

Running the machine: I suspect most machines need monitoring and adjustment. Even a computer-monitored machine, in this day and age, will have control mechanisms that we can tweak to ensure it runs smoothly. In the case of a school, we constantly need to check on elements of the machine – for example, the temperature (is everything too frantic and are people getting overworked?) and the output (are we producing outcomes, admin or otherwise, that are most efficient?). In the latter example, I have found that in headship in a small school it is important to play a central role in leading teams or individuals to steer these in the right direction. So when I talk about output and efficiency, in simple terms, I have a regular Monday morning meeting with my office manager to prioritise the admin and my workload for the week ahead. This 30-minute meeting helps both of us to steer our teams and balance our understanding of each other's team commitments.

The engineer: A friend once told me that someone who fixes the coffee machine is maintenance and repair and not an engineer. The engineer is the designer of the machine; so unless the coffee machine needs redesigning, call the maintenance person when it needs fixing. As for schools, you need to design your systems. Simple. How are registers taken? What are the timings of the day? How do we take money? How do we communicate with parents? The list is exhaustive, but it all needs to be thought of. In an established school, rather than one that is new and still growing, you can't change all those at once; but you still need to be an engineer and consider the design.

TR: I really like your analogy of the machine, Craig, and it links to a lot of the things I think we can learn from industry about how to be more effective and efficient in schools. Trying to think more like an engineer than the maintenance man in our schools when solving problems is useful. However well designed the systems are, though, leaders often feel like they are firefighting and find themselves in crisis-management situations while still trying to spin many plates. How do you handle these situations?

CJ: It's difficult at times and I know that just because I'm the head, I can't do it alone. I often call for help if I'm juggling things and this is where I rely on my relationships with staff and our team culture.

I don't get it right all the time and I'm similar to many primary heads who often find themselves in challenging situations on their own having to make quick decisions. When deciding when and where to act, I consider the cost and experience of me and others as a resource with the needs: children's safety and care first, followed by staff safety and care, teaching and learning etc.

Today I made the decision to get involved and help a child who bizarrely got trapped behind some fixed furniture. I chose to help the trapped boy ahead of answering the phone to social care (which I knew was important, but not a conversation that was urgent given that I knew the family and circumstances). As I stood for a moment looking at the circumstances in which our young boy had trapped himself, I had two or three members of staff attempt to catch me for a response on a few matters (they clearly saw what I was looking at) – none of which was pressing, aside from one which was to support an after-school event. In this case I just asked them to wait while I helped our pupil.

Someone once said to me that I should know which balls will survive if I drop any of them, before I throw them up in the air.

TR: Thanks, Craig – it's been great talking to you about how you run the operation of your school. Finally, if you had three pieces of advice to give to a new leader as to how to contribute to the smooth running of their school, what would they be?

CJ:

1. First, get to know all the jobs in your school and who does them.

2. Always continue to ask for advice and ideas from both your seniors and your colleagues.

3. Most importantly, before you start, be able to articulate the behaviours you want others – including children – to see in you as a leader. Often people rattle off values and characteristics of leadership. For me, I'd say go further than that. You need to be able to articulate,

for example, 'I'm the sort of head that you will see hold doors for others, greet parents in the morning, enjoy a joke a lunchtime and tell a member of staff that the quality of learning is not meeting expectations etc.' Then stick to the things that matter to you.

IN SUMMARY – A LEAN OPERATION

- Think Gemba – 'the real place'. How much time are you managing to spend out on the 'shop floor' versus time in the office?

- When things go wrong, does the culture allow for staff to highlight this or is there a fear of blame that keeps problems hidden away?

- To get to the bottom of problems in school, could you carry out no-blame, root-cause analysis? Consider the use of the 'Five Whys' investigation to get to the root cause so that you can put in place a long-term fix rather than the sticking plaster.

- Do you consider the cost of both time and opportunity when implementing new policies and approaches?

- Are you using technology effectively to make your school more efficient and productive? Remember that there will be an investment stage in both the technology and changing habits before you reap the rewards of technology.

FIVE FIVES GRID FOR PLANNING

FIVE MINUTES: What immediate first steps can you take?

FIVE DAYS: What short-term actions can you take in the next week to kick start or plan change?

FIVE WEEKS: What actions or follow-up meetings/discussions can you plan for in the next half-term?

FIVE MONTHS: What follow-up and follow-through activities do you need to plan to ensure that the change is not just a flash in the pan?

FIVE YEARS: What might your change look like in five years? What structures, systems and processes will you need to amend to ensure that your change becomes embedded in the fabric of your school and is not a passing fad?

Section 5

Leading with your Health

Prioritise your own health and the wellbeing of staff around you. Develop interdependent relationships within and outside your school.

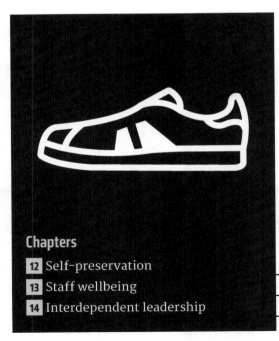

Chapters

Self-preservation

A SELECTION OF QUOTES FROM THE CHAPTER   #WholesomeLeadership

A benefit of going through difficult times is that it gives you the chance to build resilience. Those who have undergone counselling or therapy are often left with wellbeing tools and strategies that can protect against future vulnerability. But why do we wait for a crisis?

It was about 18 months into my first headship when my body finally said, 'Enough is enough.'

Above all, make time in your life for the things that bring you energy. Whether this is reading, running, yoga, playing guitar in a band or bell ringing – never give it up for your day job.

Anyone who has ever worked in a school will know how quickly the time can disappear. I can't honestly remember the last time I clock-watched. In order for school leaders to survive, let alone be effective, we have to become ruthless with our time.

As an alternative to martyr leadership, safe mode gives you the freedom to take down your expectations of yourself for a short period of time before you can regroup and get back up to full speed.

AND ONE FROM THE INTERVIEW INSIDE

Self-preservation is as essential part of leadership. You can't be the best leader if you are struggling with your own health and wellbeing, and we need to have the best and strongest teams around us in order to be most effective. Looking after ourselves helps us to look after others, and valuing health and wellbeing is an essential step.

Interview with Julia Kedwards

SELF-PRESERVATION

> " Self-preservation, nature's first great law, all the creatures, except man, doth awe.
>
> Andrew Marvell

Few would argue against the importance of personal health in our lives, yet many of us neglect this as we get swept up in the world of school leadership and school improvement. Primary schools are places where you find the most committed and caring people, prepared to go to extraordinary lengths to help children, family and colleagues – often at the cost of their own wellbeing. It's a great thing that many people see teaching as their vocation; but it is important that those in schools remember that to neglect their health is not just unwise, but irresponsible.

And I speak from personal and painful experience about what can go wrong when you try to be all things to all people and fail to look after yourself.

Burnout

It was about 18 months into my first headship when my body finally said, 'Enough is enough.' It came about a month after an Ofsted inspection – one that had been long awaited and had been the focus of our work pretty much since I started at the school. It was successful, but the process was gruelling and I felt as though the world had rested on my shoulders. I was a young head, desperate to prove myself through the challenges which had come thick and fast, including tackling underperformance, parental challenges and the pressures of trying to secure a good Ofsted judgement in a village school where the expectations were high.

Every school has its challenges and, while I would be the first to acknowledge the difficult work that goes on in more deprived communities, the raised expectations and sometimes vigorous parental engagement that come with working in a more affluent community bring about their own pressures. I was also following a successful predecessor who had been very effective in tackling certain challenges and putting systems and procedures in place. While I benefited from his organisation and thoroughness in terms of documentation and policy, they were big shoes to fill. It took me some time to realise that trying to emulate the styles of other leaders wasn't the answer and I needed to find my own way to lead.

Looking back, it was pretty obvious that I was heading for a fall. The hours and intensity just weren't sustainable, yet I was so determined to succeed and for the school to do well that I just kept adding everything to my job list and saying yes. There were lots of bad habits that I'd fallen into; it is not difficult to see why I got to the point of burnout, particularly while trying to juggle the demands of a young family at the same time.

Does any of this sound familiar?

- **Unsustainable working hours:** I was so determined to be able to cope with everything on my plate that I started getting up earlier in the morning and finishing later each night. I was setting my alarm clock for 5:00am in order to try to get some work done before the family woke up. I would get to school early, stay late and then typically work at home in the evening until 11:00pm or midnight several nights a week.

- **Broken sleep:** I was so wired when I went to bed, I found it difficult to get to sleep. As I tried to sleep, I would often remember several other things that I needed to do. Sometimes I would lie and think these over; sometimes I would be making notes on my phone for the morning; and sometimes I would get back up and go and do them. Sleep wasn't good and life was more difficult as a result.

- **Weekend working:** As a teacher, I had often worked on Sunday afternoons or evenings. This had now become so regular, it almost felt a part of my core hours. I would find myself spending parts of Sunday looking forward to the point when I could switch on my laptop and work.

- **Constant email:** These were the early days of primary school email and smartphones, and the lure of having access to email on the go was too much. I was continually online and accessible, with notifications pinging constantly, and fell into the trap of replying too quickly to everything that came in.

- **Rehearsing hypothetical conversations:** Somewhere along the line, I had developed this habit of practising future difficult conversations in the car wherever I went. For example, I could be in the car driving to work and I'd be talking out loud to an imaginary Ofsted inspector arguing the toss about something to do with Year 3 data trends. Or I'd be in the shower having it out with a parent in anticipation of a meeting that might never happen. This was one of the most unhelpful habits, looking back.

Exhaustion, anxiety and panic attacks were the price I paid: debilitating and terrifying moments that would creep in and get me at any time of the day or night. It was a difficult period and I still have a note that I wrote describing my symptoms from that time which reads as follows:

Not myself

Tired

Feel like I'm living in a bubble

Can't face things or cope

Want to stay in bed

Stomach and chest pains

Short of breath

Nothing's real

Want to switch off

No emotions/unsociable

Anxious

I keep this as a reminder of how bad things got, and a prompt to keep a healthier balance and never to take good times or wellbeing for granted. This perspective is important to me and the reason why I'll either be out on my bike or running on Sunday mornings, and not on the laptop. By no means can I say that I've cracked it (those who know me well find the irony of me writing a chapter with suggestions around balancing workload hilarious); but I love my work and am usually happy to put in long hours, with strategies in place to avoid it getting unhealthy again.

They say that what doesn't kill you makes you stronger and I believe this to be true in most cases. Thankfully, through support from my family and time with a counsellor, I learned about various wellbeing tools and techniques such as cognitive behaviour therapy (CBT) which helped me through. Although difficult, this experience helped me to build resilience to cope better with challenges in the future.

If you are reading this and recognise some of the same unhealthy habits in yourself, do yourself a favour and get some help to get it all in order – make it a priority. If you are reading this and haven't experienced it, you could do worse than to work on some wellbeing tools anyway, as everyone is vulnerable – particularly in the high-stress roles that leadership in schools can involve.

Actively acknowledging our own vulnerability to stress and working on strategies to counter this is really important – particularly when working in a challenging environment. In areas of high deprivation, when facing ongoing external scrutiny or at times of significant change, it is inevitable that the level of challenge and stress will be higher. Failing to acknowledge and work deliberately on our wellbeing in these situations is like trying to walk on the moon without a space suit; no one is superhuman.

The statistics about teachers and leaders leaving the profession are astoundingly bad. Simply too many good teachers and school leaders choose to leave before retirement age due to pressures of workload and battles with mental health. In recent years, I have also read far too many articles and blogs about colleagues leaving schools for similar reasons. It is really important that school leaders actively work on their wellbeing. In this chapter we look at the following important strategies that can help:

- Keep your mojo.
- Manage time well.
- Find space to think strategically.
- Delegate well

- Avoid the 'martyr leader' trap.

- Develop wellbeing tools.

- When all else fails, engage 'safe mode'.

> *Too much work and too much energy kill a man just as*
> *effectively as too much assorted vice or too much drink.*

Rudyard Kipling

Keep your mojo

There are times in the week and term when we naturally have energy and flow in our work. In these moments, we might feel we can take on the world and are more productive and disciplined. Like any job, however, school leadership can sometimes be a grind, where we find ourselves with less energy and motivation. Remembering that as leaders we 'set the weather', keeping our mojo is critical; it impacts not only on our own effectiveness, but also on that of everyone else in the organisation, particularly through challenging times.

Here are some tips for keeping your mojo:

- Think back to the 'to-be' list that introduced in Chapter 3. It can be motivating and energising to remember that each day you are working towards this and keep your 'why' at the forefront of your mind.

- Make sure you get enough sleep each night. They say that an hour before midnight is worth two after and it is nearly always a better deal for your staff and children if you have enough sleep. It's a false economy if we think that investing more hours will make us better leaders if we don't then have the energy to lead and support others the next day.

- Make time to eat, talk and listen with your colleagues – just because you might be in a leadership position, it doesn't mean that you have to look busy all the time. It will do your colleagues good to see this modelled by leaders too.

- Phone a colleague you used to work with one evening or at lunchtime and find some perspective from exchanging ideas. It is often quite motivational to talk to colleagues in other schools; you can leave the conversation reminded that it is a privilege to work where you work and do what you do.

■ Remember that it's impossible (and annoying) to be like Mr Motivator all the time. Try to pace yourself through the terms to keep your energy pooled and focus on bringing a sense of reassuring consistency to your school rather than peaks and troughs.

■ If keeping your mojo becomes a continual issue, could it be time for a discussion with your line manager about finding a new challenge, either within the school or at a new one?

■ Above all, make time in your life for the things that bring you energy. Whether this is reading, running, yoga, playing guitar in a band or bell ringing – never give it up for your day job. The energy and sense of identity that these things bring will make you a better leader.

Manage time well

A wizard is never late, nor is he early.
He arrives precisely when he means to.

Gandalf

Anyone who has ever worked in a school will know how quickly the time can disappear. I can't honestly remember the last time I clock-watched. In order for school leaders to survive, let alone be effective, we have to become ruthless with our time. A lot is written about time management and the many strategies that exist, and an important point is for us to remember that time is finite and we will never be able to do all the things that we would ideally like to do. Making peace with this is important and helps us to avoid the martyrdom phrase of 'There isn't enough time'.

We have enough time. We have as much time as anyone else in the world. We just have to be pragmatic about what it is possible to achieve and use our time as best we can.

Here are some time management strategies that are worth considering.

Sort out 'to-do' lists: It might sound basic and obvious, but it is this type of fundamental organisation that can help us stay afloat or, if neglected, lead down the path towards chaos and ruin. There are many different ways that people go about working with their 'to-do' lists and obviously this is one of those times when different processes work for different people.

One idea is to avoid the concept of 'to-do' lists altogether, as to write down everything you need to do can become demotivating – particularly as it is almost impossible that you will ever achieve everything on the list. Instead, try writing a 'will-do' list each day, with one or two important things that must get done (avoiding adding in things that aren't important). If time then allows you to get other things done, this will feel like you have achieved something, as opposed to carrying around a long list of tasks that are never achievable.

'Eat your frog': With a 'will-do' list in place for the day, a useful strategy is to tackle the most uncomfortable task first; this is usually the most important. If you can get this one cracked first in the day, it saves you procrastinating and filling your time with less important activities. Andy Buck calls this 'eating your frog' in the morning[55] – the concept of getting the most feared tasks out of the way quickly.

Use scheduled one-to-ones and meetings to resolve things: Often, for problems to be resolved, they need a proper conversation with the right people around the table. This is far more effective than a series of group emails that get sent back and forth while people put their views forward, which may not get resolved. Consider taking a few minutes at the beginning of the week to schedule meetings with the right people, so that you know things can move forward and decisions can be made, and can enjoy not having ongoing discussions in the background that drag on for longer than they need to.

Manage email in batches, not as an ongoing distraction: While emails are an essential part of modern life, they can become overwhelming. If you're not careful, you can spend your life reading them, writing them or simply being distracted by the various different notifications that ping up on your devices while you're trying to focus on tasks or in meetings. Consider switching your notifications off so that they don't interrupt you and then set aside some uninterrupted time when you can sit and work through them on your own terms. This is likely to be a far more efficient and effective process.

Here is some guidance that we have developed for staff in our school to help manage this:

■ It is fine to send emails whenever is convenient.

■ Emails are for when the recipient is next working and no one is expected to respond to email immediately in the holidays or during the evening.

■ Email is a great, efficient way for sharing information with a large audience, but a poor way to have difficult conversations or resolve conflict. Remember that nothing beats face-to-face communication.

---

55. Buck, A, *Leadership Matters: How Leaders at All Levels Can Create Great Schools* (John Catt Educational, 2016).

Find space to think strategically

In Chapter 6, I discussed the importance of finding time to think strategically – 'distancing yourself from the fray'. A useful tool to help plan for more strategic thinking time is the 'Eisenhower Matrix' set out in Figure 22, which is named after the former US president and Second World War commander general and plots the urgency and importance of tasks against each other.

Figure 21. The Eisenhower Matrix

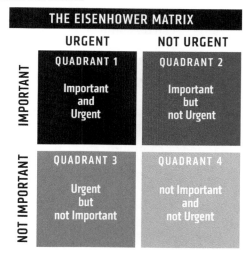

Quadrant 1: Important and urgent – do it, but decrease it: Often in schools, we can find ourselves trapped working solely in Quadrant 1, where everything is urgent and important. While there will inevitably be times and days like this, to work predominately in Quadrant 1 is chaotic; and if we spend too much of our time here, we risk burnout and neglecting other important and strategic work. Examples of Quadrant 1 activities might be behaviour and safeguarding issues, staff absence and cover, and dealing with angry parents or urgent external deadlines. In schools in the 'Stabilise' phase, it can be difficult to get out of Quadrant 1.

Quadrant 2: Important but not urgent – do it and make more time for it: Quadrant 2 is the crucial strategic space for school improvement work that is important, but not yet urgent. This includes things such as recruitment, school improvement planning, research, policy development and training and development. Making time for these activities before they become urgent is essential, as it allows the necessary space for them to be thought through and carried out properly. 'More haste, less speed' can be a painful lesson to learn, but it's a useful one. Using the 'Four stages of improving a school' model, schools in the 'Repair' stage should spend more time in Quadrant 2 to begin working more strategically. Schools in the 'Improve' and 'Sustain' phases have usually found a balance between the important work that takes place in Quadrant 1 and 2.

Quadrant 3: Urgent but not important – delegate and decrease it: The urgent/non-important things in Quadrant 3 are likely to need dealing with now, but are not important. These might include taking phone calls, receiving questions to clarify something or being interrupted to make a decision that someone else needs somewhere. Although they might seem unimportant at the time, they are usually important to someone else, so may still need dealing with. These types of activity can come about if either:

- we have not delegated well enough, so things keep coming back to us that should be sorted elsewhere; or

- things were not planned or communicated carefully enough in the first place.

I find these the most annoying, as they get in the way of more important work and could have been avoided had I been more prepared in the first place. Emails and anything with a notification on our phone often fit into this category

Quadrant 4: Not important and not urgent – ditch it: Quadrant 4 is just classic procrastination territory and involves pointless tasks or 'busyness' which simply avoids working on the right priorities. Types of activity here include taking unnecessary phone calls from salesmen, being drawn into time-consuming conflict that is going nowhere, gossip and being distracted by social media. Any Quadrant 4 activities simply need ditching – life is too short and time too precious.

Delegate well
It is common for leaders to find delegation difficult. Phrases I frequently hear that often get in the way of effective delegation go like this:

- 'I don't want to appear lazy by getting other people to do my job.'

- 'I'm worried that they won't do it the way that I would.'

- 'I can't find the time to have a conversation to delegate things.'

- 'There isn't anyone for me to delegate to!'

- 'I'm uncomfortable asking others to do things for me.'
- 'It's easier to do it myself.'

Becoming both comfortable and effective at delegation is a crucial area of leadership. A useful strategy to ensure that you don't get clogged up with other people's workload is the 'monkey management' approach in Ken Blanchard's book, *One Minute Manager Meets the Monkey*.[56] It is a short book which highlights the common problem when meetings or discussions take place with the leader or manager always walking away with all the action points. This is particularly common in schools, where time is at a premium and you often hear managers leaving a conversation saying something like:

- 'Leave that with me and I'll get back to you'; or
- 'I'll look into that and let you know.'

Of course, leaders should take actions away from meetings, but it's all too easy for some to say yes to everything. 'Monkey management', where a 'monkey' is an action or problem, highlights this trap of leaders and managers getting caught spending their time doing the work of others. A half-hour walk around school, unless careful, can result in you arriving back with several different monkeys on your back. Not only is this an inefficient use of time, it then prevents the leaders from working on their own monkeys (the 'main things').

When we fail to delegate properly, it is not necessarily good for the person we are helping out, as effectively we are saying, 'You are not capable of dealing with that problem, so I will have to.' This then prevents people around us from developing properly and builds more dependence for help in the future.

Sometimes – particularly at those frantic times in the calendar – it is easy to look at our job list and recognise a list of other people's monkeys that we have taken on. If we become aware of this, we can then go through a process of reuniting each monkey with its rightful owner.

---

56. Blanchard, K, *One Minute Manager Meets the Monkey* (HarperCollins, 2000).

In all conversations around delegation, leaders can refer to the 'Nine Levels of Delegation' identified by Tim Brighouse:

1. Look into this problem. Give me all the facts. I will decide what to do.

2. Let me know the options available with the pros and cons of each. I will decide what to select.

3. Let me know the criteria for your recommendation, which alternatives you have identified and which appears best to you with any risk identified. I will make the decision.

4. Recommend a course of action for my approval.

5. Let me know what you intend to do. Delay action until I approve.

6. Let me know what you intend to do. Do it unless I say not to.

7. Take action. Let me know what you did. Let me know how it turns out.

8. Take action. Communicate with me only if the action is unsuccessful.

9. Take action. No further communication with me is necessary.

This framework provides an excellent basis for open discussion to help achieve all-important clarity which helps leaders to be more effective in their roles.

Avoid the 'martyr leader' trap

External forces can make life in schools feel like a pressure cooker, but ultimately we are responsible for protecting our own wellbeing. If we don't spot the early warning signs, we risk allowing enthusiasm and drive for big challenges to be overtaken by frustration and dissatisfaction, which in the end can lead to disillusionment. In its worst form, this becomes one of the leadership behaviours we should try to avoid the most – 'martyr leadership'.[57]

> *When you complain, you make yourself a victim. Leave the situation, change the situation, or accept it. All else is madness.*
>
> ### Eckhart Tolle

The narrative of martyr leaders is that life is unfair, they are indispensable and there is nothing that anyone can do to make it better. See if you can recognise any of their language:

- **'My life is so unfair':** Martyr leaders like to talk about how the odds are stacked against them. Whether it's funding, time or context,

---

57. www.inc.com/les-mckeown/are-you-a-leader-or-a-martyr.html

you can spot them as they shake their heads and tell tales of woe to anyone who will listen.

- **'No one can help me – it's just an impossible situation':** Martyr leaders live in a world where nothing can be satisfactorily resolved. They spend their days in crisis management mode, battling against the daily tsunami of problems that come their way. It's all too much, but there are no real solutions so they just have to heave a big sigh and keep on going.

- **'If I could just clone myself...':** Only the martyr leader can solve the problems of the masses who queue to see them and their diary is busier than the Prime Minister's. Beneath the protests, though, they find a warm comfort in the feeling of being indispensable.

The martyr leader trap is everywhere and an easy one to fall into in a bad week. Everyone is entitled to the odd moan and offloading is an important part of dealing with stress. Unchecked, however, complaining can easily become habitual and, before you know it, you are trapped in a downward spiral of dissatisfaction, despair and martyrdom.

Coaching opportunity: To counter the threat of the martyr leader trap, consider making this a deliberate focus of coaching conversations. Start by discussing the threat – usually, it is quite easy for people to recognise the language in themselves and others – and then agree to use some of the opening coaching questions from the TGROW model (Chapter 9, Training and Development) to flip the conversation into more of a solution-focused one. Use sentence starters such as, 'So what would you see it looking like in an ideal world?' or 'What does Utopia look like on this issue?'

Leaders should act as a reservoir of hope and optimism in schools.

Stephen Tierney

Develop wellbeing tools

A benefit of going through difficult times is that it gives you the chance to build resilience. Those who have undergone counselling or therapy are often left with wellbeing tools and strategies that can protect against future vulnerability. But why do we wait for a crisis? Surely it makes more sense to develop our resilience strategies routinely, so that we are ready if and when the tough times come?

Increasingly, wellbeing approaches are becoming more than just having cake in the staffroom or the occasional shared lunch. It is our responsibility as leaders to make sure they are in place for staff and ourselves. There's no 'one size fits all' approach to wellbeing – strategies come in many different shapes and sizes to suit individuals. For some, self-help books are enough; for others, time with counsellors is a necessity.

> *It's funny how some distance makes everything seem small*
> *And the fears that once controlled me can't get to me at all.*

> *Princess Elsa (Frozen) extols the virtues of her new-found perspective after an early life crisis which resulted in her turning an entire kingdom into ice. Must we always have to get to a point of existential crisis before we learn lessons in self-preservation?*

The following are three strategies that can be considered as part of our wellbeing toolkit which have been written by cognitive behavioural psychotherapist and mindfulness teacher Nicola Smith, who works with teachers across the country (including mine) supporting mental health and wellbeing.

Mindfulness: Mindfulness is about increasing awareness so that we pay attention to things as they are, rather than how we wish them to be. Instead of ruminating on the past, which we cannot change, or worrying about the future – about things that may or may never happen – mindfulness helps to keep us grounded in what is happening now rather than being lost in our thoughts.

When our lives are very busy, we may spend our days on automatic pilot, not really attuned to what is going on in our minds, hearts and bodies. We can become accustomed to thinking, feeling and reacting in certain ways out of habit. By learning to focus on the present moment, we become better equipped to spot the build-up of stress and other difficult emotions and thoughts, so that we can deal with them more effectively. We can learn to recognise autopilot and choose when to 'shift gears' between operating on autopilot and being in present moment awareness.

Instead of subjecting ourselves to the endlessly looping tape of our thoughts and feelings, mindfulness enables us to pause. When we pause, we give ourselves the space and time to see that there may be other ways to think about situations, freeing us from the tyranny of the old thought patterns that we automatically grab onto. We may come to realise, on a deep level, that thoughts are only mental events. Thoughts are not facts and we have a choice about whether to give them power over our minds and hearts. This shift can be very liberating, giving people a sense of possibilities and choices about how to respond to old patterns of thinking and acting. This can empower people to make changes in their lives.

Cognitive behavioural therapy: As John F Kennedy once said, 'It's a good time to repair the roof while the sun is shining.' CBT can offer some ideas on 'repairing our roof' so that we have a better idea of our vulnerabilities before they catch us out at times of high levels of stress and demand. It is based on the premise that it is not a situation or event, in and of itself, that causes us distress, but rather what we make of it – our perspective and responses.

It starts by encouraging us to examine a range of challenging situations and then helps to develop an understanding of our typical responses – for example, procrastination or other avoidance behaviours. From there, you can learn to develop a range of strategies to help increase your perspective and range of responses. This can be achieved in a number of ways, in addition to meeting with an individual therapist, including group programmes, self-help books and online resources.

Sleep: Sleep is one of our most important sources of energy and helps to rebalance our energy when we have been burning up energy during stressful times. Sleep is part of the body's autonomic nervous system and regulates itself automatically as part of the body's 'homeostasis'. Often we end interfering with this process by worrying about our sleep and trying to organise or reorganise it, rather than just allowing it to happen.

Unfortunately, the harder we try to sleep, the less likely we will be able to drop off, as our bodies will activated by anxiety rather than soothed, calmed and ready for sleep.

If you can't sleep, then get up and do something instead of lying there and worrying. It's the worry that gets you, not the lack of sleep.

Dale Carnegie

So if you've been lying awake for 20 or 30 minutes or more, get up and do something calming and relaxing for a while. Listen to music, read (not work related!), doodle, draw – anything that helps to keep you soothed and relaxed. Avoid any 'blue-light' activities (eg, phone, laptop) which wake up the brain. Remind yourself that many people still function and get through the day with little sleep.

Here are a few other ideas that may help you to feel happier with your sleep:

■ Try to fit in a few mini-breaks in the daytime. This will give your head and working memory a bit of space, rather than saving up all your thoughts and worries for when you lie down in bed.

■ Have a go at some breathing exercises, especially focusing on exhaling.

■ Try some relaxation exercises, yoga or pilates stretches before bed; doing these during the day will also help to give your mind and body a break.

■ Aim to have a 'wind-down' of at least 30 minutes before bedtime – so stop working and do something relaxing and calming before you go to bed.

Aim to develop a regular pattern to your sleeping and waking wherever possible, especially the time you wake in the morning. It is much easier to balance your energy levels and build up your resilience to stress if there is routine to your sleeping (and eating) patterns.

If all else fails, engage 'safe mode'

Early on in my career, I developed this strategy to use at times when things were really stressful. It is pinched from the operating systems on PCs where, after a crash or being infected by a virus, the computer tells you it is going to work in 'safe mode' for a while. I don't know the exact science, but it feels like the computer is asking whether it can work in a mode where it does not perform all its usual functionality and can focus on a limited number of basic functions, to avoid anything else going wrong. I found myself feeling envious of my laptop that it could choose to work in this way and so have adopted a similar approach at times when I am feeling 'under the cosh'.

For me, 'safe mode' is occasionally required towards the end of a term when I am swamped with 'urgent/important' issues, staff absence and a packed schedule. It can involve cancelling non-urgent meetings, pushing back some deadlines and sending some emails to manage people's expectations of what might not get done for the next few days. I can then batten down the hatches and focus on the essentials. As an alternative to martyr leadership, safe mode gives you the freedom to take down your expectations of yourself for a short period of time before you can regroup and get back up to full speed.

Suggestion: Create your own definition of 'safe mode', depending on your particular circumstances, and use it for those occasions when everything feels overwhelming. Write it down and share it with someone you trust when you need to use it. By doing this, you are strengthening your commitment that you have temporarily readjusted your expectations of yourself.

I have found it really helpful to have someone to whom I can declare 'safe mode' – a good friend, also a head, who uses the approach too. Often, towards the end of term, an early-morning phone call will start with the words, 'Safe mode is on!'

If you find that safe mode is being used too often, take a step back and work with someone you trust, either within or outside your school, to take stock of things and be proactive in addressing your workload – particularly at pinch points in the year. Are there factors outside of work which may prompt you to engage safe mode which need addressing too?

Ultimately, to help our self-preservation, we need to become comfortable with occasionally letting things slide; it's going to happen, so get used to it.

When I admitted I couldn't be a perfect head teacher, I became better at my job. It was in my fourth year as a head and I have prioritised ruthlessly ever since. Some things can slip through my fingers now and then but I still sort out the important stuff.

John Tomsett

AN INTERVIEW WITH JULIA KEDWARDS

For some more thoughts on self-preservation, I spoke with Julia Kedwards (OBE), former head teacher and now CEO of Northampton Primary Academy Trust (NPAT). Having had the privilege to work with Julia over the last five years, there are many areas in which she has provided me with inspiration. Her commitment to the wellbeing of herself and others is one.

TR: Leadership is often portrayed as a selfless game, but how important is it for us to prioritise our own self-preservation? Are school leaders really allowed to look after themselves?

JK: Absolutely, unequivocally yes; not only are they allowed, but they should be positively encouraged to do so. Self-preservation is as essential part of leadership. You can't be the best leader if you are struggling with your own health and wellbeing, and we need to have the best and strongest teams around us in order to be most effective. Looking after ourselves helps us to look after others, and valuing health and wellbeing is an essential step.

TR: Many stresses and strains come alongside school leadership. What do you do to manage these and how do you support your own wellbeing?

JK: Staying fit and healthy is a top priority for me, as I see a strong link between physical wellbeing and mental wellbeing. Staying fit physically helps to relieve some of the pressures, as well as offering something else to think about. I've always found that running is a great physical outlet, as well as giving me space to think at the same time, and I've often come up with ideas and solutions while out running. Weights sessions in the gym are more about staying strong, and cycling needs more concentration and so is a good distraction from the day-to-day stress. However, one of the most positive decisions I ever made was to attend regular counselling sessions in order to offload the stresses and strains that as heads, we often don't get round to sharing. My weekly counselling session was more than professional supervision, as it gave me the opportunity to discuss personal as well as professional challenges, and became a lifestyle choice and as important to me as eating well, exercising and playing music.

TR: In the last 20 years, you've gone from having responsibility for a class as a teacher, a school as head and now 11 schools as CEO of a MAT. How have the pressures changed in these different situations and do they require different types of strategies to help you manage them?

JK: In some respects, the pressures are similar in that the stresses that have always kept me awake at night relate to people – whether they are the children or staff in my care or the stakeholders in my organisations. I distinctly recall waking in the night trying to work out strategies to try with a challenging child or trying to find a different way to teach something that didn't stick, and I have been stressed many times when dealing with tricky staff situations. As CEO, there are more frustrations as a result of greater bureaucracy, more essential documentation (never my strength!) and greater accountability; but these are more easily managed through better organisation and prioritisation. Ultimately, it is still the personnel issues which are most likely to keep me awake at night.

TR: Like most experienced leaders, I know you've worked through your share of stressful times, including taking on a school in special measures and eventually amalgamating it with your own. Are there things you do differently when the going gets tough?

JK: When the going gets tough, your team around you becomes even more important. Planning ahead meticulously is important, so that everyone knows what is coming up and what you are going through; this is equally important at home as at work, as support from loved ones and family is essential when times are tough. Similarly, if staff are aware of what the challenges are, they are more than often a great support and can relieve some of the pressure by keeping the ship sailing consistently. When we first started working with a second school, my first priority was to share the challenge ahead with my staff and leadership team, so that I knew they were fully on board with each step needed. The second step was to restructure the leadership team so that my existing school was fully equipped to continue on its journey while I focused some of my time elsewhere.

TR: Thanks, Julia. Finally, what three pieces of advice can you offer to school leaders to help support their own wellbeing?

JK:

1. Do everything that you can to stay physically and mentally fit and healthy; find your stress outlets and make the time to stick to them, no excuses.

2. Find good people, celebrate them, reward them and keep them. You are only ever as good as your team.

3. Be flexible and adaptable. Don't expect to have all the answers, but be prepared to go out and find them if you need to. Read, talk to others who have been there before you and ask whether you feel that you need help.

IN SUMMARY – SELF-PRESERVATION

- Have you managed to create a healthy balance so that you have enough energy to enjoy your work, family and other interests in your life?

- Can you keep your mojo throughout the weeks and terms? Can you ride the rhythms of the school year?

- Do you have effective time-management tools which you can use to manage your workload and stay productive?

- Are you finding space to think strategically? Can you adjust your working patterns so that you make sure you spend enough time in Quadrant 2 – working strategically on non-urgent/important things before they become urgent/important and therefore are unlikely to be done well?

- How effective is your delegation? Usually, this is an area in which all school leaders can become more effective.

- Can you notice the language of the martyr leader in yourself and others? How can you flip from seeing only the problems to being solution focused?

- Do you have some wellbeing tools which you can use to keep yourself positive and to safeguard against the dangers of problems with mental health?

- Do you have resilience strategies such as 'safe mode' that you can use when you are in danger of being overwhelmed?

FIVE FIVES GRID FOR PLANNING

FIVE MINUTES: What immediate first steps can you take?

FIVE DAYS: What short-term actions can you take in the next week to kick start or plan change?

FIVE WEEKS: What actions or follow-up meetings/discussions can you plan for in the next half-term?

FIVE MONTHS: What follow-up and follow-through activities do you need to plan to ensure that the change is not just a flash in the pan?

FIVE YEARS: What might your change look like in five years? What structures, systems and processes will you need to amend to ensure that your change becomes embedded in the fabric of your school and is not a passing fad?

Staff wellbeing

13 CHAPTER PREVIEW

Sometimes, discussions about wellbeing in schools can be at a superficial level, focusing on things such as hand cream in the toilets, passes for the gym or new furniture in the staffroom. These are all nice touches and while the TNTs are not to be dismissed, they are unlikely to contribute significantly to better wellbeing of staff. Although these are relatively easy for leaders to implement, they can give an appearance of doing something about wellbeing without tackling thornier issues.

One of the most challenging things I have experienced was breaking the news to a class that their teacher had died suddenly.

Despite the obvious irony of the DfE and Ofsted leading campaigns around workload and wellbeing, there is no doubt that their influence is a useful lever for schools to take this important issue more seriously.

Looking back, I think that in my first few years of leadership, my focus was very much about trying to get people to do new things and more things; now more often it's about trying to get them to avoid new fads and do less. The government call this 'eliminating unnecessary workload'; I call it 'cutting the faff'.

Excessive workload is a destroyer of wellbeing; teaching and school leadership need to become jobs that you can do full time within a reasonable number of hours and still have a life beyond.

Interview with Stephen Tierney

STAFF WELLBEING

> " Connect the dots between individual roles and the goals of the organization. When people see that connection, they get a lot of energy out of work. They feel the importance, dignity, and meaning in their job.
>
> Ken Blanchard

It is the morning of the 2017 marathon and three of us from school are in the car on our way down to London. This is my first marathon and to try to take my mind off the race, I am flicking nervously through the programme in the back, reading more about the mental health campaign led by the 'young royals' – William, Kate and Harry.

In a radical shift from the previous stoic and reserved image of the royal family, all three of them open up about difficult periods in their life. As we pass round the Lucozade, I read more about Prince William's struggles as a child following the death of his mother. He says he wants today's event to be remembered as the 'Mental Health Marathon'. He hopes that by high-profile people talking freely about their battles with mental health, it will encourage others to be open with theirs.

I turn the page and read the statistics around mental health in the UK. I'm taken aback that approximately one in four people experience a mental health problem each year[58] and in England, one in six people report that they experience a problem such as anxiety

---

58. McManus, S, Meltzer, H, Brugha, TS, Bebbington, PE, and Jenkins, R, 'Adult Psychiatric Morbidity in England, 2007: Results of a household survey' (NHS Information Centre for Health and Social Care, 2009), digital.nhs.uk/data-and-information/publications/statistical/adult-psychiatric-morbidity-survey/adult-psychiatric-morbidity-in-england-2007-results-of-a-household-survey

or depression each week.[59] These are shocking figures which mean that in a typical-sized primary school with 50 staff, we can expect around a dozen to experience struggles with mental health every year and around eight in any given week.

Just two hours later, I am standing in the starting pen along with 50,000 other humans. It is an extraordinary and moving experience. I observe the different ages, shapes and sizes of people taking part. I shake hands with strangers, hear stories of inspiration and read the names of many loved ones who are being remembered today on the T-shirts of runners.

As the race begins, we inch slowly towards the start line, wishing each other luck. Moved by the humanity of the moment, I think again of the scale of the mental health problem. I'm inspired by the number of well-known people who have been so open and honest about their own battles with mental health. As we pass the start line, I look out for the royals without success. I resolve that I will do more back at school to help staff to be open about any problems they may have and to seek help when they need it. The pace picks up. I realise that in a position of responsibility and as someone perceived as being confident, it might also help others if I am open about having faced my own challenges too. It might make it more acceptable for others to find help.

The marathon is incredible; I lose myself running through the streets of London to the sounds of steelpans, jazz bands and cheering crowds. I look out for Wills and Kate as I run the final few yards on the Mall, but they are otherwise engaged.

59. McManus S, Bebbington P, Jenkins R, Brugha T (eds), 'Adult Psychiatric Morbidity Survey: Mental Health and Wellbeing, England: 2014' (NHS Digital, 2016), digital.nhs.uk/data-and-information/ publications/statistical/adult-psychiatric-morbidity-survey/adult-psychiatric-morbidity-survey-survey-of-mental-health-and-wellbeing-england-2014

Consideration of staff wellbeing has always been at the heart of good school leadership. As leaders, we are only as successful as the quality of teaching that takes place in our classrooms every day – this is where the value is created in our schools. It is of paramount importance, therefore, that we do all we can to create a place where our staff enjoy working and stay well.

There are several compelling reasons why we should always consider further investment in the wellbeing of our staff:

- Healthy teachers and support staff who are well motivated are more likely to provide better learning opportunities for children.

- Staff absence rates – both occasional and long-term sickness – are likely to be lower when staff wellbeing is good.

- Good staff are less likely to leave schools where wellbeing and morale are positive.

- It is easier to recruit to a school which has a reputation of being a good place to work.

- Avoiding conflict between staff, or managing conflict well, prevents time being spent on potentially time-consuming distractions.

- As leaders, we have a moral, legal and professional duty of care towards the staff in our school.

But all is not 'well' in the world of teaching.

Trouble at t'mill

While the picture around mental health across the country is concerning in itself, recent research suggests that this problem is more prevalent within the teaching profession than we may have realised. A study carried out by Leeds Beckett University in 2018 found that, according to a survey of 775 teachers, 54% reported poor mental health, with 52% of this number saying that their illness had been identified by a GP.[60] Figures from the annual Health and Safety Executive survey in 2017[61] paint a similar picture, with 2,460 cases of work-related stress per 100,000 workers in the teaching profession – twice the average rate in other industries over a three-year period.

---

60. Teachwire.net, 'Pupil progress is being held back by teachers' poor mental health', 23 January 2018, www.teachwire.net/news/pupil-progress-is-being-held-back-by-teachers-poor-mental-health
61. Health and Safety Executive, Annual Survey, November 2017, www.hse.gov.uk/statistics/causdis/stress/index.htm

Although it is convenient for policy makers and regulators to dismiss such statistics and simply demand a stiff upper lip, these findings resonate with my own experiences leading in schools. The number of staff struggling with the challenges of anxiety and depression is alarming. It is important that we do more to help both the symptoms and causes.

DEFINITION

well-being[62]

noun: well-being;

■ the state of being comfortable, healthy, or happy.
"an improvement in the patient's well-being"

These different synonyms of comfortable, healthy or happy have different meanings and there are many interpretations of what wellbeing 'is'. For some, it's about relationships with colleagues; for many, it's about trying to stop their workload spilling into every evening and weekend; for others, it's simply about pay and conditions.

WELLBEING ON THE AGENDA

Staff wellbeing has become a much bigger focus of national discussion in recent years and is now trending in education. This is probably partly in tune with wider attitudes in society towards health, wellness and lifestyle, but also a reaction to the challenges of recruitment and retention discussed in Chapter 9. The government has finally joined the conversation, openly acknowledging some of the issues and commissioning the Teacher Workload Challenge with a brief to reduce unnecessary workload. Ofsted has also come to the party, acknowledging its role in driving unnecessary workload (sort of) and leading its myth-busting campaign. This has been helpful for schools to revisit processes that exist 'for Ofsted', but play no helpful part in improving teaching.

It is positive that lots of discussion is now taking place around wellbeing in schools and great that more leadership teams across the country now have this higher on their agenda. Despite the obvious irony of the DfE and Ofsted leading campaigns around workload and wellbeing, there is no doubt that their influence is a useful lever for schools to take this important issue more seriously. The ball is now in our court; we need to understand more about what staff wellbeing really is and how we can make meaningful improvements to it.

62. Google Dictionary: www.google.co.uk/search?q=Dictionary#dobs=well-being

Superficial, transactional or deeper?

Sometimes, discussions about wellbeing in schools can be at a superficial level, focusing on things such as hand cream in the toilets, passes for the gym or new furniture in the staffroom. These are all nice touches and while the tiny noticeable things (Chapter 10) are not to be dismissed, they are unlikely to contribute significantly to better wellbeing of staff. Although these are relatively easy for leaders to implement, they can give an appearance of doing something about wellbeing without tackling thornier issues.

At other times, the focus can be at a transactional level, on issues such as pay and workload – perhaps with leaders looking to reduce contact time or cut workload associated with marking. These changes are significant and can make a genuine difference to working hours, giving more opportunity for staff to enjoy precious family or leisure time.

But a focus at this transactional level without a deeper sense of connection to the school's purpose can feel hollow. Many choose to work in a school because of the sense of service and enjoyment of education that goes with it. This deeper connection is more than simply working hours and financial reward. These three aspects of wellbeing form the basis of our challenge to create a culture and ambition that people feel connected to at a profound level: healthy accountability, sensible systems and fair rewards at a transactional level, along with some nice touches around the edges.

Figure 22. The three aspects of wellbeing

More than workload and pay

Wider research supports the view of wellbeing as more than just superficial or transactional approaches. In 2014, a significant government paper published findings on the links between wellbeing and performance in the workplace.[63] According to extensive literature, it was identified that wellbeing tends to be higher when employees have:

63. Bryson A, Forth J and Stokes L, 'Does worker wellbeing affect workplace performance?' (National Institute Of Economic and Social Research, 2014), www.gov.uk/government/uploads/system/uploads/attachment_data/file/366637/bis-14-1120-does-worker-well-being-affect-workplace-performance-final.pdf

- autonomy over how they do their job and a measure of control in relation to the broader organisation (eg, participation in decision-making);

- variety in their work;

- clarity over what is expected of them, including feedback on performance (eg, via appraisals) and opportunities to use and develop their skills (eg, via the provision of training);

- supportive supervision;

- positive interpersonal contact – with managers and co-workers, but also with customers or the general public (where the job requires it);

- a perception of fairness in the workplace, in terms of both how the employee is treated and how co-workers are treated, with disciplinary and grievance procedures being one way for employers to address this;

- higher pay – although this relationship depends not only on the absolute level of pay, but also on how this compares with other workers' pay;

- physical security, including the safety of work practices, the adequacy of equipment and a pleasant working environment;

- a sense of job security and clear career prospects; and

- a perception of significance, in terms of both the significance of the job for the worker and the perceived value of the job to society.

These factors suggest that we should consider a much wider view of wellbeing than simply reducing workload. These factors cannot be tackled simply through reducing marking policies or planning expectations (although these are good things to consider), but through wholesome and compassionate leadership, where staff feel valued and are engaged as professionals in the purpose and development of their school.

Real questions that matter to staff include the following:

- What is it like to work here?

- Are the staff treated well?

- Is there flexibility for those with families or other commitments or conditions?

- Will I be looked after if things go wrong?

*Work is love made visible. And if you cannot work with love
but only with distaste, it is better that you should leave your work and
sit at the gate of the temple and take alms of those who work with joy.
For if you bake bread with indifference, you bake a bitter bread that
feeds but half man's hunger.*

Kahlil Gibran

AN INTERVIEW WITH STEPHEN TIERNEY

For some thoughts on this issue, I spoke with Stephen Tierney, head teacher and CEO of Blessed Edward Bamber Catholic MAT, and author of *Liminal Leadership*.[64] Having read Stephen's book and blogs, I was interested to find out more about his views on how we can develop approaches to more authentic wellbeing for staff in our schools.

TR: As someone who's responsible for many people in the schools across your trust, I know that looking after your staff is something you consider to be really important. What approaches do you employ across your schools to support wellbeing?

ST: When you look at someone's behaviours, it is also important to look behind to see what drives them – the beliefs they hold that lead to them behaving a certain way. In terms of people's wellbeing, some leaders are largely driven by beliefs about maximising effectiveness and efficiency; wellbeing has a place in ensuring that the organisation works well. Others are driven by a fundamental belief about humanity and how this can be supported and lived out within the organisation. These are not mutually exclusive and there are tensions between them that ultimately need to be managed.

When a leader's thinking is rooted in a view of humanity, they are arguably more likely to see the whole person: their work inside school and their life at home and beyond. The needs and wellbeing of the person can then be held in tension with the needs of the pupils they teach or support. It becomes a cultural thing rooted in the ethos and relationships, as well as workload management.

---

64. Tierney, S, *Liminal Leadership: Building bridges across the chaos... because we're standing on the edge* (John Catt Educational, 2016).

The little things matter. Time off to attend appointments with loved ones or funerals of those we cared about, but aren't included in any version of the *Burgundy Book*; being able to take your child to their first day at school, seeing them in the nativity play or sports day or being with an elderly relation at key moments. I've tended to find that whatever you give as a leader almost invariably comes back many times over. Say yes to as many little things as you can; teachers have often gone as far as organising cover arrangements with a colleague (December Nativity season allied with staff illness can be a pinch point), making the 'yes' that much easier. It's in these little moments that your humanity as a school leader shines through or not.

Excessive workload is a destroyer of wellbeing; teaching and school leadership need to become jobs that you can do full time within a reasonable number of hours and still have a life beyond. Our work now is about doing fewer things better – the whole trust's five-year development plan is on two sides of A4, and the next stage will be looking at and simplifying our systems and processes. I think that some of what we do is far too complicated for the purpose it serves; it creates unnecessary workload. School leaders also need to look at things which have little impact and start stripping them out. Our performance management system is minimal and focused on professional development and learning; annual performance-related pay we never implemented; and marking requirements have been stripped right back, with associated monitoring processes stopped.

It's always more time that people want: give teachers a significant amount of time for collaborative planning of schemes of learning and professional development. For over a decade now, we have finished half an hour early on a Thursday afternoon to give staff two hours of development/meeting time. We've tried various things over the years and settled on over half of the Thursdays during term time being spent in departments developing schemes of learning. This year we decided to reduce all teachers' contact time by an hour a week in return for each teacher identifying an aspect of personal professional development they wanted to focus on.

TR: Wellbeing has become a big issue in education in the last few years. The government has acknowledged this through the DfE Workload Challenge and now Ofsted is very vocal about reducing workload and supporting wellbeing. What do you think the reasons are for such an issue in the teaching profession?

ST: My challenge in answering this question is that the two organisations mentioned are a massive part of the problem: their current strategy is to try to blame others rather than having a cold, hard look at themselves. The Education Select Committee Report on workload is well worth a read. In short, far too many ill-thought-through, unnecessary or poorly implemented changes with unrealistic timescales by the DfE and the impact of a high-stakes, cliff-edge, punitive accountability system are driving up workload and impacting negatively on wellbeing. These are root causes that are leading to such poor retention in the profession.

By way of balance, the third component of the unholy trinity is school leaders. Collectively, we have too often added to the problem rather than seeking to mitigate or minimise it. Using our freedoms as academies, we have increased the number of Inset days in recent years to meet the demands of substantial concurrent curriculum change; as leaders, we can make a real difference even if we have little time for reports, posters or myth busters.

TR: There's a well-rehearsed caricature of the 'moany teacher' who has long and frequent holidays and I often walk into my local to be greeted by the standard heckles around how many more weeks it is until half-term. Do you think that the stresses we face in schools are any worse than those in the majority of other jobs?

ST: It's important to remember that only part of the stresses that affect our wellbeing come from our work; personal, economic, health and family demands also have an impact. No profession or group of workers is exempt or has a monopoly on these other varied factors, which can impact on our wellbeing at different times in our lives. I sense that life is becoming more out of balance for many people, for a variety of reasons.

The unusual challenge in teaching is that the hours worked, which in total are possibly similar to those in many other professions, are squeezed into a more condensed period of time – 38 weeks per year. Are teachers more likely to take their work home and suffer to a greater extent by the inflexibility of needing to be in front of a class on a set day at a particular time? Over my career I've also worked many hours in what are termed holidays and at weekends. People outside of teaching remember their school days and the long holidays that they could spend enjoying themselves; transferring their experience as a pupil, imagining that it is the same for a teacher leads to a common misconception that feeds the standard heckles. Delighted you are getting down to your local.

I wonder how often that is on a Monday to Thursday evening during term time (rhetorical question!)?

TR: Thanks, Stephen – it's been great to talk to you about this important subject. On a final note, if you had to give three pieces of advice to school leaders to help them look after their staff, what would they be?

ST:

1. The only way to reduce workload is to do fewer things; you're then challenged with what to stop doing. Stopping low-impact time wasters saves time and money; be ruthless and systematic.

2. The small kindnesses are the big things that many staff remember; they cost next to nothing, produce massive discretionary returns in effort and model the behaviour you want throughout the school. Be as kind as you can as often as you can.

3. Root your decisions in the long-term health of people and your school; ethos, relationships and culture will outlast the next Ofsted visit or current financial challenges.

MENTAL HEALTH

With mental health and wellbeing such important issues, here are some suggestions as to how we can go about supporting staff better in the future.

Talk about wellbeing and mental health openly

Thankfully, the taboo of mental health is slowly being dismantled in society and it is much more acceptable for people to talk about challenges they might be facing. In our schools, we can do more to make the culture more accepting. Simply talking about the prominence of mental health concerns and reminding staff of the help and support available is a start. It is a potentially life-changing strategy and the impact should never be underestimated.

Clarify people's roles

One area that is often neglected in the search for better staff wellbeing is simply to clarify roles:

- Are staff clear about their job purpose and responsibilities?

- Are they clear on how well they are doing and how they can improve?

- Is there clarity on where the school is heading next and what changes are coming?

- Are the feelings and opinions of all staff clearly understood so that they feed into decision-making and policy change?

Unfortunately, discussions that focus on role clarity might be limited to annual appraisals and clouded by accountability. In these situations, communication for clarity is crucial.

Collect wellbeing data

If you don't have it to hand already, dig out and analyse data which gives you indications of the impact of your work on wellbeing. Specific data may include staff absence rates (look at different aspects of this, such as individual days, long-term absence and patterns with specific days of the week or times of the year), staff turnover rates and exclusions, physical restraints and staff injuries. All of these are useful pieces of a jigsaw that, once complete, helps you to understand more about the overall wellbeing of your staff.

Another important source of data is a simple staff wellbeing survey which can be completed anonymously by staff at the same point each year. For leaders, this may feel threatening, as you open yourselves up to potentially uncomfortable messages; but it is a great way to take the temperature of wellbeing in your school. Resist the temptation to 'gamify' the results of this by choosing the timing of a survey. As we have learned from Jim Collins in *Good to Great*, we lead better when we confront the brutal facts.

Regular supervision

Staff who are regularly exposed to stressful or challenging circumstances should be entitled to regular supervision in the same way that colleagues in areas of the health service, social workers or counsellors are. Monthly or half-term 'supervision' allows staff in these key positions to offload and talk anonymously with trained professionals about either specific or general issues. The usual barriers of time and money can crop up when trying to implement this, but making mandatory attendance part of policy and costing it into the budget is a wise investment.

Give time

The best present we can give is time. Whether or not this is additional non-contact time built into the weekly timetable or days around particular pinch points in the year, the answer to many challenges can lie in finding ways to allow staff additional time to balance their workload and get ahead of the game before the next week or half-term.

Keep the balance

While focusing on wellbeing, we must also make sure this doesn't become self-indulgent. In the words of head teacher John Tomsett, 'None of us working in schools goes underground to dig coal. In relative terms, our working conditions are pretty good. We have long holidays.' There are staff cultures I have come across where it feels like it's about the staff first and children second.

Measuring success

Working on wellbeing is something that is not entirely tangible. While statistics such as absence, turnover and complaints give an indicator of where things are really wrong, these are rarely recognised through the existing accountability systems. It is time consuming, emotional and expensive for leaders dealing with difficult wellbeing issues; but occasionally you hear from people or see things that remind you how important it is.

Dear Tom

I thought I'd get back in touch, as it's been a while, to let you know what's happened since I left last summer. I continued with the counselling (I told you I would!) and it was the best therapy I've ever had. For the first time in ages I feel 'normal' again and ready to finally put the past behind me.

I took the huge step of getting back in touch with all the colleagues from my previous school. I was so nervous, but have already had an email back inviting me for dinner with them in a couple of weeks. They said they missed me and it made me feel so relieved. I'm really looking forward to meeting up with them, as I think it will help to bring some closure to the past.

I will always be so grateful. You kept me at the school at a time when it would have been much easier for you not to and the support of everyone there means an awful lot. If it hadn't been for that conversation in my classroom and the help that followed, I don't know what I would be doing today. I certainly wouldn't be teaching.

It's so difficult for someone like me to open up about mental health and if I'm honest, I spent years avoiding facing up to it.

Thanks for everything, Tom. The school was instrumental in my recovery from what has without doubt been the most difficult two years of my life. I may be a stone heavier, but I'm medication free and feeling mentally strong!

Take care

Sam (not real name)

CUTTING THE FAFF

Although there is more to wellbeing than just the transactional elements, we shouldn't underestimate the importance of cutting out unnecessary work to free up staff for the things that matter most. In my experience, there is a lot that we could be doing more efficiently or just stop doing altogether.

Looking back, I think that in my first few years of leadership, my focus was very much about trying to get people to do new things and more things; now more often it's about trying to get them to avoid new fads and do less. The government call this 'eliminating unnecessary workload'; I call it 'cutting the faff'.

DEFINITION

faff[65]

British informal verb

verb: faff; third person present: faffs; past tense: faffed; past participle: faffed; gerund or present participle: faffing.

■ spend time in ineffectual activity.
"we can't faff around forever"

Ten timesavers in primary schools

Remembering some of the principles of lean working from Chapter 9, here are some questions to consider in order to kick the faff and free up time to work on the most important things..

1. Communication: Do briefings, emails and meetings provide clarity and avoid confusion? As I have said already, clarity is everything in a primary school. Clear communication avoids timewasting conversations about logistics and keeps people's headspace clear to focus on teaching.

---

65. Google Dictionary: www.google.co.uk/search?q=Dictionary#dobs=faff

2. Feedback, not marking: Have you revisited your marking expectations and policy with staff? This is 'low-hanging fruit' for most schools in terms of trying to free up more time to work on the important things.

3. Time-costing: Do you capture information from teachers on how many hours they report it takes them to complete assessment tasks such as data entry, school reports or marking? Consider using this as a starting point to identify where to invest efforts to save time.

4. Assessment points: Are the processes for data collection slick and time efficient? A common concern from teaching staff is time-consuming processes of data entry, including 'double data entry', where the same information must be entered into different spreadsheets or systems. Could you invest more in these processes to try to make them lean?

5. Lesson plans: Have you revisited expectations of planning with staff to make sure there aren't time-heavy processes where teachers write out plans for external audiences rather than themselves? While some less experienced teachers may well need to write more detail, after two or three years most teachers will be able to do this with much less written down. Is planning from previous years 'recycled' and are there schemes of work in place to avoid teachers starting from scratch each year?

6. Planning and resourcing: Are there clear agreements on when planning and resources will be shared with each other in a timely way? The most effective way I have seen year groups working together in primary schools is when the bulk of planning and resourcing is complete and shared across the team, so that they can leave on a Friday night prepared for the week ahead. With the weekend free, this avoids the habit of Sunday evenings spent exchanging emails about what is happening in the week ahead.

7. Support staff: Is good use made of teaching assistants whenever possible to carry out administrative tasks such as data entry? Sometimes paying overtime to these staff is a smart investment to free up valuable hours of teacher time.

8. Meetings and briefings: Do you ensure that meetings always start and finish at the agreed times? Managing meetings so that they don't get hijacked or go off on tangents is important – particularly when we consider both their financial and opportunity costs.

9. School reports: Have you revisited the formats and processes for children's end-of-year reports? These are a hugely time-consuming element of workload for teachers and yet there is no correlation I have ever seen between more detailed reports and higher achievement in schools. Parents appreciate a personal comment, so focus on this and make sure they are done well. I would avoid having senior leaders or the head making comments too, as a large opportunity cost comes from the time invested in this process – usually at a really busy time of the year.

10. Assemblies: Do they always overrun? The classic issue in almost every primary school that I have visited is assemblies running over time, which has an impact on the rest of the day. Get strict on the timings, apologise when you get it wrong and make sure that these events don't eat into precious curriculum time, which causes stress for teachers.

DEALING WITH THE TOUGH TIMES

However hard we work on staff wellbeing issues, there will still be challenging times that hit every school and I have experienced my share of these over the years. The most difficult is the death or serious illness of a child, parent or member of staff. When these things happen, nothing else matters other than supporting individuals and the school community.

One of the most challenging things I have experienced was breaking the news to a class that their teacher had died suddenly. As a young leader, this was a moment I felt wholly unprepared for; nothing can really prepare you for these moments. Sadly, these events are facts of life which can happen in schools at any time.

Inevitably, when tragedy occurs, it causes us to see life from a different perspective and question everything. It is an incredibly difficult balance to strike, as these situations mean that staff may feel demotivated; there may also be staff absence to contend with. If and when this type of situation arises in your school, remember that there will be many others who have been through similar situations.

- Talk to other leaders about the situation – it is surprising how many other people around you either are battling with similar challenges or have been through them recently. They can help to offer you support.

- Slow down your pace – walk slower and try to exude a sense of calm and order around school. Make time to talk with staff and, most importantly, time to listen.

- Communicate clearly, carefully and with compassion – in these situations, while your intentions will always be good, it is easy to unwittingly cause upset or distress to others with a careless comment or poorly worded email. Just take an extra few moments with everything you do and get other people to look over your communications before they go out.

■ If you have to deliver bad news yourself, make time to prepare for these conversations carefully. Consider writing down what you need to say, so that you can use the script if you need to; be compassionate and be prepared for silence after you have spoken. Sadly, there is no way to dress up bad news; but you can deliver it carefully, compassionately and accurately.

■ Get professional support – there will be networks available to your school to help with these situations and other critical incidents. I have found educational psychologists invaluable in these situations, as they are well trained in giving advice and counselling to staff and children. Your union is also a good place to find advice and support on the end of the phone.

■ Make sure that you prioritise your own wellbeing and self-preservation. Your staff need you more than ever at this time, so take good care of yourself and don't burn the candle at both ends.

IN SUMMARY – STAFF WELLBEING

- Does a wellbeing ethos exist in your school that goes further than superficial 'nice' things and addresses root causes around work-related pressures, mental health concerns and dealing with stressful situations?

- Are you already collecting and analysing data which relates to staff wellbeing and benchmarking this across different schools over several years? If not, could you develop this, starting with wellbeing questions as part of an annual staff survey?

- Are clear systems and pathways in place for staff to talk to someone when they have mental health concerns? Do you have access to counsellors who can facilitate either individual or group sessions to work on supporting positive mental health?

- Could you improve opportunities to communicate with individuals in school to achieve further clarity of role? Implementing good one-to-ones for quality time with line managers is a great starting point.

- Is regular counselling supervision in place for those staff who routinely deal with emotionally challenging situations, such as child protection or with high-profile children and families?

- When the really tough times come your way, are strategies and systems in place to support staff through these?

FIVE FIVES GRID FOR PLANNING

FIVE MINUTES: What immediate first steps can you take?

FIVE DAYS: What short-term actions can you take in the next week to kick start or plan change?

FIVE WEEKS: What actions or follow-up meetings/discussions can you plan for in the next half-term?

FIVE MONTHS: What follow-up and follow-through activities do you need to plan to ensure that the change is not just a flash in the pan?

FIVE YEARS: What might your change look like in five years? What structures, systems and processes will you need to amend to ensure that your change becomes embedded in the fabric of your school and is not a passing fad?

Interdependent leadership

14 CHAPTER PREVIEW

Everyone loves a team player. But how much do we understand about the mechanics behind good teamwork? And how good are we at developing this in ourselves and others?

Those with an abundance mentality are more likely to welcome competition, seeing it as an opportunity to improve rather than a threat.

Competition in education should not be a game of one-upmanship between individual schools, local authorities or trusts. We should not be trying to beat each other; rather, we should be working together to beat the many inequalities in the system around underfunding and underachievement for those in the poorest communities. Poor ideas; shoddy accountability; the erosion of a broad, rich and rigorous curriculum.

Diminishing local authority control and the increased autonomy of schools in recent years have been both liberating and petrifying at times. In this increasingly fragmented and unpredictable world, it is critical that schools work together to take on the big challenges in the system.

AND ONE FROM THE INTERVIEW INSIDE

It might sound crass, but surround yourself with likeminded people – people whom you trust, who constantly give above and beyond because they believe in you, themselves and the 'why?'. They might not necessarily be your best friend or think like you, but they've got your back, are at the top of their game and love what they do.

Interview with Andrew Morrish

INTERDEPENDENT LEADERSHIP

> **"**
>
> Alone we can do so little; together we can do so much.

Helen Keller

The second marriage

I remember clearly the moment I first set eyes on Northampton Primary Academy Trust (NPAT) in 2012, a few months before I took up post at Simon de Senlis. I had read the story of five schools in Northampton in the local press that had started working together to form a MAT as equal partner. I was inspired by the ambition and drive of the partnership.

These were all great schools, led by the types of go-getter heads that I aspired to be. In those early days, the MAT scene was uncharted territory and NPAT was a trailblazing partnership. Built on the foundations of collaboration and strong leadership, it had a child-centred ethos and a serious commitment to sport and the arts.

The early days

Before too long, we had entered into conversations about partnership working and were quickly involved in various school improvement projects together. This 'friends with benefits' stage made a real impact, helping us at Simon de Senlis to move from the trials of 'Requires Improvement' through a good Ofsted inspection with the challenge and support of experienced leaders. I have described us as friends here, but the challenge was the most robust and astute I had ever experienced – having five heads in your school trumps Ofsted any day of the week in terms of finding the true strengths and weaknesses.

Getting serious

I remember clearly the awkward conversation about 'who asks who' in these situations with two of the other heads as it became inevitable that we should solidify the partnership by joining the trust. I also remember questioning with governors and directors whether we needed to 'get married' in order for us to work together, or whether we could just join the partnership outside of the MAT and carry on all the good stuff without legally becoming part of one. As time progressed, it became clear that the legally binding bit was the right call, cementing the many commitments that we believed. 'My school is your school; your children are our children' has become a mantra for us and captures the sense of shared ownership that we all feel for each school at times such as inspections or results day.

Of course, at this stage in any relationship comes the inevitable power struggle; only in this relationship, it was more about positions on the board and whether we had to fall into line with particular curriculum approaches rather than creating joint bank accounts and whether it's still OK to play football on a Sunday. Many important questions must be asked and answered before making that commitment and we learned a lot about being completely honest and candid with each other.

Tying the knot

In April 2015 we officially converted to become part of NPAT. This was a very unceremonious occasion, as somewhere in Whitehall official paperwork was updated and filed while the 420 children in a Northampton suburb continued learning as normal. To continue the metaphor, it was very much the low-key registry office affair with witnesses only and then back to work in the afternoon with no honeymoon, as we simply couldn't afford the time off work!

Then came the relief that all the decision-making, consultation and paperwork that came from academisation alongside the day job was finally over and we had a clear road ahead. Of course, this void was soon filled with the waves of different challenges that appear in schools every day.

Keeping the magic alive...

As Henry Ford once said, 'Coming together is the beginning, keeping together is progress, working together is success.' This is now the challenge for schools in MATs as we continue to find common ground and adopt shared approaches where they make sense, while keeping a degree of individuality and character at a local level. The trust has now grown to 11 schools, including three special units, with all schools rated either 'Good' or 'Outstanding' by Ofsted. We have always tried to keep an unwavering focus on teaching, learning and outcomes; but with over 3,000 children and around 500 staff based across ten sites, it is hard. As much as we wanted to avoid becoming tied up in the issues that come with being a MAT – such as red tape, policy development, HR strategy plans and endless risk management – these are all important and necessary parts of a successful organisation and so inevitably take their turn in the spotlight.

DEFINITION

Interdependent[66]

adjective: interdependent;

■ (of two or more people or things) dependent on each other.

The previous two chapters in this section on the Health of wholesome leadership related primarily to the physical and mental wellbeing of ourselves and others. This final chapter considers the health of our working relationships with others. 'Interdependence' – a mature state of leadership – can shift our thinking from self-effectiveness to cooperation, collaboration and a wider impact on the system. Interdependent leadership captures how we work effectively within and across teams to achieve synergy, where the output of a team is more than the sum of its component parts. Many ideas in this chapter are built on Stephen Covey's work around synergy, interdependence and abundance thinking.

---

66. Google Dictionary: www.google.co.uk/search?q=Dictionary#dobs=interdependent

No man is an island,
Entire of itself,
Every man is a piece of the continent,
A part of the main.
If a clod be washed away by the sea,
Europe is the less.
As well as if a promontory were.
As well as if a manor of thy friend's
Or of thine own were:
Any man's death diminishes me,
Because I am involved in mankind,
And therefore never send to know for whom the bell tolls;
It tolls for thee.

John Donne

Together everyone achieves more

The importance of working well in teams has long been recognised as one of the most important factors in successful organisations. Everyone loves a team player. But how much do we understand about the mechanics behind good teamwork? And how good are we at developing this in ourselves and others?

It can be easy to fall into a trap of thinking that simply by recruiting good or outstanding individuals, we will create a high-performing team. While a capable and skilled staff is clearly desirable, success in any organisation is realised only when individuals recognise that they are working towards something that is bigger and more worthy than their own success.

Put the team ahead of one's personal statistics and recognition.
One brilliant character who does not put team first can
destroy the entire team.

Sataya Nadella, CEO, Microsoft

| DEFINITION |

Synergy[67]

Synergy noun [U]

■ The combined power of a group of things when they are working together that is greater than the total power achieved by each working separately:

"teamwork at its best results in a synergy that can be very productive"

We see synergy around us in many areas of nature. Birds preserve energy by remaining in formation as they migrate or fly longer distances; trees and plants grow taller in copses and woods than they would do as an individual organism. My favourite analogy of synergy and school leaders is that of a cycling team working together in groups or as part of the peloton.

Cyclists know that up to 30% of their energy can be preserved by riding with the pack rather than at the front, and so swap in and out of position to exert and preserve energy at different times. Often, particular riders are protected so they will have energy left for the sprint or perhaps for the next day's stage. It is a good example of where the right strategy, tactics and discipline within a team can lead to great synergy.

In cycling, if a rider pushes ahead too quickly and leaves his team behind, he risks not only using up unnecessary energy himself, but also – more importantly – letting down his team-mates, who are unable to benefit from the cover. Likewise, if a team pushes ahead too quickly, leaving others behind, it is almost impossible for them to catch up (this is known as 'being dropped'). These principles of team cycling apply in our school setting: effective leadership occurs as leaders set the right pace, pushing ahead carefully at times and making sure that others come with them. Effective leaders also make sure that they pull their own weight and support the success of others at different times. Winning teams are a group of capable individuals who all recognise and play their role as required – whether this is leading at the front, playing 'second fiddle' to someone else or covering and supporting in the background or from the side.

---

67. Cambridge Dictionary: dictionary.cambridge.org/dictionary/english/synergy

Synergy is what happens when one plus one equals ten or a hundred or even a thousand! It's the profound result when two or more respectful human beings determine to go beyond their preconceived ideas to meet a great challenge.

Stephen Covey

Stephen Covey (as usual) has lots to say on the subject of synergy, which he includes as one of his *Seven Habits of Highly Effective People*[68]. Covey describes the 'leadership maturity continuum' as the journey from dependence to independence and then to interdependence.

Figure 23. The leadership maturity continuum

Stages of human development are a useful analogy to help explain the leadership maturity continuum. When a child is born, it depends on others to feed, change and wash it. Through childhood, lots of these skills are learned and become automatic, so that by their teenage years, adolescents are capable of functioning pretty independently. But maturity does not end here and it is not until we reach adulthood that we often understand that the world works better when we have others around us to look after each other. This realisation of the world as interdependent is important: it allows us to appreciate other people and realise that we can become more than the sum of our parts if we work in partnership and synergy with each other.

Similarly, in our careers, we start off needing lots of help and guidance from others. Once we have been shown the ropes, we can grow from this dependence on others into a more independent state. As we continue to mature professionally, we start to develop more interdependent relationships with each other, resulting in us being more effective at what we do. If these interdependent relationships are healthy, they are immensely powerful and can help us to realise synergy – where together we achieve more than the sum of our collective parts.

---

68. Covey, S, The 7 Habits of Highly Effective People (Free Press, 1989).

Figure 24. Towards interdependent leadership

Dependent Leadership	What's my bag?
Independent Leadership	This is my bag; that's your bag
Interdependent Leadership	All these bags are ours!

AN INTERDEPENDENT MINDSET

Interdependence is and ought to be as much the ideal of man as self-sufficiency. Man is a social being.

Mahatma Gandhi

Key to achieving powerful interdependent leadership is for individuals within the team to develop an 'interdependent mindset'. In Figure 25, I offer four elements of an interdependent mindset that need securing within a team as the conditions from which synergy can then flow.

Figure 25. Key elements of an interdependent mindset

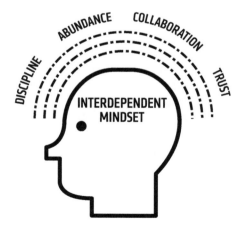

Abundance thinking

Covey writes the following to introduce us first to the 'scarcity mentality':

> Most people are deeply scripted in what I call the Scarcity Mentality. They see life as having only so much, as though there were only one pie out there. And if someone were to get a big piece of the pie, it would mean less for everybody else.

> The Scarcity Mentality is the zero-sum paradigm of life. People with a Scarcity Mentality have a very difficult time sharing recognition and credit, power or profit – even with those who help in the production. They also have a hard time being genuinely happy for the success of other people.

In contrast, an abundance mindset is where we believe that there is enough success to go around for everyone, where we stop seeing ourselves in competition with others and see those around us as partners in shared success. Those with an abundance mentality are more likely to welcome competition, seeing it as an opportunity to improve rather than a threat. Without an abundance mindset, it is likely that behaviours associated with self-protection and unhealthy competition will creep in. In these situations, it is almost impossible to achieve the power of interdependent working.

Check your abundance mentality by observing your reaction next time the successes of others are announced – this could be a promotion for someone in school or the success of another teacher or school, such as a win in a sports competition or the announcement of school results. Do you notice the language of an abundance or scarcity mindset in your initial thoughts?

Table 16. Scarcity language versus abundance language

Scarcity language (Defensive/resentful)	Abundance language (Congratulatory/open)
■ They only achieved that because they had more opportunities or are favoured.	■ That's brilliant – they worked so hard for that.
■ I could never do that because I don't have enough time.	■ I'd be really interested in learning more about how they achieved that.
■ We can't do that because of finances.	■ That's really inspiring/motivating for me.
■ We couldn't do that here because of our context.	■ What a brilliant thing to happen in our school/area/education system.

Abundance thinking is an important concept – not just within a school, but across schools. Our goal should be for every child in every school to get a better education, not just those children in our class or school.

Collaboration and cooperation

Although the word 'collaboration' is widely used to describe the process of working together, in many cases it is used to describe cooperative work. Both words derive from Latin synonyms which translate to mean 'work' – *operates* ('cooperate') and *laborare* ('collaborate') – and so broadly can be interpreted to mean 'co-working'. Their meanings in today's world have subtle but important differences, which can be defined as follows:

Cooperation – two or more people working together or helping each other to achieve their own separate goals.

Examples:

- English subject leaders sharing approaches and ideas around the teaching of spelling, so that they can write a new spelling policy for their individual schools.

- Staff from different schools attending a TeachMeet to share ideas on reading approaches at Key Stage 2.

- Head teachers attending a meeting with the local authority to share challenges faced around in-year transfers and to discuss possible solutions.

Collaboration – two or more people working together to achieve a single shared goal.

Examples:

- English subject leaders working on a single approach to spelling which they will then use across their separate schools.

- Teachers within the same school working on a lesson-study triad as part of the process of implementing a new approach to reading within the school.

- Head teachers committing to being part of a working party in order to develop a code of practice that they will agree to follow and then review on an annual basis, to try to reduce the number of in-year transfers across schools within a town.

Although comparing definitions such as these may appear pedantic, the distinction is important, as it is through genuine collaboration that we achieve synergy in our work; whereas cooperation – although helpful to us as individuals – ultimately outputs towards more selfish goals and can create 'silo working'.

If, as school leaders, we can understand the subtle but powerful difference between cooperation and collaboration, we can ensure that our impact can be much greater as a whole and that 1+1 can equal more than 2.

Discipline

In Chapter 2, we discussed the importance of discipline within teams as part of the professional culture of a school. Both disciplined thought and action are essential for leaders as we 'make the weather' within teams and organisations.

> *Greatness is not a function of circumstance. Greatness, it turns out, is largely a matter of conscious choice, and discipline.*
>
> ### Jim Collins

When leaders with the right mindset are also self-disciplined in their thoughts and actions, these are powerful ingredients at work with the potential to release the power of synergy.

Trust

The final element in the interdependence mindset is trust: the firm belief in the reliability, truth, ability or strength of someone. Trust is the cornerstone of authentic leadership and the invisible glue that holds all effective teams together.

Trust can be built among colleagues when, over time, we become more certain of both the actions and intentions of others around us. There is no shortcut to building trust, but it can be achieved when people have the discipline to collaborate regularly, demonstrating abundance thinking. In schools, it is a critical element, as there are often times when we have to make decisions while others are unavailable or pick up on the work of others because they might be unavailable or teaching.

Trust takes time to develop in any organisation, but can be nurtured through the following types of behaviour:

■ Walking the talk – simply doing what we say we will do is the first step in building trust in us as leaders.

■ Not over-promising – in order to walk the talk and be able to follow through on our word, we should be careful not to over-promise and set ourselves up for failure. It is preferable to under-promise and over-deliver, despite how enthusiastic and ambitious we might feel at times.

■ Remaining non-judgemental of others when things go wrong – particularly if they are not present. People who are not present when the conversation takes place are always the easiest to blame and it is too easy sometimes to point the finger at someone who is not there. This can undermine relationships and so it is important to avoid.

■ Delegating can indicate to others that you have faith in them, as opposed to leaders always hanging on to important tasks because they don't trust anyone else to do them as well as them.

Trust is not something that can be established overnight. It can take a long time to build up and can be dismantled instantly; it is a vulnerable yet critical element of an interdependent mindset.

INTERDEPENDENCE IN PRACTICE

In primary schools, an example of interdependence could be how well a head teacher and deputy work together – perhaps one is more effective at handling difficult parents or particularly emotional conversations with certain staff, whereas the other is better at analysing situations and picking the right strategy going forward. Or perhaps one is more suited to leading from the front in staff meetings or briefings, while the other is better at ensuring that changes are captured in written communications or policy changes.

Interdependence must also exist in any effective middle leadership team, where typically different leaders may have responsibility for subjects across the school, such as English and maths, or phases such as Early Years, Key Stage 1 or Key Stage 2. While individually, these separate leaders may be capable (independent), unless their work is properly joined up, it is unlikely to be as effective as it could be.

This is particularly important for staff who may receive different messages from different leaders at different times, as conflicting messages from a leadership team undermine everyone's credibility. As with the first example, the same principle may exist in a team of middle leaders, where one may perhaps be better at understanding the trends and implications of data while another may be more confident leading training to staff. No leader can be all things to all people, so dovetail working of this kind is well worth developing.

A specific role in primary school where interdependence is everything is that of SEN and inclusion coordinators (SENCos), where one person has responsibility for the provision for SEN throughout the school and is entirely dependent on colleagues at all levels to make this provision effective. An effective SENCo will have interdependent relationships with almost everyone in the organisation, including children, parents, support staff, teachers and leaders (in my experience, they are often the people with their fingers on the pulse of what is going on across school).

In all these examples, the important part is not necessarily which particular skill the individuals have, but how aware they are of the importance of their own strengths and weaknesses and those of the team around them.

INTERDEPENDENT SCHOOLS

As well as creating interdependence within our own setting, we can benefit significantly from relationships and partnerships with other local schools and those further afield. Diminishing local authority control and the increased autonomy of schools in recent years have been both liberating and petrifying at times. In this increasingly fragmented and unpredictable world, it is critical that schools work together to take on the big challenges in the system. Only through interdependent working across schools is there is a possibility that we can significantly improve standards across the system. The depressing alternative is schools and trusts being drawn into competition with each other for pupil numbers, funding and teachers, creating a 'zero-sum' game where nothing really gets better.

Competition in education should not be a game of one-upmanship between individual schools, local authorities or trusts. We should not be trying to beat each other; rather, we should be working together to beat the many inequalities in the system around underfunding and underachievement for those in the poorest communities. Poor ideas; shoddy accountability; the erosion of a broad, rich and rigorous curriculum: these are the real enemies to education that should be 'beaten'. I believe that we will only win if different parts of the system work together rather than in opposition.

And in the end, the love you take is equal to the love you make.

Lennon/McCartney

MATs

MATs have become a focal point of the educational landscape in recent years, with more schools either choosing to become part of a MAT or being forced to as a result of a poor Ofsted inspection. Let's be clear: like academies and free schools, a MAT is no silver bullet to improving a school. Some have become worse off as a result of takeovers by trusts which have been allowed to assume control of fragile settings in difficult communities with no real understanding of the challenges or strategy for improvement.

We should not shy away from the things that are wrong with this part of the system at the moment. There is no doubt that some are motivated to join MATs primarily by money, ego and power; while others join for self-preservation or to 'preserve their autonomy and individuality' – a concept opposite to the essence of a MAT in my opinion.

But I believe that these negative stories represent a small minority of trusts these days. It is worth considering that, despite the stereotype of the MAT leader on a six-figure salary overseeing an empire of schools, just 12 of the existing 1,178 MATs consist of 30 or more schools, with 776 consisting of fewer than four.[69]

The reality of MATs is that they primarily consist of authentic and committed people searching for answers in this brave new world – often just with fancier-sounding titles!

Having been very much a part of the 'academies scene' for the last four years, and now seeing the landscape evolve through work as part of the regional head teacher board, I am more convinced by the potential of the MAT model to improve schools at scale across the country where they are set up and run well. With sharper lines of accountability, less interference from local government and more freedom to collaborate, the conditions for finding innovative and authentic answers to some of education's most pressing problems are being established in some cases. In recent years, I have seen genuinely exciting work taking place in important areas such as curriculum and assessment through visits to free schools and MATs. The next important challenge is for schools within MATs to develop more effective ways of working with each other interdependently.

---

69. Education Policy Institute, 'Quantitative Analysis of the Characteristics and Performance of Multi-Academy Trusts' (Ambition School Leadership, November 2017), www.ambitionschoolleadership.org.uk/documents/999/Quantitative_analysis_of_the_characteristics_and_performance_of_multi-academy_trusts.pdf

Confused governance

Despite the changing picture, structures of local governance have remained relatively unchanged in many schools, and I believe that one of the biggest potential benefits of the academy system is that it affords a fresh opportunity to look at this. I have always thought it odd that ultimately, the biggest decisions in a school are made by a group of non-specialist volunteers, and in recent years have seen how the challenges of recruitment to local governing bodies alongside the confusion and lack of training caused through the changing landscape have led to weak and ineffective governance at a number of schools.

That isn't to say that there aren't effective governing bodies or individual governors out there – of course there are. But I believe the premise that a group of volunteers from the community is the best way to hold head teachers and leaders to account is fundamentally flawed. In my experience, it is often in the most deprived communities that this problem is most acute, as there are fewer community members with the time and professional skills to become effective at providing the effective challenge and support necessary.

AN INTERVIEW WITH ANDREW MORRISH

For some more thoughts on the power of collaboration across schools, I spoke with Andrew Morrish, CEO of Victoria Academies Trust and author of *The Art of Standing Out*. Having visited Andrew's schools in Birmingham and seen his authentic approach to collaboration in action, I was keen to learn more about his thinking as someone who really personifies the 'system leader'.

TR: You've worked across many schools and seen thousands of different teachers working in different ways over the years. What are the benefits of collaboration and effective teamwork among your teachers?

AM: I always remember the day when we first became a MAT. One of the heads in the local cluster that I chaired was surprised by my decision to break away from the local authority, as I was always the one leading the charge. She had entirely missed the point, of course, as there was this perception at the time – this was four years ago – that academy heads want to pull up the drawbridge and go it alone; a sense that they don't want to work collaboratively any more. This is, of course, completely wrong, as never before since I became the leader of a MAT have I worked so tirelessly to continuingly scan the horizon and reach out to other schools, organisations and leaders – be they MATs, single academy trusts, teaching school alliances, school centred initial teacher training providers (SCITTs), local authority schools, organisations, social enterprises, charities, housing associations and so on. The difference now is that we get to choose who to work with, as opposed to it being opposed by geographical local authority boundaries.

Perceptions have changed now, though, and more heads are beginning to see the advantages of being in a MAT. There are, of course, other ways of achieving a similar end result in regard to working collaboratively – teaching school alliances, formal partnerships, federations and so on. So it is not just a case of being pro-MAT. But I do feel that the days of working alone have long gone and it is inevitable, sadly, that a time will come when the last school standing in a local authority will be required to turn off the lights. What I find really exciting at the moment is the ability to continually re-invent yourself to adapt to the shifting sands. It's as if we've been given licence, to a certain extent, to create and define the system – whatever that might look like. I am, of course, understandably cautious about this, as potentially we have 20,000 schools all trying to huddle up and get themselves in groups without anyone overseeing how it's done on a national level. Even now, as a MAT leader, I have grave concerns as to how the system will end up. Presumably, with a MAT being as small as only two schools, we could end up with almost 10,000 MATs, each with its own systems, services, back-room staff and so on.

Regardless of the political restraints, this does not stop a school leader from taking the decision to get out there and partner up with likeminded schools. The word 'likeminded' is critical here, because where collaboration hasn't worked so well, this has been on the basis that there has been no 'likemindedness' at all. I am often asked to go and support MATs in the early start-up phase and it still amazes me at the number of schools that seek to 'work collaboratively', but without any sense of shared purpose, mission or values. Collaboration works well only if there is buy-in of the 'why?' I suspect that this may be why many schools have not yet formed a MAT, because they have been unable to find the perfect partners or likeminded schools. One thing that I feel we have worked hard on is making sure that we have a strong sense of purpose and reason for being. Without that, we just become a cluster of schools.

Even without cross-school collaboration, the benefits of creating a culture of teamwork in a school are significant. When I was head of a four-form entry primary in London, I got into very good habits in regard to team-building, running the school very much on a secondary school model. This has served me well ever since; and even in small one-form entry schools, the creation of teams is essential, especially in regard to capacity building, sharing best practice, wellbeing and succession planning. By doing this, and by doing it well, it almost by default lends itself to the creation of a culture of collaboration and a school ethos where synergies and powerful partnerships allow the forces of change to have a more effective impact.

TR: When I visited you at Victoria Park a couple of years ago, I sensed a really open mindset among your staff to both sharing and learning from others. Was this something that was always a natural trait of these individuals or was it the result of conscious development in this area?

AM: It was very much a conscious decision. As I said before, it's a strategy that has served me well – especially when it comes to re-culturing a school. The school at the time had been in special measures for several years, was earmarked for closure as a 'fresh start' and basically consisted of two separate staff groups as a result of the recent unsuccessful amalgamation of the separate infant and junior schools. Staff soon saw the benefits of working collaboratively, having been given permission to take risks and try new ideas. There was a tangible and palpable desire to improve and to become an outstanding school. Intrinsic motivation was high because staff were given the time and support to always 'be up to something'. What they most valued at the time was that I was there to stay. Staff crave stability and are far more likely to buy into a vision if they know you are in for the long term and it's not just a vanity project. This, of course, is one of the problems with the so-called 'super-head' syndrome – especially in local authority schools, where a consultant head is airlifted into a school, rapidly pulls up loads of trees, plants a few new ones and then clears off. I've always been determined to see the job done – even more so as a trust leader, as it's our name on the tin.

Several years ago, we started our own SCITT and now train a number of new teachers each year. Part of their training includes growth mindset, learning behaviours, critical thinking, the importance of feedback and so on. This means that when our trainees begin their teaching careers with us, they do so from a very strong platform, as they have a good understanding of our values, ways of working and school culture. On the rare occasion when we need to recruit NQTs from beyond the SCITT, we need to make sure that we ask the right questions at interview to ensure that their values and beliefs are aligned with ours. When they do, it makes teamwork and collaboration so much easier. If they don't, we don't hire them.

TR: You've taken on many schools in difficulties over the years in challenging circumstances and I know that battening down the hatches and becoming inwardly focused is an easy thing to do in these situations. Have you always managed to remain outward looking during these turnaround times or has collaboration beyond your own school been a challenge?

AM: To start with, it was very difficult as we only had the one school in the trust – the sponsor academy. In many ways, we had to asset strip the school in order to provide capacity and support for the school that was in special measures. It's so much easier now, as we have more schools that can share the load, so we are less reliant on a single school. One of the expectations now for a new sponsored school joining the trust is that within three to four years as a capacity taker, the academy becomes the capacity giver and passes it on. We find that this model works well as it not only creates the necessary integrity for those providing the support – been there, done that – but also motivates those receiving the support, as they know that in a couple of years, through leadership development and investment, they can become the future leaders supporting new colleagues in difficulties.

So yes, I have always been outward looking; but I have to work hard at it. I see this very much as one of my key roles as a CEO. One of the challenges that didn't exist several years ago is that there is an ever-expanding market for this and schools are forever bombarded by companies providing the solutions to all their problems – MATs especially. As gatekeeper, I need to be very careful as to whom we choose to partner up with – be they schools, other MATs or consultants. We've benefited a great deal from being part of other networks and have sent staff to a number of their member schools and events to learn from best practice. All of this is greatly valued and appreciated, but it can become a bit of a challenge when you have to pay it back! As a result, we have a continual stream of schools contacting us wanting advice or to visit.

TR: Now in your role as a trust CEO, what are the important things that you have to put in place to make sure that schools across the trust benefit from being part of your MAT? How do you make sure that 1+1 equals more than 2?

AM: Being a head teacher is the best job in the world. It was with such a heavy, heavy heart that I stood down from all exec head duties last year, as I love the buzz that being a head gives. In particular, I knew that as CEO I would lose the day-to-day contact with parents and pupils. As a result, I try to make a real effort to work with children and parents across the schools – if nothing else, to keep my eye in. It's also a wonderful way of staying grounded and keeping contact with the real people that matter. Having a good understanding of the issues that schools face is important, as it's my job to remove all the stuff that heads have to needlessly deal with so that they can focus on the important things. We have worked hard to build a strong central team that acts almost as a one-stop shop for schools to go to with any issues, and we try to solve them. This is where we can add real value – especially in regard to additional discretionary spend and buying power as a family of schools.

Getting good governance right is essential. All governance now flows through the board and we are in the process of replacing local governing bodies with academy councils. Again, this now frees up school governance to focus only on education, safeguarding and the local community – the board deals with the rest, such as finance, procurement, contracts, estates and HR. As CEO, it is entirely my responsibility to keep the board informed and see that they are well placed to discharge their duties, which are as far reaching as ever. I had never heard of fiduciary duties a couple of years ago; but now, I can't get enough of them. So we have a really effective and skilled board which provides just the right level of challenge and support. The scheme of delegation is essential here and we've worked hard to refine and simplify this so that we can add value.

One of the things the board takes very seriously is the duty to serve as custodians of the vision, values, beliefs and ethos of the trust. We revisit these at every meeting, ensuring that alignment continues as best as possible across the trust – especially when new schools join. Ensuring a sense of commonality versus individuality is incredibly difficult, particularly with schools at different stages of the journey and across a number of local authorities. We've averaged two new schools a year since we started and would have more than doubled this if we'd said yes to every school that wanted to join. But we've allowed our values and sense of purpose to guide us well, and have resisted the urge to expand too quickly. So my job as CEO is to manage this continued organic growth while at the same time ensuring that the trust doesn't stagnate. In particular, I need to ensure that we maintain the right level of balance of capacity givers and takers. As tempting as it may be to build an empire of schools that are all high performing, it was never my intention to do so. The whole point of forming a MAT was to support local schools; so typically 50% of our schools either are in or have been in special measures at one point or another.

One of the main advantages of being a MAT is the notion of being a single employer. This means that we can move staff around the schools, refreshing and revitalising as we go. We have a very clear succession plan in place linked to a CPD entitlement programme, in which we invest heavily in our future leaders. This allows me to plan ahead in terms of bringing schools in, in the knowledge that we have ready-made leaders waiting in the wings to run them. While it's not always a bad thing to refresh an organisation from beyond the schools themselves, the aim of setting up the trust was to always build from within – to grow our own. This begins, of course, with the SCITT, where already we are seeing future heads emerge at an early stage of their career. I find this a particularly rewarding element of my job and look forward to the day when one of our SCITT trainees becomes a head of one of our academies. I'm sure it won't be long.

All of our schools have adopted similar approaches to teaching, learning, curriculum, behaviour and so on, while at the same time retaining local uniqueness. When it comes to evaluating how effective we are as a family of schools – in other words, what is it that we can now do as a trust that we couldn't previously with the local authority – we now measure only what we value. This means that we have a number of layers of self-evaluation, some more granular and nuanced than others. It's about wearing different lenses. These include internal school-led peer review, external peer review, external quality assurance visits, in-school self-evaluation and trust-wide self-evaluation. Neither of these last two refers to Ofsted; instead, they are based on the impact of our values on all that we do. This then generates a detailed annual strategic plan, complete with published key performance indicators that allow us to hold each other to account, all based on the right things.

As CEO, I'm also very conscious of the need to look after the best interests of the current schools. Whenever a new school wants to join, we invariably get asked what we can provide to it – school support, finance, HR and so on – all the usual questions, including the cost of membership. All of these are perfectly valid; but I always flip it round and ask the school what it is bringing to us in terms of added value. This occasionally results in a puzzled look, which is all I need to know in terms of it perhaps not necessarily being right for the trust. Being part of a MAT is about giving back as much as taking, so when a school expresses an interest to join but isn't aware of the need to add value and bring something to the table, invariably we part company at that point. This may seem harsh; but in terms of building synergies and ensuring the long-term security of the trust, it's very important indeed. We've all worked hard to build something very special here and we can't run the risk of letting a school in that doesn't go with this. That said, our entry requirements are very simple: 'If you subscribe to our values, you're in.' Oh, and having a healthy surplus balance helps.

TR: As your group of schools has grown, how have the approaches changed that you have had to employ across the trust? What mistakes have you learned from on this journey?

AM: The approaches haven't really changed that much, to be honest – they've just been fine-tuned a bit, that's all. The real difference – and one that makes it so much easier – is that there's more of us to share the load, as opposed to having to rely on the same individuals or schools. We've also been able to pool a lot more in terms of 'what works well', so that we can adapt and refine what we do so that we get some degree of consistency across the schools. Although we want each school to retain its individuality, at the same time we need some commonality. It needs to be no different from moving a teacher in a school from Year 5 to Year 2: you don't want there to be a completely different planning or assessment format; you want a common approach throughout the school, while at the same time giving the teacher freedom to exercise their own individuality. The same applies across the trust. This is one of the biggest challenges when a new school joins. It's not so bad for a sponsored school, as we take immediate control of running it. Where it's a lot harder is when an established high-performing school – a school with a successful head teacher who quite rightly has earned the right to become autonomous. How do you then persuade them to change tried-and-tested systems to suit the trust? This is where 'buy-in' right from the outset is crucial. Quite often, compromise is king and it's knowing where your bottom line is. For example, in the early days I would have insisted on a re-branding, especially of signage, logos and so on. I'm past that now and no longer see this as an issue, provided that the school is prepared to buy into our ways of working.

As we've grown, we've moved away from a flat structure of governance to one that is hub-based. This ensures that accountability systems remain fit for purpose and that each hub is led by an executive head teacher, so it is easier to promote consistency as well as sharing best practice across all the schools. As exclusively a CEO – and not tethered to a school, so to speak – I'm now in a better place to be able to operate more strategically across the trust, ensuring that all elements of our work complement each other – operations and education in particular.

In terms of making mistakes in the earlier stages, this would have been something I wished I'd got right earlier: getting the operational part in place right at the start. But looking back, I didn't have the capacity to do anything about it, as it was only me plus a couple of heads and we were all busy running our schools, a new sponsored academy included. In essence, I was OK doing the CEO and executive head teacher role; but combining that with a chief operating officer or finance director role – that was way out of my comfort zone. But we learned quickly; and as more schools joined, the increased top-slice amount meant that we could afford gradually to employ a finance and operations team, including an experienced director of finance and operations, someone from outside the education sector.

We still continue to struggle with management information systems, finance included. Across the eight schools, we cover five local authorities, each with its own ways of working – finance systems, safeguarding, contracts, IT and so on. Trying to assimilate these new schools seamlessly into the trust is a continual challenge. Our approach is far more laidback now, as we know that we can get it right in time rather than rushing something through and making mistakes with it. Having an established team in place, who know exactly what needs to be done, is vital. Take the conversion process, for example: this is so much easier and smoother than it was previously, as we've refined and developed our due diligence processes almost to a fine art.

Other mistakes? I wish there'd been a course called 'Being a MAT CEO: A Guide for Dummies'. As with most tasks required of a school leader, you tend to operate in a state of unconscious incompetence, being in a seemingly continued state of crisis management – especially in the early start-up phase. I'd often get a call from the DfE asking for this return or that, not having a clue that the return was required in the first place. But I'd put down the phone, take a deep breath, turn to Google and knock the form out.

There's so much more out there now for new MATs, which of course is how it should be. I mentioned due diligence earlier and we certainly made some mistakes along the way with this – not least because we weren't always sure of what we were looking for. And even if we were, we had no markers or benchmarks against which to compare it. But if you had to ask me what is the number one thing that needs to be done when setting up a MAT, it's to be sure that you have in place a CEO and a finance director who both know what is required of them. We knew that we needed a finance director in the early days, but couldn't afford one, so I bumbled along in the role as best I could. Good directors of finance are worth their weight in gold.

TR: Andrew, it's been brilliant talking to you. Finally, if you had to give three pieces of advice to school leaders around how to collaborate effectively with others in the system, what would they be?

AM:

1. Build powerful networks. Either get yourself on social media or get yourself out there – go to courses, events, conferences. Take a pile of business cards, wear a big smile and get connected.

2. Know your 'why?' Make sure you know your vision statement, purpose, USP inside out and can quote these word for word to anyone willing to listen. If you don't know them off by heart, don't expect anybody else to. And when you've done that, make it your mission to ensure that everybody else around you knows them as well.

3. It might sound crass, but surround yourself with likeminded people – people whom you trust, who constantly give above and beyond because they believe in you, themselves and the 'why?' They might not necessarily be your best friend or think like you, but they've got your back, are at the top of their game and love what they do.

IN SUMMARY – INTERDEPENDENT LEADERSHIP

■ Is there an understanding of synergy and interdependent leadership within teams in your school?

■ Do leaders in your school share an 'abundance mentality'? Is this evident in the way that they respond to the success of others? Can you notice the language of abundance mentality rather than scarcity mentality in your school?

■ Can you identify projects and activities where cooperation and collaboration exist in your school? Can you identify where making the shift to collaboration can bring more benefits to your organisation?

■ Are leaders in your school disciplined in their thoughts and actions? Do people do what they say they will? Can they say no when 'too good to be true' projects or opportunities spring up mid-year?

■ Is trust evident across staff and leaders in your school? Are conversations open and honest? Are people supportive of each other and do they remain non-judgemental of those not present when things go wrong?

■ What informal or formal collaboration exists across schools and how is this effective? Does the time invested in these partnerships equate to impact in school? Does 1+1 equal more than 2?

FIVE FIVES GRID FOR PLANNING

FIVE MINUTES: What immediate first steps can you take?

FIVE DAYS: What short-term actions can you take in the next week to kick start or plan change?

FIVE WEEKS: What actions or follow-up meetings/discussions can you plan for in the next half-term?

FIVE MONTHS: What follow-up and follow-through activities do you need to plan to ensure that the change is not just a flash in the pan?

FIVE YEARS: What might your change look like in five years? What structures, systems and processes will you need to amend to ensure that your change becomes embedded in the fabric of your school and is not a passing fad?

THE END

Tom Rees
Author

So there you have it: my take on school leadership, with some help along the way from some tremendous teachers and leaders from across the country. I hope that you have found it useful.

Writing *Wholesome Leadership* over the course of the last year has taught me many things. Committing my opinion and beliefs to paper has made me question everything, and has been both challenging and reaffirming to my values and beliefs. Although, in writing about the 'whole' of leadership, I have attempted to capture the breadth of leadership activity, as I got closer to the final manuscript I realised that there is still so much to say. I could write for another two years and still not be satisfied that I have said it all.

So I have come to realise that this the book is not a definitive publication of 'the way it is', but rather a snapshot at a moment in time of what I currently think. Perhaps it's the start of even more conversations that I will enjoy about school leadership in the future.

Through writing *Wholesome Leadership*, I have revisited many processes and theories from different stages of my own leadership journey. It has allowed me to reflect how over time, it is inevitable that we will lose important skills and forget successful processes as we face new challenges.

Becoming an accomplished leader does not necessarily mean that we will be at the top of our game across every aspect of leadership at all times; more that we will commit to a process of continual self-renewal and being open to relearning and refreshing our knowledge and approaches over time.

If you would like to talk to me about school leadership, you will often find me on Twitter at @tomrees_77. Of course, you're welcome to agree, disagree, praise or suggest improvements to anything I have written. I look forward to any debate that might come as a result; who knows, it might help me to write *Wholesome Leadership 2.0* in a year or two!

The only thing left to say is that I remain fiercely hopeful about education and in awe of the role that teachers and leaders play every day in making their schools great places to work and learn.

If nothing else, I hope that Wholesome Leadership has made you think, perhaps allowing you to reflect on the work you do every day as a school leader and the important role you play in our society.

You're all clear, kid; now let's blow this thing and go home.

Han Solo

#WholesomeLeadership

ACKNOWLEDGEMENTS

Writing *Wholesome Leadership* has been possible only through the support of a number of people, to whom I will always be grateful.

To begin, I should thank Alex Sharratt and John Catt Educational for giving me the opportunity to write a book in the first place. With no real credentials to become an author other than my school experience and an occasional blog, I was surprised when Alex offered me this opportunity 12 months ago. With original plans to write it over the summer holidays, I missed my own deadline by six months and so, among other things, I've appreciated Alex's unhurried and patient approach.

Thanks also to Oliver Caviglioli, who has become far more than just the illustrator of *Wholesome Leadership*. Oliver has a truly special talent and it has been my privilege to have worked with him. I will miss our energetic Skype calls and Oliver's enthusiasm for magazines as much as his sage advice on writing and design. A particular thanks to the 14 interviewees who feature within *Wholesome Leadership*. The book is a much richer one for their fabulous contributions and it has been an honour to feature so many of my educationalist heroes.

I'm also indebted to a number of friends and colleagues who have taken the time to offer me support, advice and critique throughout this process. There are too many to thank them all by name; but in particular Craig Jones for his ongoing critique and Andrew Morrish and Andy Buck, who both generously shared their own writing experiences with me and have nudged me along throughout these last 12 months.

There are many things in life that I find myself becoming increasingly grateful to my parents for, and this project is no exception. In particular, my mother deserves even more appreciation than usual for her dedicated proofreading and editorial advice. Thanks Mum!

The process of writing *Wholesome Leadership* has been torturous and at times ridiculous – taking up countless hours of writing late into the night and over holidays that I look forward to reclaiming. For this reason, I'll finish by both thanking and apologising to my wife and children. Adele, Freddie, Stanley and Ellen, I love you all. Thank you. Sorry. It's finished now.